Dorothy Lee

# Dorothy Lee

## The Life and Films of the Wheeler and Woolsey Girl

JAMIE BROTHERTON *and*
TED OKUDA

Foreword by Nick Santa Maria

McFarland & Company, Inc., Publishers
*Jefferson, North Carolina, and London*

*Frontispiece:* A glamour portrait of Dorothy from the mid–1930s.

LIBRARY OF CONGRESS CATALOGUING-IN-PUBLICATION DATA

Brotherton, Jamie, 1978–
Dorothy Lee : the life and films of the Wheeler and Woolsey
girl / Jamie Brotherton and Ted Okuda ; foreword by Nick Santa Maria.
p.    cm.
Includes bibliographical references and index.

ISBN 978-0-7864-3363-6
softcover : acid free paper ∞

1. Lee, Dorothy, 1911–1999.
2. Actors — United States — Biography.
I. Okuda, Ted, 1953–    II. Title.
PN2287.L2899B86 2013    792.02′8092—dc23    [B]    2013004421

BRITISH LIBRARY CATALOGUING DATA ARE AVAILABLE

© 2013 Jamie Brotherton and Ted Okuda. All rights reserved

*No part of this book may be reproduced or transmitted in any form
or by any means, electronic or mechanical, including photocopying
or recording, or by any information storage and retrieval system,
without permission in writing from the publisher.*

Front cover image: Dorothy Lee, circa 1934

Manufactured in the United States of America

*McFarland & Company, Inc., Publishers
Box 611, Jefferson, North Carolina 28640
www.mcfarlandpub.com*

To John Cavallo, who loved Dorothy as much as we did — and do.
To Nick and Nina Clooney, whose enthusiasm never waned.
To Grandma Josy, who loved Dorothy since childhood.
To Marjorie Millsap, for sharing her life with us.

# Acknowledgments

Our sincere thanks to Dorothy Lee, who gave us her blessing and provided a wealth of material; to John Cavallo and Scott and Jan MacGillivray, who graciously helped to fill in gaps in Dorothy's personal and professional timeline; to film historians Mark A. Miller and James L. Neibaur, for their valued assistance and advice; and to Nick Santa Maria, for his heartfelt Foreword.

For their unflagging support, we are indebted to our families, the Brothertons (Josephine, Tania, Anthony, Juana, Linda, Maria, Richard, Thomas, James and Anthony Jr.) and the Okudas (Sakiko, Scott, Belinda, Cheryl and Christopher).

For their encouragement, our appreciation goes to Terry Alvarado, Alex Bartosh (*A-1 Video Service*), the Bersbach family (Betsy, Brent, Dick, Mary, Stacy), Marlena Bielski, Fran Blasing, Eric Bradley, Shirley Cameron, Scott Campbell, Mark Clark, Nick and Nina Clooney, Gary Cohen, Brad Conner, Mary and Steve Cooper, Steve Darnall (*Nostalgia Digest, Those Were the Days*), Eddie Deezen, Deborah and Carl Del Vecchio, Marshall Duffield, Jr., Susan Duffield, Robert Feder, Greg Glienna, Nils Hanson, David Harnack, Marian Marsh Henderson, Tom Hofbauer, David J. Hogan, Bill Jackson, Steve Jajkowski (*The Video Veteran*), Gloria Jones, Karen Knapstein, Leonard J. Kohl, Joe Konrath, Rich Koz, Erich Kunzel, Laura LaRocca, Deana Martin, David Maska, Sam Mastromauro, Alan Matthes, Rob McKay, Maureen Miller, Teresa Miller, Jim Mueller, Marcia Opal, Jorie Purvin, Terry Reynolds, Lynn A. Robinson, Rosario Roller, Laura Roman, Samuel K. Rubin (*Classic Film Collector, Classic Images*), Ralph and Kathy Schiller, the Schneiders (Blake, Brent, Carrie, Darren, Todd), Suzanne Scott, Ben Sears, Madeleine Short, Susan Sliwicki, Fred C. Smith, Bing Spitler, Stella Stevens, James Toback, Doris Eaton Travis, Mike Tynus, Gary Wegner, Mort Walker, Stanley Wernz, Pam White, Mark York, Mark Yurkiw, Bill Zehme, and Jacklyn Zeman.

For more about Wheeler and Woolsey movies, we highly recommend *Wheeler and Woolsey: The Vaudeville Comic Duo and Their Films, 1929–1937* by Edward Watz (McFarland, 1994).

# Table of Contents

| | |
|---|---|
| *Acknowledgments* | vi |
| *Foreword by Nick Santa Maria* | 1 |
| *Preface* | 3 |

| | | |
|---|---|---|
| 1 • | Do Something: Presenting Marjorie Millsap | 5 |
| 2 • | I Want the World to Know: Broadway Baby | 13 |
| 3 • | Sweetheart, We Need Each Other: Boys Meet Girl | 21 |
| 4 • | Whistling the Blues Away: The Star Treatment | 37 |
| 5 • | You've Got What Gets Me: Parting Company | 57 |
| 6 • | Niagara Falls to Reno: A Star Without a Studio | 69 |
| 7 • | Keep on Doin' What You're Doin': Back with the Boys | 83 |
| 8 • | Isn't Love the Grandest Thing? Marriage Between Movies | 97 |
| 9 • | My One Ambition Is You: Motherhood, Matrimony and Retirement | 113 |
| 10 • | I Love You So Much: Kindred Spirits in the Autumn Years | 123 |
| 11 • | Dilly Dally: An Unexpected Rediscovery | 133 |
| 12 • | Dance and Let the World Dance with You: A Final Bow | 139 |

| | |
|---|---|
| *Afterword* | 143 |
| *Filmography* | 147 |
| *Chapter Notes* | 179 |
| *Bibliography* | 181 |
| *Index* | 183 |

# Foreword
## by Nick Santa Maria

I had a strong feeling I should call. It was almost a premonition. I was in the habit of telephoning Dottie at least once a month, but due to my heavy work schedule I had neglected to make my regular call. Yet something told me I should call at that particular point in time.

I had first encountered Dorothy Lee while watching the Wheeler and Woolsey film *Half Shot at Sunrise*. It was 1980, and VCRs were still fairly new to the general public. I had rented a bad public domain print of the film and, having grown up with Leonard Maltin's book *Movie Comedy Teams*, I was eager to sample the work of Bert, Bob and Dorothy. In New York, where I was born and raised, the local television stations never showed Wheeler and Woolsey films. Before Maltin's book I never even knew they existed. Watching the movie, I was enthralled. Soon afterward I got hold of another public domain title, *Hook Line and Sinker*, and that was a great deal of fun, too. I liked Wheeler and Woolsey, and I found Dorothy Lee to be funny, cute as a button, and the epitome of the baby-voiced female comic actresses of the early sound era.

Not long after my introduction to the trio, I attended a screening of *Rio Rita*, the film that had started it all for Wheeler and Woolsey. Although it creaked as most early talkies tend to do, the antics of Bert, Bob, and Dorothy drew hearty laughter and applause from the full auditorium. My appreciation became set in stone.

Since then, I've collected all of their films on DVD, and have read whatever material I could get my hands on regarding these wonderful troupers, little knowing that one of them would become a very good friend of mine.

Some like-minded friends and I had decided that the unjustly forgotten Wheeler and Woolsey needed more recognition than they were receiving. We'd decided that they deserved their own organization, something akin to the Sons of the Desert, the organization that honors Laurel and Hardy. We settled on the name "The Diplomaniacs" (based on the title of one of the better W&W films) and proceeded to set the wheels in motion. A newsletter was the first order of business, and we thought, "What better way to inaugurate the first issue than to feature an interview with Dorothy Lee?" I wrote and asked if she would mind being involved in our efforts to keep the memory of Wheeler and Woolsey alive. Imagine my surprise when less than two weeks later I heard her voice coming from my answering machine. The voice was a far cry from the "baby talk" she'd used in her early films, but it was unmistakably Dottie and I eagerly returned her call. She graciously allowed me to do an extensive interview with her over the phone, and offered her undying support to the organization. That became the start of our monthly phone correspondence.

Alas, the Diplomaniacs never came to pass. Shortly after our interview, I was shunted off for a year on the national tour of *Grease!*—yes, I'm in show biz, a fact that Dottie greatly enjoyed—and any hope of my continuing plans for the organization fell by the wayside.

My relationship with Dottie remained rich and loving. She was a concerned and generous friend. She wanted to know every detail of my career, my relationships, and my life in New York City. When I married, her beautiful card arrived before any of the others. When I debuted on Broadway, she was just as excited as any parent or grandparent could be. (She always wanted me to call her "Granny," although I could never bring myself to do so.) We shared thoughts on her films, her relationships with co-stars, and we even sang her old songs together. She also put me in touch with Jamie Brotherton, who became a wonderful friend of mine. Dottie had always encouraged Jamie to be a writer, and I know she would be extremely proud to know that Jamie and author-historian Ted Okuda, another of Dottie's dearest friends, are responsible for the book you are reading.

On the day I was hit with that incredible urge to give Dottie a call, I couldn't possibly have known that it was to be the last time I would ever speak to her. Her nurse answered, and after informing me that Dottie was gravely ill, she graciously allowed me to speak with her. Poor Dottie sounded very weak. Each sentence she uttered was done with extreme effort. Her breathing was very strained. After a brief conversation, I said goodbye, adding for the first time, "I love you, Dottie." She said, "I love you too" and that was it. She passed away peacefully a few hours later. It's strange to know that my phone call might have been the last she ever received.

I think of Dottie often. Her films are a constant reminder of the vitality and spirit that lived on long after her retirement from show business. She shared her light with all who knew her, and I'm proud to have been one of those people. To paraphrase Bert Wheeler from *Hips, Hips, Hooray!*, "Gee, she was a swell kid!"

*Nick Santa Maria is an actor, author, composer and historian who lives on the West Coast.*

# Preface

If Dorothy Lee is remembered at all, it's for her co-starring appearances in thirteen feature films with the comedy team of Bert Wheeler and Robert Woolsey. Bert and Bob were among the most popular movie stars of their era (1929–1937) and the exposure Dorothy received from these pictures made her a familiar name and face both on the screen and in the press. After Bob died in 1938, Wheeler and Woolsey faded into memory. Dorothy retired from show business in 1941 to settle down and raise a family. End of story.

Well, not exactly. Not as far as we're concerned, anyway.

While the Wheeler and Woolsey movies were undeniably Dorothy's chief claim to fame, other facets of her career and private life were no less notable. She went from being a struggling vaudeville performer to the female vocalist in one of the most popular bands in the country to a star in the new-fangled "talking pictures" all within the span of a few short years. During the Great Depression, she lived a fairy-tale existence, rubbing shoulders with Hollywood luminaries and earning the type of income that most people could only dream of. She retired and balanced domestic life with charity work. And she saw, to her amazement, a revived interest in the movie career she had written off long ago.

Although Dorothy was unimpressed by her acting abilities, with the proper guidance and the right material, she could rise to the occasion and display the sweet, natural charm that Bert Wheeler, who chose her to play his leading lady in *Rio Rita*, found so beguiling. She always felt she went as far as she did only because of a series of lucky breaks, yet others saw her potential even if she didn't. (There's no telling how much more she could have accomplished had she not voluntarily cut her career short.)

This book is based on twenty-four years' worth of conversations between the authors and Dorothy, or "Dottie" as we called her. (For the sake of consistency, however, she's "Dorothy" throughout the main text.) The majority of these conversations were casual chit-chat and not formal interviews, which she was never entirely comfortable with. She wasn't shy about talking, that's for sure, but with formal interviews she was under self-imposed pressure to come up with something the other party might find interesting. In time, her interviews tended to cover the same ground, like a musician playing the anticipated greatest hits line-up. And there was nothing wrong with that. Her stories were fascinating no matter how many times you heard them. Yet under less guarded circumstances, when there was no agenda, Dottie relaxed and her candid memories and opinions flowed with greater ease. Very often, a photograph or the mere mention of a name would trigger a long-dormant memory and she would recall details with a clarity that surprised even her.

It wasn't until Dottie's final years that it occurred to us to write her biography. She offered her wholehearted approval: "No one has really told my story and maybe it isn't even worth telling. But if anyone does, I'd like it to be the two of you." It took several years to complete the research and writing process but we finally got around to telling Dottie's story and we'd like to think that, somewhere on high, she approves of the result. We hope you do too.

The discerning reader will note that we selected the titles of songs Dorothy performed in movies and on stage for the chapter titles because we felt they best reflected the content and mood of each chapter, while still being relevant to our subject.

We've done our best to curb our obvious affection for our subject and appraise her life and career with a reasonable degree of clear-eyed objectivity. Yet if sentimentality permeates our text, it's because when we watch her films or look at her photographs, our minds cannot completely separate the images before us from the woman who was our dear friend. For us, viewing a Dorothy Lee movie generates emotional responses that often have little to do with the movie itself. Nevertheless, we have made every effort to maintain a critical perspective.

Dottie passed away in 1999 and there hasn't been a day since she hasn't been a fixture in our thoughts. Writing this book served as a reminder — though none was needed — of the impact she had on our lives and how much we miss her.

# Chapter 1

# Do Something
## *Presenting Marjorie Millsap*

*"I'll always be thankful that my parents instilled me with a great sense of self-confidence. They raised me to believe that there wasn't anything I couldn't accomplish just because I was a girl."* — Dorothy Lee

Dorothy Lee was born Marjorie Elizabeth Millsap on May 23, 1911, at one o'clock in the morning at 1460 West Adams Street in Los Angeles, California. Because her mother feared the possibility of having her child switched with another baby while at the hospital's maternity ward — a very real concern during that era — Marjorie was delivered at home by family pediatrician Dr. M.L. Moore. Delivery went without complications, and the little girl became the pride and joy of her middle-class parents Homer and Bess Millsap, who were both 30 years old.

Homer originally hailed from Iowa, as had his father before him. The Millsaps were of English descent, the name deriving from the word "milksop" (a piece of bread soaked in milk) and often used to describe a farmer who dealt in milk products. At the age of sixteen, Homer passed the state bar exam, making him the youngest attorney to be admitted to the Iowa state bar, although he was unable to practice until he turned eighteen. He would thrive at his profession, running a successful law firm in Los Angeles. At one point in his career, his clients included comic legend W.C. Fields and celebrated race-car driver Barney Oldfield. His wife, Bess, nee Chaney, originally from Ohio, listed her occupation on Marjorie's birth certificate as housewife. Her father had been recognized as a Civil War veteran, and she maintained a close relationship with her mother Elizabeth Chaney, who had given birth to ten children before the age of 29 (although only eight survived).

Bess doted on Marjorie, who was affectionately nicknamed "Midge." With big brown saucer-shaped eyes, a cherubic face and golden curls, Marjorie was a precursor to Shirley Temple in looks, and at a very early age she became enthralled with show business. As Dorothy remembered, "When I was little I loved going to see the silent movies. My parents would take me, and I used to drive them and the audience crazy because I kept on asking my mother each time the title card came up, 'What's that say, what's that say?' I wasn't even old enough to read the captions."

Live theater left just as indelible an impression on her: "My mother took me to the Orpheum once when I was a little girl, and I was just crazy about it. When I left I said, 'Momma, that's what I want to be ... I want to be a show lady!'"

The opportunity to be a "show lady" arose sooner than anyone thought. Frank Eagan, a family friend whom Marjorie called "Uncle," owned and operated a large song-and-dance studio that produced theatrical revues. One day when Bess and two-year-old Marjorie visited, they watched a rehearsal for an upcoming production. Entranced, Marjorie asked her mother, "Why don't you put me up there [on the stage]?" In recalling the incident, Dorothy commented, "My mother said, 'She will go out there and become so frightened.' But Uncle said, 'Why not let her go out there and see what she can do?'"

Marjorie's first stage "routine" consisted of a little ballet dance, which received rousing approval. She never forgot that experience: "After I got out [on stage] they practically had to get the hook just to get me off, I loved it so much!" Marjorie was a hit, and she even received a write-up in the local newspaper. Bess was so proud of her daughter that she had her dance shoes bronzed—a memento that Dorothy would proudly display for the rest of her life. From this point on, young Marjorie was determined to become a performer, and her parents remained supportive. Bess started and maintained a scrapbook of Dorothy's showbiz achievements (and private ups and downs) for the duration of her career.

Two-year-old Marjorie Millsap in 1913.

Dorothy continued to hang around the dance school and became everyone's "pet." The teachers and pupils enjoyed showing her dance steps, and she would observe the students as they were being instructed. This experience was the totality of her dance training, as she never took any formal lessons.

The Millsaps relocated and Marjorie grew up on Gower Street, just around the corner from Paramount Pictures. (She remembered she was able to watch the famous Ambassador Hotel being built.) Her neighborhood playmates were all boys—a group of twelve, to be exact. The gang frequently played at an athletic field that was constructed behind the Millsaps'

## 1. Do Something

home. Marjorie developed into quite a tomboy, excelling in such strenuous, male-dominated sports as football, baseball, pole-vaulting, and long-distance running. She became so proficient at these activities that she found she could beat her best friends at any game or sport. She recalled: "It's not that I was so strong, but I kept a terrific pace. I grew up right next door to the Rothert boys, Harlow and Lory. I played with them for years, and they later became the Stanford athletes. We used to have fights to a standstill — glorious battles."

Bess Millsap filed for a divorce in March 1918. In her petition, Bess cited cruelty and desertion as grounds, stating that Homer had beaten her on several occasions, and that he had deserted the family some fifteen months earlier. Both parents would marry new mates within a year's time. Marjorie lived with her mother and grandmother (who were more strict about her upbringing) and her new stepfather, whom she would come to adore. With his second wife, Homer had two more children, a daughter and a son. Marjorie maintained a

**A young tomboy at age twelve in 1923.**

close relationship with her father, stepmother and half-siblings. "Even though my parents got divorced, I never felt unloved or ignored by either one of them," Dorothy recalled. "I remained close to my father after my mother got custody of me. The problems they had between themselves were never thrust on me. I was never used as an emotional pawn."

Marjorie's mischievous streak would sometimes drive the adults up a wall. In a May 1931 issue of *Screenland* magazine, she asked her childhood pal and cousin, "Remember that time we were caught smoking cigarettes? My uncle was so mad! That night after dinner he pulled out some cigarettes and made each one of us smoke one. The others cried. They were so sick they had to go to bed. But, I got to laughing and just sat and blew smoke through my nose!" In the article, the unidentified cousin chided with a smile, "Oh, she was always the bad one! Father was so particular about the way we acted at the dinner table. He'd tell Midge to put on her napkin and she'd say, 'No,

I won't!' So he'd tell her not to dare to, and she'd tie it around her neck so tight, she almost choked."

Marjorie's fascination with motion pictures persisted. After every trip to the local theater, she rushed home and kept her grandmother awake all night as she enthusiastically re-enacted the movie she had seen, exclaiming, "I know I can act if I ever have the chance."

Gloria Swanson and Norma Talmadge were among her favorite movie stars. But it was the dashing, athletic Douglas Fairbanks on whom she developed a big crush. "I was so star-struck!" she remarked years later. "While stuck in bed with the mumps, I wrote him a fan letter, asking him to send me an autograph. And he actually did send me an autographed photo, signed 'To Midge.' I kept that photo for years. Ironically, after I began appearing in movies myself, I became good friends with his son, Douglas Fairbanks, Jr."

Her love of Fairbanks and his thrilling daredevil stunts led to situations in which she attempted similar feats of derring-do. When Marjorie was about twelve, she ventured with a group of friends, to her father's downtown L.A. law firm so that she could collect her allowance. Her friends dared her to walk on the professional building's twelve-story ledge, never dreaming she'd actually go through with it. To their astonishment, Marjorie managed her way up and walked across the ledge (which was only about a foot wide) to the window where her father was holding a meeting. Upon seeing her, Homer Millsap froze, instructing her not to move a muscle. Once she was safely inside, Marjorie wasn't subjected to her father's wrath. Instead, he gave her a big hug and more allowance than what she had expected.

During one of Marjorie's regular weekend visits with her father and stepmother, half-sister Melissa and a few other children challenged her to climb down a narrow chimney, just like Santa Claus. Marjorie accepted the challenge, although this stunt wasn't performed as smoothly as she hoped. On her descent, she became wedged so tightly that she wound up getting stuck. The frantic adults called the fire department, who rescued her by pulling her out, dirty but unscathed, from the chimney top.

With her mind on movies and other non-academic pursuits, Marjorie still maintained good grades (B and C averages) while attending Romana Convent, although she had difficultly adhering to the strict rules and regulations set down by the nuns who served as teachers. Marjorie wrote with her left hand, so she endured severe discipline to train her right hand when one of the nuns tied her left hand behind her back. As a result, she became ambidextrous, and would amuse her friends with her ability to write with both hands, and write in cursive, forward and backwards, with equal legibility. (In later years, she was still able to write "Dorothy Lee" with both hands simultaneously, and both signatures would be identical.) It also gave her a greater advantage in playing sports, though she favored her left hand for playing tennis and her right hand for golf.

Homer taught Marjorie how to drive when she was fourteen years old — lessons of the open road, minus the formalities that are required today. Marjorie quickly learned how to handle the wheel. She drove herself all the way to Santa Monica after spotting

## 1. Do Something

a newspaper ad calling for girls to try out for the U.S. Lacrosse Team. Her athletic prowess caught the attention of the coaches and she easily landed a position, becoming the smallest player on the team. When the United States battled Canada at the Coliseum in a Lacrosse tournament, it was little Marjorie who scored the final points, securing the U.S. victory. She was hailed as the team's star player and received a lot of publicity; newspapers featured photographs of her in midair, triumphantly taking down her opponent. "Because of the publicity I got, I made a personal appearance at one of the West Coast theaters and did some running and high-jumping. I loved being on stage."

That same year, 1925, Marjorie's showbiz career officially began when vaudevillian Homer Dickinson, a family friend, came to dinner. During his visit, he lamented that Florence Tempest, his wife and performing partner, was very ill and could not perform with him in his upcoming engagements. As Dorothy later recalled: "Homer said, 'Oh, I don't know what to do. Here I am booked six or eight weeks and my wife is so ill. I'm trying to find someone to take over.' I said, 'I can do it!' He sat down at the piano and played a few things. After hearing me sing, he said to my mother, 'Gee, she would be great for my show!'"

Dorothy, age 14, as she appeared opposite Homer Dickinson in 1925.

Dickinson offered Marjorie the job, and her parents felt at ease with placing their daughter in the fatherly Dickinson's charge. Dickinson and Tempest's stage act was similar to the George Burns–Gracie Allen partnership (comic patter laced with song and dance), with Dickinson serving as straight man to Tempest's "Dumb Dora" character. Tempest's role was modified to suit Marjorie's abilities — and the fact that she was barely a teenager — so Marjorie played the part as a dumb little girl whose nonsensical comments had a skewered logic behind them. (Q: "Did you put fresh water in the fish bowl?" A: "No ... the fish hasn't finished drinking the water I gave him last week.")

It was thrilling for the impressionable youngster to launch her career on the

Orpheum Circuit, which was known for premier vaudeville entertainment. Dorothy recalled, "I was lucky to have begun where I did. The Orpheum Circuit was A-class, what they considered in those days as top drawer. And I was the greatest ham in the world. I also tried out for things at the Saturday matinee, but I sure didn't get away with a thing on that vaudeville tour. We were doing four shows a day. Imagine being just fourteen years old and doing four shows! I loved it! Throughout the tour we would stay in hotels and rooming houses. I couldn't go out of my hotel room except with my partner to dinner. If a boy came to see me, he sat across from us in the lobby."

Marjorie toured with Dickinson on the West Coast vaudeville circuit for about six months. Her salary was $30 a week. The experience made her more determined than ever to pursue a show business career: "I was supposed to go back to school in the fall, but once I had the taste of the stage, I had no interest in school. I had been attending West Lake School for Girls, a snobby finishing school. They were trying to make a lady out of me. *No way!*"

On occasion, Marjorie would get homesick after reading letters from friends telling her about parties and proms that she had missed. "I'd think, 'Do I want to go home or stay on the stage?' I made my choice to stay in show business, and when I made it big, I went to plenty of proms."

Despite her waning academic interests, Dorothy completed her education through the mail, receiving and returning her homework while she was on the road (having attended Virgil Junior High School and Los Angeles High, prior to Westlake).

To help create a stage presence, Marjorie Millsap decided a name change was in order: "I chose Lee from my darling grandmother and Dorothy I just came up with on my own. It was later that my father helped me to legally change my name to Dorothy Lee."

Homer and Dorothy signed with Fanchon and Marco, a brother-and-sister team (their real names were Fanny and Mike Wolff) who, in addition to operating dance studios, were stage promoters, producers and managers of a number of West Coast circuits. They would be instrumental in launching the careers of such future stars as Joan Crawford, Doris Day, and Cyd Charisse.

Dorothy described Fanchon and Marco as wonderful people to work for, and she enjoyed appearing in their "prologues" (stage shows presented between scheduled screenings of motion pictures). Dorothy toured with them for six months doing four shows a day. Since they would do a variety of "theme" prologues, Dorothy fit in well when called upon to do collegiate roles or perform athletics — such as the time they had her kick a football into the audience.

Typical of the Fanchon and Marco prologues was "Bugs," presented at the Loew's State during the week of May 21, 1927. Billed as the "Hollywood Bugs," Homer and Dottie performed their song-and-patter act amidst a lavish setting of oversized flowers, trees and mushrooms. The "Hollywood Beauties" and members of the chorus were gorgeously costumed as ladybugs, spiders, and butterflies. The show-stopping finale featured a huge white spiderweb set against a black velvet drop. The chorus, dressed as

## 1. Do Something

bright red spiders, climbed up the web and performed the closing dance number in semi-suspended positions. The *Los Angeles Times* found moments like these "startling," adding that the entire presentation was "the most pretentious, elaborate and wholly enjoyable [prologue] that has ever appeared on the Loew's State stage." (This prologue made a lasting impression on Dottie. For the rest of her life, she favored ladybug images on clothing, personal stationery, ceramics, etc., so much so that in some circles her nickname became "Dottiebug.")

When her apprenticeship with Homer Dickinson ended, Dorothy continued to work for Fanchon and Marco. Now she was allowed to sing with whomever the master of ceremonies was for that particular evening, like the time she joined Rube Wolfe for an engagement at the Loew's State Theatre in downtown Los Angeles. At one point, she took over the emcee chores herself.

During a San Francisco tour with the Fanchon and Marco unit, Dorothy met Robert Boothe, who performed an adagio-dance act with his sister. Dorothy described him as a "society boy from Pasadena who took up dancing for exercise due to his being overly health-conscious." Boothe and the sixteen-year-old Dorothy became inseparable, to the chagrin of her parents: "My parents didn't approve of me getting involved in a serious relationship at a young age. Definitely not. But eventually my mother told me, 'The two of you are always together, so you might as well get married!' And that's what we did."

Dottie married Boothe in 1927. Life on the road may have been exciting for the young newlywed couple, but they soon learned it wasn't a road paved with riches. Dottie recalled:

"We struggled financially. When you're young and in love, you don't think about tomorrow. But we didn't even think about *today*. Robert was a nice guy, really, but he wanted to live a lifestyle that was beyond our income, as though we were big Broadway stars making big salaries. I can't say we didn't have fun, but we weren't smart about handling what little money we had. I say *we*

**Dorothy with her first husband Robert Boothe in New York in 1928.**

because I allowed Robert to make decisions that weren't in our best interest. I was his wife and back then I thought a wife should support her husband 100 percent. Yeah, I was pretty dumb."

At one point, the couple showed up at Bess' house, broke, tired and hungry: "We ran out of money and we were starving, so we headed to my mother's place. As we sat there wolfing down the meal Mom prepared for us, I looked up and she gave me a dirty look, as if to say, '*I told you so!*'"

Fanchon and Marco were hired by Paramount Pictures to stage a revue number for *Take Me Home* (1928), a silent film starring Bebe Daniels and directed by Marshall Neilan, one of the studio's leading directors. Standing a petite five feet tall, Dorothy was placed at the end of the chorus line. Neilan noticed the smallest and most energetic of the dancing girls, and singled her out. Dorothy said:

"Marshall — or 'Mickey' as everyone called him — called me 'Peanut' because I looked so tiny standing next to all the other chorus girls. One day Mickey said, 'Come here, Peanut. How would you like to do a scene in the picture with Bebe Daniels?' So I said, 'Oh, wouldn't I!' It turned out to be a short scene, but who wouldn't want to make their film debut with Bebe? [She] was one of Hollywood's biggest stars at that time. And she was so sweet to me. Of course neither of us could have imagined we'd be in two more films together [*Rio Rita, Dixiana*] only a couple years down the road.

"Mickey boosted my confidence by telling me that I had talent. And he said, 'When you're in show business it's a tough life, but don't be afraid. Just always do your best.' That inspired me."

Also in the cast was an ex-vaudevillian who was trying to get established in motion pictures: Joseph Evans Brown. Within two years, with the advent of "talking" pictures, Joe E. Brown became one of the screen's most popular comedians, and Dorothy would be his co-star in *Local Boy Makes Good* (1931).

Dorothy continued to do chorus work, but her bit part in *Take Me Home* whetted her appetite for movie roles. She began haunting studio casting offices, to no avail: "I would come home after auditioning and say, 'I knew I could do it, but I didn't get the part.' My grandmother was so sweet; she would say to me, 'Don't forget, when it's your turn, you will get it.'"

At one of the casting offices, Dorothy met George Choos, a producer of musical revues. Impressed by her personality and drive, he told her that he was preparing to produce a collegiate musical-comedy and he assured her she would be a member of the cast. Dorothy felt Choos was just trying to cheer her: "I thought it was the usual foolish air-castle promise, so I never gave it another thought. A full year went by after I had met Choos, when suddenly I received a wire from him, asking me to come to New York."

Dorothy auditioned for Choos, whose "college show" would star prominent band leader Fred Waring and his group, the Pennsylvanians. Dorothy remembered, "By this time, I was fortunate to have quite a lot of experience behind me. There were 250 girls that showed up to try out, and out of all of them, I was one out of two lucky enough to be chosen for the show, *Hello Yourself*."

# Chapter 2

# I Want the World to Know
## *Broadway Baby*

One of the biggest hits on Broadway during the 1927 season was *Good News*, an energetic and tuneful musical-comedy that capitalized on the era's obsession with collegiate life. Its success prompted producer George Choos to mount his own high-spirited college-themed show, *Hello Yourself*, starring one of the nation's most popular bands, Fred Waring and his Pennsylvanians.

Frederick Malcolm Waring was born on June 9, 1900, in Tyrone, Pennsylvania. As a teenager, Waring formed the Waring-McClintock Snap Orchestra with his brother Tom and his friend Poley McClintock. They became local favorites by appearing at a variety of functions, mostly college-oriented. Waring took architectural engineering courses at Penn State University, but gave up his studies when his band — by this time calling themselves Fred Waring's Banjo Orchestra — became successful enough to begin touring.

By the early 1920s, Waring's Pennsylvanians, as they were now known, were one of the most sought-after acts in show business. They were hugely popular on radio and the theatrical circuit, and their RCA Victor recordings were consistent best-sellers. While bandleader Paul Whiteman had been crowned "The King of Jazz," Waring struck a chord with the youth culture of the decade. He was the first bandleader to introduce such props as the megaphone and raccoon coats, further emphasizing his clean-cut college image. With Waring's Pennsylvanians as the main attraction, *Hello Yourself* was a guaranteed hit.

Dorothy packed her bags for New York, bid her husband farewell, and boarded the train with Evalyn Nair, the only other girl selected during Choos' auditions. Dorothy and Evalyn became fast friends and wound up sharing a small apartment on Fiftieth Street.

Dorothy found herself auditioning before Fred Waring without any musical accompaniment to backup her singing or dancing. "I must've had some nerve, but I did it. Fred was just wonderful. I had seen him on stage before working with him, and he was marvelous. I never thought that I had much talent. It was Fred who saw my potential and thought I had personality. He took me under his wing and coached me, taught me phrasing because I didn't think I could sing. He brought me forward and I credit him for my success."

According to Dorothy, the production demanded rigorous training: "Before the opening of the show, we would rehearse for it all day long. Then at nighttime, we would rehearse our dancing. We worked from eight until midnight. Evalyn and I would walk home after rehearsal because we couldn't afford a taxi, and there were times we had to walk barefoot because our shoes were worn right down to the heels due to all our tap dancing practice."

The two women heeded the cautions of their mothers and knew better than to be picked up by strangers, especially Stage Door Johnnies — men who hung around theater exits in hopes of picking up impressionable chorus girls. So Dorothy and Evalyn kept to themselves until they became better acquainted with members of Waring's band, who would drive them home after that point. During her off-hours, Dorothy attended several Broadway shows. "I was lucky to see many of the great Broadway productions of the time. Especially, I will never forget seeing [Florenz] Ziegfeld's great *Show Boat*, which also starred Edna May Oliver whom I would later work with. Fred Waring had bought me a ticket and I went to a matinee by myself. I had never been so thrilled in my life to see a show like that. It was something and I was very impressed. I later got to meet Ziegfeld and he was a very nice man."

*Hello Yourself* opened on October 30, 1928, at the elegant 875-seat Casino Theatre, located at 1404 Broadway (at West 39th Street). The setting for this "musical in two acts" was a college campus, with scenes listed as Gymnasium, Library, and

**Dorothy with Fred Waring, her mentor and the love of her life, in 1928.**

## 2. I Want the World to Know

Grounds of the Westley University. There was more premise than plot — it was simply a excuse for a parade of musical numbers centering on co-eds, frat boys, and Waring's Pennsylvanians. Richard Myers and Leo Robin wrote the songs and Dave Gould handled the choreography. Gould later won Academy Awards for Best Dance Direction for his work on *Folies Bergère* (1935) and *Broadway Melody of 1936* (1935), and was choreographer on *Hips, Hips, Hooray!* (1934), a Wheeler and Woolsey picture that co-starred Dorothy.

Dorothy made her Broadway debut as Sue Swift, a wisecracking co-ed, and led her fellow students in the opening production number, "We Might Play Tiddle De Winks." Her second-act showcase, "I Want the World to Know," involved a peppy high-kick dance that echoed the rhythmic movements of Ann Pennington, who was often called the "consummate flapper." Pennington was known for her "snake hips" routine, a shimmy dance in which her grinding hips mimicked the side-winding movement of a snake. Dorothy recalled, "I loved Ann's snake-hips bit and copied it. I worked it into my stage routines and did it in movies and personal appearances later on."

On opening night, as Dorothy was breezing through her dance number, one of her stocking garters snapped. Due to censorship regulations, displays of bare legs were deemed unacceptable on stage, and Dorothy frantically fidgeted with the stocking to keep it from rolling down, while trying to remain in character and not to disrupt the performance. The audience, however, thought it was part of the act and maintained steady applause during the entire number. "I had no idea my stocking was going to fall," Dorothy said. "It certainly wasn't planned, but when it happened, the audience went crazy. They loved it so much that every night after that I had to keep doing that bit, which wasn't easy. That unmanageable stocking became the hit of the show — more than me!"

Artist John Held, Jr., captured the essence of the Roaring Twenties and the Jazz Age with his illustrations and caricatures of flappers and collegiate types. His work was featured in a variety of high-profile publications, including *The New Yorker*, *Vanity Fair* and *Harper's Bazaar*. Dorothy later remarked, "Since my real name is Marjorie, I became interested in Held's cartoon 'Merely Marjorie, An Awfully Sweet Girl.' So I became Merely Marjorie, with one stocking continually falling down."

Another scene in *Hello Yourself* relied heavily on Dorothy's athletic prowess: "We did a scene where I go into the fraternity house, and the other college kids haze me by putting me in a blanket and throwing me way up, so high in the air I went plain out of sight. I almost touched the ceiling's very hot stage lights. It became one of the biggest hits in the show and the audience practically tore up the seats. They eventually put a little flag up there for me to grab on to so when I came back down, I was waving the flag. It brought down the house.

"One night when they tossed me and I landed, the blanket wasn't large enough to catch me, and I fell six feet. I hit my neck, landing in the sand on my neck, knocking it out of place, and bit not only my tongue but clear through my lip."

Dorothy's hijinks made a favorable impression on audiences and she was eventually given an additional number in the show. *New York Times* drama critic Brooks Atkinson praised her in his review from October 31, 1928: "Miss Dorothy Lee, skilled in Ann Pennington gyrations and gesticulations, a scintillating little person, was a roving spot of light."

The age of silent cinema was rapidly drawing to a close. There had been attempts to produce sound films from the inception of motion pictures, but these experiments had been written off as short-term novelties. However, with the premiere of Warner Brothers' landmark *The Jazz Singer* on October 6, 1927, the idea of "talking" pictures could no longer be dismissed. When Al Jolson, the film's star, uttered the immortal line, "You ain't heard nothin' yet," he served notice to Hollywood and the movie-going public that the recording microphone was here to stay.

*The Jazz Singer* was actually a silent movie with only a handful of sound sequences, but that didn't matter to audiences. The film was a box-office smash, and its follow-up, *The Singing Fool* (1928), another part-talkie starring Jolson, enjoyed even greater success. The overwhelming popularity of Warners' *Lights of New York* (1928), the first "100% All-Talking Picture," triggered a flurry of activity as studios and movie houses scrambled to adapt to the new technology.

RCA (Radio Corporation of America) had developed Photophone, an optical sound (sound-on-film) system, but found that the major motion picture studios had already signed agreements with Western Electric, a subsidiary of A.T.&T. (American Telephone & Telegraph), for sound equipment. So in 1928, RCA acquired a substantial interest in FBO (Film Booking Offices of America, Inc.)—a low-rent distribution-production company that had been churning out inexpensively made westerns, comedies and melodramas—with the intention of producing an all-talking film that would showcase the new Photophone system.

*Syncopation*, FBO's first talkie production, was filmed at the Pathé Studio on Long Island, New York. Fred Waring and his Pennsylvanians were still appearing in *Hello Yourself* when director Bert Glennon signed them to perform musical numbers in *Syncopation*. Glennon also encouraged Dorothy to do a screen test, which landed her a supporting role.

Production began in November; *Syncopation* was shot during the day to accommodate the evening performances of *Hello Yourself.* Despite the technical difficulties associated with early sound recording—the microphones were so sensitive that the slightest clank of a woman's bracelet or a creak in the floor would require a scene to be re-shot—the film was completed within a four-week shooting schedule. Much of the script was written during production, and Dorothy's minor role was expanded as shooting progressed.

Based on *Stepping High*, a novel by Gene Markey (who also wrote the dialogue), *Syncopation* was pretty old-fashioned and lugubrious even by the most undemanding standards of the era. Benny Darrell (Bobby Watson) and his wife Fleurette "Flo" Sloane (Barbara Bennett, the younger sister of actresses Constance and Joan) are an adagio dance team who split up, personally and professionally, when the social-climbing Flo abandons the underachieving Benny for millionaire playboy Alexander Winston (Ian Hunter).

In their comedy-relief supporting roles, Morton Downey plays Lew Lewis, a happy-go-lucky crooner, and Dorothy plays Peggy, Lew's flapper girlfriend; like their castmates, they give clumsy, unpolished performances. Downey was never much of a thespian, Dorothy was still a neophyte, and both deliver their lines in an overly emphatic fashion, as though they're projecting their voices to the back row of a cavernous theater. Nevertheless, their lighthearted antics provide a welcome and much-needed respite from the aggressively maudlin proceedings. Dorothy's ding-a-ling character harkens back to her apprenticeship with Homer Dickinson, as Peggy remains clueless to the tormented melodramatics swirling around her, much to Lew's exasperation.

One scene added during production was the song "Do Something," composed specifically for the film by Bud Green and Sam H. Stept. Dorothy sits atop a piano and sings to Downey, delivering the number in the style of the quintessential coquettish flapper. Downey joins in, and their cute duet is easily the highlight of the picture.

It's hardly Dorothy's best film, but *Syncopation* gives us an idea of what she was like on stage in *Hello Yourself*: a kewpie-doll charmer whose exuberance won over audiences and critics, rendering them charitably blind to the very rough edges of her acting abilities.

Making *Syncopation* was an experience Dorothy never forgot: "I was so excited to be in my first picture. Morton Downey fell in love with Barbara Bennett while on the set. They got married [on January 28, 1929] and had a number of kids. [One of them, Morton Downey, Jr., became a controversial TV talk-show host during the 1980s.] Downey used to use the most awful language, every four-letter word you could imagine. Even though I was in show business, I didn't

**Dorothy and Morton Downey sing "Do Something" in *Syncopation* (1929).**

know all the bad language yet. He was older than I was and, knowing I was a naïve kid, he did it on purpose just to shock me, and boy, did he. I would go to Fred and tell him about it. Fred told me, 'Don't let it get to you.' Eventually I learned to let it just roll off. Downey could be difficult to work with, but he was a really nice man."

After *Hello Yourself* closed on Broadway on January 12, 1929, after 87 performances, the show went on the road, touring in Chicago and Detroit before returning to New York. "I owe a great deal to Fred for getting as far as I did," Dorothy enthused. "When I started making good, nearly every manager in town wanted me as their client. Fred told me, "Don't pay attention to any of them." Then he got his own manager, John O'Connor, to manage me, and I always got marvelous constructive criticism."

It was becoming obvious to everyone that Waring's interest in Dorothy was not limited solely to career counseling, nor did she look upon Fred as just her mentor. Their open displays of affection revealed a serious love affair, one that had developed in spite of their respective marital commitments. In 1923 Waring had married socialite Dorothy McAteer, whom he met while his band was performing at a party. Her aristocratic family was vehemently opposed to their relationship so they postponed their nuptials until he became better established. By that time, however, Waring had misgivings about solidifying his union with McAteer. Nevertheless, he abided by his promise and married McAteer, who took zero interest in his career.

With his marriage already on shaky ground and his romance with Dorothy blossoming, Waring divorced McAteer in 1929. Dorothy found herself in the same predicament. Her time away from Robert Boothe had taken its toll on their relationship: "I had fallen madly in love with Fred, as he did with me, and our feelings transcended the fact that he still had a wife and I still had a husband. Most people would say that a marriage vow is a marriage vow, and that cheating is cheating, but when Fred and I started getting serious, we were up front about it with our spouses.

"Robert had stayed out in California when I was in New York. He did come to visit with me, but by then it was too late. We had our differences, but I can't fault him because I'm the one who fell in love with somebody else. I

In this 1930s publicity shot, Dorothy is wearing the engagement ring Fred Waring gave her a few years previous.

know it hurt him terribly, but he realized that it was only a matter of time before we would have gotten divorced anyway, regardless of what had developed between me and Fred. We did manage to part on good terms, all things considered, and we did remain friends. He went on to become a professor in San Luis Obispo [California]. Could you have imagined *me* being married to a professor? It wasn't long after I divorced Robert that Fred and I got engaged."

Dorothy's engagement ring from Waring was handcrafted by the jeweler to their specifications. It consisted of blue Lapis and green Onyx lined with diamonds. It was a ring that Dorothy treasured and wore for the remainder of her life, despite subsequent marriages. She can be spotted wearing it in publicity photographs and, mostly, in her later films.

*Syncopation* premiered on March 3, 1929, a later date than originally scheduled. After the film had been completed, RCA merged with the Keith-Orpheum theater circuit, forming RKO Radio Pictures. Finalizing the business arrangements meant delaying the release of *Syncopation*, and Metro-Goldwyn-Mayer's *The Broadway Melody* wound up beating it to theater screens by a month; this made *Syncopation* look even shoddier by comparison. (*The Broadway Melody* also wound up being the first musical to win a Best Picture Academy Award.)

The critics hardly greeted *Syncopation* with open arms. *Variety*'s review was typical: "As a story picture it isn't so good, as the tale is the usual one nowadays of the film musical comedies.... The star of the picture, were performance naming the star, is [Morton] Downey.... [H]e is the picture's natural standout ... Downey kicks in with [comedy relief] through cracks to a dumb-dora sweetheart (Dorothy Lee)."

Regardless of its delayed release and lukewarm reception from critics, *Syncopation* was embraced by the movie-going public. It broke all house records at New York's Hippodrome Theatre, where it played for two weeks. The novelty of seeing (and hearing) an all-talking, all-singing picture is what attracted audiences. Quality had nothing to do with its success.

*Syncopation* exemplifies the drawbacks inherent in many early talkie productions. The camerawork is static (there's no hint of the fluid cinematography that graced silent cinema), the editing is choppy, and the performances are hopelessly stilted, although the actors are ill-served by the cliché-ridden, overwrought dialogue and plot. Waring's Pennsylvanians receive prominent billing, but are only seen in two sequences, performing a total of seven numbers. This footage was photographed crudely and unimaginatively, and none of it is integral to the storyline. Yet these shortcomings were readily dismissed by audiences enthralled by these newfangled talking pictures. Dorothy recalled, "Some people felt talkies were just a fad and that the public would tire of them once the novelty wore off. I can't say that I instinctively knew talkies would last, but even in those early days I knew that you couldn't give an audience a taste of something they like and then immediately take it away from them. The audience, not the critics, determines what's going to stick around."

Lackluster reviews didn't put a damper on Dorothy's excitement about her first significant movie role: "I'll never forget how thrilled I was when *Syncopation* premiered. I was so proud to take my grandmother and the rest of the family. They got a big kick out of it."

Another person who got a big kick out of *Syncopation*—primarily Dorothy's performance in it—was Broadway star Bert Wheeler, who was preparing to appear in the film adaptation of the hit musical-comedy *Rio Rita*.

# Chapter 3

# Sweetheart, We Need Each Other
## *Boys Meet Girl*

Of the many people who provided Dorothy with advice and opportunities, three in particular had the greatest impact on her professional career. The first was Homer Dickinson. Next was Fred Waring. Last, but certainly not least, was Bert Wheeler.

Albert Jerome Wheeler was born April 7, 1895, in Paterson, New Jersey. Although he came from a non-theatrical background, he developed a keen interest in show business at a very young age. Bert, as he was called by his aunt, worked his way from being usher at the Paterson Opera House to performing in Gus Edwards's *Kid Kabaret*. Edwards, a New York–based vaudeville impresario, specialized in revues that showcased young talent and he played a pivotal role in launching the careers of such future stars as Eddie Cantor, Groucho Marx, and George Jessel.[1] By the age of sixteen, Bert was already a seasoned veteran with notable singing and dancing abilities. He appeared in New York stock company productions such as *Mutt and Jeff* (1912) and comic operas from *The Firefly* (1913) to *When Dreams Come True* (1914).

In 1915 he married a pretty chorine named Margaret Kudner Grae; as Bert and Betty Wheeler, they devised a fifteen-minute act that included a routine called "Charlie Chaplin and a Girl," highlighting Bert's uncanny impersonation of the comic legend. Chaplin himself was so taken with Bert's impersonation that on a photograph of Bert (wearing Chaplin's Little Tramp garb) he inscribed, "To my worthy imitator, Mr. Wheeler. I can hardly tell myself from you. Sincerely yours, Charlie Chaplin." Bert used the photograph as a promotional item, reprinting it in the form of flyers to pass out to theatergoers. Warmly received by audiences and critics alike, Bert and Betty established themselves as vaudeville headliners.

But by 1918 the sameness of their act resulted in dwindling bookings. Bert sent Betty to Chicago to spend time with her family while he teamed with Tom Moran for an act called "Me and Mickey" and toured the Orpheum Vaudeville circuit. The partnership allowed Bert to hone his improvisational skills as a full-fledged comedian. When he sprained his ankle during a rehearsal, Bert hit upon the idea of delivering his routine while lying on his stomach. The impromptu bit went over so well with audiences that it became a staple of Bert's repertoire.

Bert's professional relationship with Moran began to deteriorate due to Moran's heavy drinking, and in less than a year, their partnership came to an end. Bert reunited with Betty and incorporated audience-tested "Me and Mickey" material into their new routine, "Bits of Everything." This time, the Wheelers became a hugely popular vaudeville attraction. Harold Lloyd, one of the biggest movie stars of the silent era, took notice of Bert and wanted to sign him to a contract. Bert turned down the offer, preferring to keep his partnership with Betty intact.

Bert and Betty caught the eye of Ned Wayburn, the influential choreographer of *The Ziegfeld Follies*. Spearheaded by famed impresario Florenz Ziegfeld, each production of the *Follies* (1907–1931) presented the cream of the crop of Broadway entertainment, wrapped in eye-popping, opulent settings that had become the Ziegfeld trademark. Stage performers of the era felt that they hadn't truly "made it" in the business until they secured a coveted position in a Ziegfeld show, and few acts were deemed worthy of the Ziegfeld stamp of approval. Thanks to Wayburn, the Wheelers were now among the elite, signed for the 1923 edition of the *Follies*. This guaranteed their star status for the next couple of years.

During a 1926 vaudeville tour, Betty abruptly dissolved the act and the marriage, leaving Bert for another man. A dejected Bert could have not had any idea that this break-up would set the stage for the beginning of a new, even more successful professional partnership.

With ordinary looks and a smart-alecky style of delivery, Robert Woolsey was the polar opposite of cute, lovable Bert Wheeler, which is what made them an ideal pair. Robert Rolla Woolsey was born on August 14, 1888, in Carbondale, Illinois (for years, his birthplace was cited as Oakland, California, but recently uncovered documents indicate otherwise). He grew up in poverty; the deaths of his father and four siblings forced Robert and his younger brother Charles to take odd jobs to support their mother. While working at a stable, a jockey named Wee-Wee Higgins introduced Robert to the world of horse racing. A broken leg ended Woolsey's days as a jockey; ironically, the horse that threw him, Pink Star, went on to win the Kentucky Derby in 1907.

From 1908 to 1909 Robert worked as a bellboy at the Hotel Sinton in Cincinnati, Ohio. It was there that he was brought into contact with actors, one of whom asked the lanky, homely young man, "What are you doing here? You have the face of a comedian!" Woolsey began honing his craft as an actor, touring in vaudeville across the country and overseas (trips to the British Empire and the Orient), and working his way up from stock company productions before establishing himself as a musical-comedy headliner on Broadway. By then, Robert had taken to wearing horn-rimmed glasses and smoking cigars, which would become his trademarks. He had appropriated the glasses-and-cigar look from fellow comedian Walter Catlett; there were similarities between both men, despite the fact that Catlett was about a half-foot taller and possessed a larger frame than Woolsey's slight build.[2]

## 3. Sweetheart, We Need Each Other

Woolsey's role in the Broadway musical *The Right Girl* (1921) garnered good reviews. That same year he married a dancer named Mignonne Park Reed. "Mignonne was as homely as Bob," Dorothy remembered. "They were a perfect pair. Mignonne was a wild gal when she got drunk occasionally at parties. Although she had been long retired from show business, she would think she was a dancer again, and get on top of the tables and do real high kicks. Bob would say, 'Don't mind her, the old gal is just stewed to the gills.' She was a riot!"

Woolsey appeared in Broadway shows ranging from *The Blue Kitten* (1922) to *Poppy* (1923) starring legendary funnyman W.C. Fields. Then Woolsey was cast in Florenz Ziegfeld's stage production of *Rio Rita*, which teamed him with Bert Wheeler.

*Rio Rita* opened at the brand-new Ziegfeld Theatre on February 2, 1927. Critics and audiences were captivated by the music and hijinks presented in the uniquely extravagant Ziegfeld fashion. Set in Mexico and Texas, the escapist storyline, typical of '20s Broadway musicals, dealt with Texas Ranger Jim Stewart's (J. Harold Murray) pursuit of a notorious bandit known as "The Kinkajou." Along the way, Stewart falls in love with Rita Ferguson (Ethelind Terry), a.k.a. Rio Rita, a señorita whose brother (Walter Petrie) may very well be the criminal he's looking for. A lighter subplot involving Wheeler and Woolsey was loosely intertwined with the main story: Bootlegger Chick Bean (Wheeler) marries his new love, a cabaret girl named Dolly (Ada May), only to be notified by his shifty attorney Ed Lovett (Woolsey) that the divorce from the previous Mrs. Bean (Noel Francis) is not final. All of this was simply an excuse for a series of comic set pieces and music interludes. Freed from the responsibility of having to propel the major plotline, Wheeler and Woolsey incorporated surefire bits of business they had honed (separately) from their stage experience. Bert and Bob established a rapport that made it seem as though they had been partners for years.

The play created the template for the characters Wheeler and Woolsey continued to portray for the remainder of their partnership: Bert was the genial, not-so-innocent innocent (parodying the musical-show juvenile leads of the era) whose affiliation for and friendship with the cigar-chomping, wisecracking Bob wound up landing both of them in hot water. (Bob would punctuate the predicaments they got into with his trademark cry of "Whoa-ohhhh!") To offer a concise description of the team, it was like pairing Eddie Cantor with Groucho Marx. It is unfair, of course, to generalize these four distinctive talents in such an offhanded manner, yet the comparison is valid. More to the point: Wheeler and Woolsey weren't a traditional straight man-comedian combo. They were two comedians whose comedic styles and personalities complemented each other perfectly. That both were adept at singing and dancing was the icing on the cake.

After moving to the Lyric Theatre on December 26, 1927, and finally to the Majestic Theatre on March 12, 1928, *Rio Rita* closed on April 7, 1928, after 494 performances. It was popular enough to have run for another year, yet Florenz Ziegfeld opted to sell the motion picture rights to Joseph Schnitzler, the president of RKO Radio Pictures. Out of the entire Broadway cast, Wheeler and Woolsey were the only ones recruited to repeat their roles for the film adaptation, which was to be produced on a lavish scale (with the final third of the film photographed in the early two-strip Technicolor process). For the title role, production chief William LeBaron selected Bebe Daniels, a choice that surprised many in Hollywood.

Earlier in the decade, Daniels was one of Paramount's top stars. With the coming of sound, however, the studio lost interest in her; they kept her inactive and didn't even bother to test her for the new medium, so she bought out her contract. At the time LeBaron signed Daniels for *Rio Rita*, she was considered a has-been. But LeBaron, a former producer at Paramount, knew something about Daniels that other Hollywood insiders didn't: She possessed a lovely singing voice. (LeBaron had heard her sing at private gatherings and knew her soprano voice would be perfectly suited for the musical.)

During pre-production for *Rio Rita*, Wheeler saw *Syncopation* and was captivated by Dorothy Lee's performance. He became dead set on having her play his leading lady. Dorothy recalled, "I had heard of Bert Wheeler before because he was already a big [Broadway] star, more so than Woolsey, although I had never seen either of them perform. Bert sat through a screening of *Syncopation*, and caught my name in the credits. He thought, 'I have to find this little girl for my picture.' For the longest time he couldn't find me and wasn't sure how to go about it. One night while he was standing up at one of those bars where all the actors hung out—'speakeasies' as they were called back then—Bert got into a conversation with a gentleman: 'I've just seen the cutest little girl named Dorothy Lee in *Syncopation*, and I've got to find her to play opposite me in *Rio Rita*.' The other fellow told him, 'Why, no kidding, I do a big number with her in *Hello Yourself*.'

"So Bert came over to meet me and we had lunch together to discuss it. Bert told me how he had just been signed to star in this picture, and how I should tell my agent to contact RKO because he had just found the perfect girl to be his leading lady. I had to finish the run of *Hello Yourself* first, but after that I went to Hollywood and signed a contract with RKO, with a starting salary of $450 a week which later increased to $1,000. [That] was pretty darn good in the Depression days. I also requested that a special clause be added to my contract, so that while I wasn't making pictures, I could still do live stage work with Fred Waring. They allowed that, and it was just great!"

When *Hello Yourself* concluded its run, Dorothy and Fred temporarily parted company as she headed to her home state: "I had been recently divorced when I started with RKO, so I moved in with my mother, stepfather and grandmother. It was much more fun to be at home with them than on my own, plus they took excellent care of me, cooking my meals and everything else. It was so nice, and it made me happy to be with them. RKO [located at 780 Gower Street in Hollywood] was only about a 15-minute drive from where they lived, which made my commute to the studio very convenient for me."

Upon her return to California, Dorothy experienced one of the perks of being part of the film community: "My agent took me to my first big Hollywood party—it was at Buster Keaton's Italian-style mansion which he had built for his wife Natalie

[Talmadge]. Even by Hollywood standards, this house was *huge*. I was only eighteen years old and still pretty green, so I was very intimidated. I was surrounded by all this luxury and all these fancy people, and I never felt so out-of-place in my life. I tried to hide out in the women's bathroom, only this was no ordinary bathroom. It was a separate room unto itself, with a waiting area filled with those plush, circular seats you see in hotel lobbies. It was all so overwhelming that I started to cry. A woman took pity on me and asked me what was the matter. I told her that I was a nobody who really didn't belong at this party, and she began comforting me, assuring me that no one there was judging me. That helped calm me down, and as I started to regain my composure, I realized that this nice woman was Fay Wray.[3] She asked me about myself and I told her about my experiences on stage. She wound up coaxing me to do my 'snake hips' dance, and before long, I was teaching it to her and other women in the bathroom! It was a riot, and I can never thank Fay enough for treating me with such kindness and compassion.

"I'll never forget Buster Keaton. He was the sweetest, nicest man that you could ever know. He was famous for being the Great Stone Face, but in private he would be very funny. At the party, we all gathered in the family room. For Buster's grand entrance, he appeared at the top of the stairs. Then he fell all the way down the entire flight! Everyone just about fainted from shock — you would have thought he was killed. But then he leapt to his feet, perfectly fine, and said, 'Gotcha!' And then he roared with laughter, having fooled us. He loved to laugh and his smile would light up the room, but the minute anyone started taking photos, he'd get that frozen look on his face. He didn't want to spoil his public image.

"I thought Natalie was a bit on the snooty side. But not Buster. He was remarkably down-to-earth for someone who was such a big star. I loved him, and we would become very close friends."

Production on the film adaptation of *Rio Rita* began June 26, 1929, with Daniels and John Boles (on loan from Universal) essaying the lead roles and Bert, Bob and Dorothy providing comedy relief. Budgeted at $675,000 — an ambitious gamble for the young studio — the film would capture the opulent pageantry of the Ziegfeld production. Content-wise, however, it was not an exact replication of the stage show; some of the original musical numbers were deleted including Woolsey's first-act intro "The Best Little Lover in Town"; Wheeler's second-act closer "Moonshine"; and "The Jumping Bean," a number performed by Ada May (as Dolly) and the Ziegfeld Dancers.

The role of Dolly was a much better showcase than the role of Peggy in *Syncopation* had been; she had three song-and-dance numbers and the chance to share comedic exchanges with Bert and Bob. Onscreen and off, Dorothy recalled, they shared a genuine camaraderie: "I met Bob Woolsey for the first time on the *Rio Rita* set, and he was nice, but a bit of a feisty fighter, the caustic type like you see in his pictures. He always had to be in control and wanted to run the show. When you were in a scene with him, you kind of just did it his way. He made a pass at me once and I rebuffed him. He caught on that I wasn't one of those gullible bimbos he was used to conquering, and we got along fine after that. He would still make passes at me but they were in a joking manner and we would both laugh about it.

"Bert was a very sweet and dear man, and much more laid-back than Bob. He and I would collaborate on our songs and dances, and discuss the best ways to do them. We would ask each other, 'What do you think? Should we do it like this or like that?' So we always worked it out to where we were in perfect agreement with what we did, and it was a lot of fun to do. I really liked both of them. They were very talented, and it was an honor for me to be able to just work with them. As soon as we became friendly with each other, we were on a first-name basis. To me, Bert was always Bert, but I frequently called Bob 'Woolsey.' I don't know why, exactly; it might have been because I felt closer to Bert. Bert always called me 'Lee,' and after a while so did Bob. Then the Hollywood crowd began calling me 'Lee' instead of Dorothy, Dottie or Dot. Bert, Bob, everyone called me Lee. It just stuck."

Dorothy's scenes opposite Bert are quite charming, with Dorothy proving to be a winsome romantic foil, ably setting up the punchlines for Bert to deliver. "I owe a great debt of gratitude to Bert for coaching me with my lines and helping to put me at ease," she recalled. "Our director, Luther Reed, left the handling of the musical numbers to others, but when it came to dialogue, he wanted us to stick to what was in the script. He didn't want any deviation. I certainly appreciated what a big opportunity this was for me, but I also realized we weren't performing Shakespeare either. I could understand if it was a joke or the set-up to a joke because those sort of things have to be exact in order to work. But I didn't see what the big deal was if I said, 'I'll see you in a minute' instead of 'I'll be right back.' It sure made a difference to [Reed], because he wanted it word for word."

Even though he was on the opposite coast, Fred Waring also offered his assistance. Dorothy revealed, "While Fred remained in New York, he helped me so much with my singing. I still don't think that I can sing, but every night he would call me on the telephone and I would rehearse with his pianist for the next day's shooting. He also taught me phrasing. It was just wonderful!"

In sharp contrast to the primitive, studio-bound production techniques of *Syncopation*, much of *Rio Rita* was filmed on location, a grueling experience for Dorothy and other participants: "For the opening [sequence], I had a darling song-and-tap dance number titled 'The Kinkajou.' A great big set was built out on location in the San Fernando Valley where it was hot as the devil. It felt like [it was] 120 degrees! Why they didn't allow us to work in an indoor set, I'll never know. They built a wooden stage for us to dance on and because sound recording was new they placed this black powder on the dance floor, which was to muffle the impact of the sound of our feet hitting the floor. With the huge lights above our head, it made it even hotter. I did the number about 15 times. They kept a nurse on the set because four or five of the chorus girls had already fainted. I never fainted, thank God. I don't know why, I guess because I was so young and healthy.

"My cousin was always around the set. Her boyfriend, Homer Watson, was the

## 3. Sweetheart, We Need Each Other

**Dorothy (front row, center) and the Pearl Eaton Girls perform "The Kinkajou" in *Rio Rita* (1929).**

prop and costume man, and to make matters worse, he played a dirty trick on me. Part of my outfit included a cowboy hat, and he gave me one that was too large for my head. He made me so mad. I can still remember it falling in my face and how I struggled to keep it up. It was all fun once it was through, and afterwards Homer told me, 'Now you'll never forget me.' And I never have."

No one viewing the finished product would have suspected how the dancers really felt: "When we were done dancing and the director shouted 'Cut!,' we were dripping with sweat and our arms and legs were covered in that black powder. How it did not show up on the screen I'll never know."

Dorothy's second number was a duet with Bert, "Are You There?," in which the lovers, occupying separate hotel rooms, lament that they can't be together until Bert's divorce becomes final.

In the Technicolor portion of the film, Bert and Dorothy perform "Sweetheart, We Need Each Other," which they deliver with lyrical earnestness before bursting into a rousing acrobatic dance routine. It remained one of Dorothy's favorite numbers, especially since she and Bert partially choreographed it themselves: "That was a darling number. Bert was good at physical comedy and he knew I was a bit of a tomboy, so we worked all these stunts into the routine. Bert had performed a similar version on stage but the one we did together we worked out the dance ourselves, especially the part at the end where we tumble over each other and I support him on my back and we sing the last line of the song. It was cute!"

Bert, Bob, Dorothy and Helen Kaiser later reprise the song; Dorothy recalled with anguish: "We had a hell of a time shooting that scene. We were all sitting atop a ledge on the set of what is supposed to be a ship, and at the end of the number we fall backwards, overboard into the water. I will never forget that scene because we had to do it over and over again, at least four times straight — in the middle of the night! You see, from 8 P.M. to 6 A.M. was the only time that RKO could rent Warner Brothers' Technicolor cameras since [Warners] was one of the first studios to own a color camera. A third of *Rio Rita* was shot in color, so we would work all night long.

"After we had finished our song, we fell backwards into a man-made, four-foot ditch of ice cold water. Since it was filmed once again outside — at night when the temperatures dropped as dramatically as they rose in the day — the temperature was only 35 degrees! They had four duplicate costumes for each of us in case we had to redo the scene and, boy, did we. We had to dry off and do it all over again. I remember it so well because each time I hit the water I thought, 'I'm never going to live through this.' It was that cold."

Production was completed on July 20, and *Rio Rita* opened in theaters on October 6, garnering overwhelmingly favorable reviews. *Photoplay* raved, "In practically every respect it is the finest of the screen musicals.... Despite very strong competition Bebe Daniels, in the name role, is the most glowing personality.... John Boles' glorious tenor is heard to advantage.... Comedy is of the sure-fire, riotous type. Bert Wheeler and Robert Woolsey are principal funmakers.... George Renavent, Don Alvarado and Dorothy Lee are also outstanding." *Variety* found the film to be "perfect," with special praise for the comedy element: "In comedy it's Bert Wheeler [with] Robert Woolsey ... while Dorothy Lee, not so long ago in pictures and formerly with Waring's Pennsylvanians stands second to Miss Daniels."

The critical and box-office triumph of *Rio Rita* was a boon to its participants. For RKO, it proved that the neophyte operation could successfully compete with the other Hollywood studios. For Bebe Daniels, it brought her back to the front ranks of movie stardom. For Wheeler and Woolsey, it firmly established them as popular film comedians. And for Dorothy, it gave her more exposure and recognition than she had ever dreamed of.

On October 29, three weeks after *Rio Rita* was released, the Wall Street stock market crashed. During the decade, playing the stock market was considered an easy way to get rich quick and everyone jumped on the bandwagon. The investor only needed to put ten percent down in order to purchase stock shares ("buying on margin" as it was called), but building a financial empire based on a shaky foundation of borrowed money created a system that was doomed to collapse — and it did. On "Black Tuesday," interest rates soared and investors who had believed they were solvent found themselves bankrupt. "The stock market crash was horrible," Dorothy remembered. "It ruined so many lives and triggered the Great Depression. I was fortunate in that I didn't play the market because I didn't start making big money until after the crash. And I was lucky enough to work steadily during a pretty bleak period in this country."

Despite the Wall Street catastrophe, *Rio Rita* went on to become one of the highest-grossing movies of the year. Encouraged by this box-office response, William LeBaron suggested that RKO find another vehicle to showcase Wheeler and Woolsey. *The Ramblers*, which ran on Broadway for 289 performances in 1926 and '27, was an ideal property for the new comedy team: A frothy romp with just enough plot

Dorothy's first Hollywood publicity portrait, sent to fans who requested a picture of the new movie star.

upon which to hang comedy routines and song-and-dance numbers (the music and lyrics were by Bert Kalmar and Harry Ruby, seasoned tunesmiths who were equally adept at composing both romantic and comedic songs). *The Ramblers* starred Bobby Clark and Paul McCullough, Broadway favorites whose style bore a certain resemblance to Bert and Bob's partnership, although Bobby and Paul were an established team long before Bert and Bob appeared in *Rio Rita*.

The storyline was restructured to bring the comedy relief characters (called Professor Cunningham and Sparrow in the play) to the forefront, providing greater opportunities for tomfoolery. The book for the play had been written by Guy Bolton, Bert Kalmar and Harry Ruby. It was adapted for the screen by Cyrus Wood, with unaccredited contributions by Roscoe "Fatty" Arbuckle, the once-popular silent-screen comedian whose career was derailed by a murder scandal in 1922. (Arbuckle was acquitted, but his career never fully recovered.) Some of the original songs were dropped, while others were added to better suit Bert, Bob and Dorothy's prominence in the picture.

With the title changed to *Radio Revels* ("Radio" referring to "Radio Pictures"), production began on January 27, 1930. Since the romantic leads were not the main focus, it was pointless to cast someone of the stature of Bebe Daniels or John Boles in those parts, so the studio recruited lesser-known contract players June Clyde and Hugh Trevor. Dorothy later recalled, "The happiest thing about casting June in that role was that we became best friends for life. She was the sweetest, most loyal gal I ever knew."

The plot, such as it is, finds Professor Cunningham (Woolsey) and his cohort Sparrow (Wheeler), penniless con artists passing themselves off as fortune tellers, trying to gain favor among the wealthy socialites vacationing near the Mexican border. As the Professor zeroes in on a particularly gullible target, Fannie Furst (Jobyna Howland, serving as Margaret Dumont to Woolsey's Groucho Marx), Sparrow becomes smitten with Anita (Dorothy), an American girl who has been raised by gypsies.

Fannie tries to push her niece Ruth Chester (June Clyde) into a relationship with the oily Baron de Camp (Ivan Lebedeff), but Ruth only has eyes for Billy Shannon (Hugh Trevor), a struggling aviator. When the baron hires gypsies to kidnap Ruth and take her across the Mexican border, Billy, Sparrow, and the Professor ride to the rescue.

Compared to *Rio Rita*, Dorothy's participation this time around is minimal (she's off-screen for long passages), although she does appear in two key musical numbers. "I Love You So Much," written for the film, is a charming Bert-Dorothy duet with a sly streak of humor. Dorothy refuses to kiss Bert until he gives her a bite of his apple; when he finally does, she gives him a passionate kiss, prompting Bert to grab an entire basket full of the fruit. By the conclusion of the song, Bert and Dorothy are physically spent, surrounded by a pile of apple cores. The song became a hit, and Dorothy's picture appeared on the sheet music. In later years, Bert Wheeler noted that "I Love You So Much" was a song that people would often associate him with.

The film contained Technicolor sequences, among them Dorothy's main number, "Dancing the Devil Away." Reprimanded by the gypsy queen (Marguerita Padilla) for associating with Sparrow, Anita is brought before the gypsy camp to purge herself of evil influences. The scene switches from black-and-white to color as Dorothy, now wearing a skimpy, shimmering outfit, launches into an invigorating dance number, displaying her agility and high-kicking skills. Presented in the style of a stage revue (echoing Dorothy's days with Fanchon and Marco), it's an exhilarating interlude that comes out of left field — in a motion picture where practically everything comes out of left field.

One of Dorothy's most vivid memories of the production involved a scene in which Julius (Mitchell Lewis), the leader of the band of gypsies, hurls knives at Anita: "I was leaning against a wooden board, and Mitchell was supposed to be throwing knives at me. The knives weren't actually being thrown at me. There was a professional knife-thrower on set and they had it all rigged to make it look real. While we were coming off of a lunch break, I met up with the professional. He engaged me in conversation, and facetiously said, 'I bet you're afraid to let me throw these knives at you.' Being the crazy nut that I am, I have never turned down a dare and shot back, 'Oh no,

## 3. Sweetheart, We Need Each Other

"Dancing the Devil Away" was Dorothy's big solo number, filmed in Technicolor, in *The Cuckoos* (1930).

I'm not! Why don't you go ahead and throw them at me?' So he did. Our producer, Bill LeBaron, just happened to walk on the set and saw what was going on. He just about hit the roof: 'What the hell is the matter with you? Don't let me catch you doing anything like this again!' I'm sure he was very concerned about my safety, but the producer in him probably thought, 'If she gets killed, we've wasted all that footage.' By the way, the knives never touched me."

Although advance press announcements still referred to it as *Radio Revels*, the film's title was changed to *The Cuckoos* by the time it was released on May 4, 1930. While not as lavish as *Rio Rita*, *The Cuckoos* is a better representation of a typical 1920s Broadway musical comedy, the sort that tickled the funnybone and didn't overtax the brain cells, sending the audience home humming some of the tunes. It was well-received by critics; the *Photoplay* review echoed the general sentiments of others: "Check your critical goggles and roar at this nonsensical musical comedy.... It's a big show, too, with all the trimmings.... Great for spring fever." Dorothy was singled out in several reviews, despite (in some instances, *because* of) her limited screen time. *Variety* enthused: "She has an incisive manner of putting her voice over whether speaking or singing and it just fits the screen, besides the girl has ginger and personality." The *Hollywood News* stated: "Little Dorothy Lee almost runs away with the feminine acting honors as a petite little gypsy girl."

The reviewer for *Film Spectator* felt she was the most noteworthy aspect of the film: "Fairly good entertainment.... However, not by any stretch of the imagination could it be called a motion picture. The advent of sound in motion pictures has produced many strange anomalies, and *The Cuckoos* is one of them.... The hit of the picture, to me at least, was Dorothy Lee, who had a part in *Rio Rita* very similar to the one she had in this. However, in *Rio Rita* she danced and sang; in this she is merely present in the picture [where was this reviewer during "I Love You So Much" and "Dancing the Devil Away"?].... [H]er personality is such a compelling one that she is an outstanding member of the cast. RKO could do no better than build up this girl to a place where she would be making them a great deal of money."

RKO was indeed interested in making "a great deal of money" and signed Bert, Bob and Dorothy to long-term contracts. Before starting their next picture, Dorothy exercised the clause in her contract to work again with Fred Waring: "Fred brought his whole orchestra from New York to California to do a wonderful show called *Rah Rah Daze*, which was written specifically to feature me. I was thrilled and we had a great time."

Written by Francis Drake "Pat" Ballard and Waring, *Rah Rah Daze* relied heavily on the collegiate theme that had worked so well in *Hello Yourself*. It was set at "Wooster College" and Waring starred as Freddie Frey, a freshman who aspired to become the leader of the college orchestra. As the female lead, Dorothy played co-ed Dorothy May, the "vivacious pepster" who romances Freddie.

*Rah Rah Daze* opened at the Mason Opera House in Los Angeles. There was a sellout crowd for the whole week, breaking the house record of $27,000. It garnered favorable reviews; the *L.A. Evening Express* called it "entertainment calculated to be fast, melodious and devastating." However, the best review Dorothy received came from one of her childhood idols: "I never forgot the day Gloria Swanson, whom I idolized, came to see the show, and sent a note back that she wanted to meet me. It was the thrill of my life, and I was so stunned. She came backstage and said, 'I just loved the show, and had to tell you how cute and adorable I think you were.' Can you believe it? I had admired her for years and now here she was admiring me! Fred and I were practically falling over each other. We were amazed."

On March 24, 1930—two days after *Rah Rah Daze* opened—production began on *Dixiana*, which reunited Bert, Bob and Dorothy with *Rio Rita* castmate Bebe Daniels and director Luther Reed. However, it was not the film that was originally planned. As Dorothy explained, "Our next picture was supposed to be *Babes in Toyland*, based on the [Victor Herbert] operetta. I was going to appear with Bert and Bob, of course, and the studio was thinking about having Irene Dunne [as the feminine singing lead] and Edna May Oliver in it too. Edna would have made a great Mother Goose. I would have loved to have played a character like Little Miss Muffet."

The basic problem with the operetta, in terms of adapting it for the movies, was that it had no plot. It was a three-act revue featuring storybook characters and Herbert's musical score. Dorothy remarked, "Anne Caldwell was going to adapt the script, but RKO never followed through with it. Instead, they brought us together for *Dixiana*, which turned out to be a real bomb! [*Babes in Toyland*] had such a beautiful music score. Whenever I hear 'Toyland,' I can't help thinking about what might have been."[4]

In an attempt to recapture the successful elements of *Rio Rita*, RKO unfortunately settled for a poor carbon copy. Although great care was lavished upon the physical aspects (it's an exceptionally handsome production and is cinematically more proficient than *Rio Rita* and *The Cuckoos*), the soggy script undermined the entire endeavor. It's set in New Orleans during the 1840s, with top-billed Bebe Daniels as Dixiana Caldwell, a circus performer who falls in love with plantation heir Carl Van Horn, played by Metropolitan Opera star Everett Marshall. Dixiana is shunned by Carl's wealthy society circle, and their romance is further complicated by the treachery of no-account gambler Royal Montague (Ralf Harolde), who has designs on Dixiana. Mired in this maudlin plotline are Bert and Bob, who are given the thankless task of providing comedy relief. The stale material with which they're saddled could hardly be considered relief from the hackneyed melodramatics.

Dorothy felt the main problem stemmed from the studio's choice for the male lead: "*Dixiana* was intended to be this big, over-the-top production like *Rio Rita* had been and they even cast Bebe Daniels as the lead. But instead of bringing back John Boles, RKO chose Everett Marshall for Bebe's love interest. At the time, other studios were recruiting opera singers like Lawrence Tibbett and Grace Moore to appear in films, so RKO brought in Marshall from the New York Metropolitan Opera. He had never made a picture before and, well, that just ruined everything. He was a very good-looking man with a beautiful operatic voice, and he was such a nice person, too, but nobody helped him to learn how to act before the camera. When he'd sing in that big, booming voice, his mouth would get all contorted and his facial expressions looked comical on the screen. He didn't know how to face the camera properly and they never photographed him correctly. And he wasn't coached on his dialogue delivery.

"Our director, Luther Reed, was never much help in that department anyway but I was surprised that nobody took him aside to give him a few pointers. I didn't realize how much trouble he was having until I saw the rushes and by then it was too late. So it was a sad situation. He was the main love interest, a very important character, and he blew it, which ruined the whole film."

While Marshall's inadequate performance is certainly a liability, it's doubtful that even a seasoned actor could have done much with the role as written. And Marshall's acting is by no means the film's sole problem. Unlike *Rio Rita* and *The Cuckoos*, the score for *Dixiana* is largely forgettable, a fatal flaw for a movie that is first and foremost a musical.

Bert and Bob as Pee Wee and Ginger Dandy, Dixiana's circus cohorts, aren't as funny as they could have been. There's virtually none of the tried-and-true comic set pieces they relied upon previously, and their scenes are awkwardly grafted onto the main story. A secondary love triangle develops when Pee Wee and Ginger vie for the attention of Nanny (Dorothy), a fickle Southern belle who can't choose between them. Dorothy's screen time is limited, due to her involvement with *Rah Rah Daze*, but she does get to perform a duet with Bert, "My One Ambition Is You," one of the film's very few bright spots:

"We did that song and dance in sort of a unique way. Bert came up with all the staging himself. In those days, the studio let you do a lot of your own stuff, at least RKO did. Bert and I were on a winding staircase, he was [standing] outside the banister while I was on the inside. When Bert sang his portion of the song, we slowly walked up the stairs that way. Then when I sang, I cascaded down the stairs. I was wearing the cutest little hoopskirt dress with pantaloons and ballet slippers, so it was easy to glide down on. When we came to the bottom of the stairs and sang our last line, Bob is jealously hiding behind a curtain. As we do our little dance, Bob kicks Bert in the behind. Then when Bert and I switch, Bob inadvertently kicks me. I think that Bert did it and slap his face, so he gets upset and pushes me on the floor. Then he helps me up and my hoop skirt falls off. He and I don't even pay attention and dance off together. It was so cute.

"How we came to do it like that was when we were rehearsing one day and my hoop skirt fell off on its own. Everyone became hysterical and wouldn't stop laughing, so they told us to keep that bit in the routine. We had to do at least four takes of me unfastening the skirt to make it look spontaneous because it was very hard to do. The clasp was so hard to unhook that I thought I'd break my wrist! And you can still tell that I was unhooking it, then we danced off smiling arm in arm. It gives the wrong idea about what just happened — and what's going to happen. But I love the song and that is the one number that's always been my favorite."[5]

As in *Rio Rita*, the finale of *Dixiana* was photographed in Technicolor, and this section provides two more highlights, Bob's amusing rendition of "A Lady Loved a Soldier" and a dance solo by the legendary Bill "Bojangles" Robinson.

By the time *Dixiana* wrapped on April 26, *Rah Rah Daze* had closed. Fred Waring had sunk a fortune into the show and planned to take it on tour. But after a successful opening week, the box office take tumbled to a dismal $2,700 during the second week. Then Dorothy became ill and had to miss a couple performances. At the end of the four week engagement, Waring had lost an estimated $160,000. Waring and others involved tried to figure out how such a seemingly surefire project could have been such a resounding failure. Some concluded that, despite its merits, it was no longer the type of show Depression-era audiences wanted (or could even afford) to see.

Throughout their relationship, Fred and Dorothy had a string of very public lovers' quarrels. Every other week the newspapers reported that the couple had either split up or were engaged. Dorothy reflected, "We loved each other dearly but the plain truth is that we could get on each other's nerves if we spent too much time together. Only a loved one knows how to set your temper off and during our arguments we knew exactly

## 3. Sweetheart, We Need Each Other

**Dorothy (center) at the Fox Carthay Theatre for the premiere of *Dixiana* on September 4, 1930. The other attendees are unidentified.**

how to get under each other's skin. People used to wonder how Fred and I could bicker so much one moment then seem so lovey-dovey the next." After *Rah Rah Daze* closed, Waring headed back east to regroup while Dorothy continued with her movie career.

Around this time, Mary Treen, Dorothy's cousin, began making fleeting appearances in films. It wasn't until the mid–1930s that Mary landed acting roles with greater frequency; once she did, she turned up constantly in movies and on television for over fifty years. Mary—who, like Dorothy, had attended the Westlake School for Girls—never became a lead actress, but she was an always-reliable supporting player whose face may have been more familiar than her name. Mary is best remembered for her role as Cousin Tilly, who worked at the Bailey Savings & Loan, in Frank Capra's enduring classic *It's a Wonderful Life* (1946).

*Dixiana* opened on September 4, 1930, to mixed reviews. *Variety* assessed it with clear-eyed accuracy: "The whole affair runs along as though misjudged in every respect.... With four comics of established rep in the cast, the comedy is the worst of the lot.... Accordingly, the blame must go on the script, if excepting that the early rushes must have been seen by some one.... Radio will have to put plenty of work behind this picture to recover its extensive investment, for the picture cost a great deal from its looks."

"*Dixiana* was a horrible dog," Dorothy often stated. "It was a flop and deservedly so." *Dixiana* reportedly lost $300,000 for RKO, and it was apparent that the novelty of sound was no longer enough of a draw to guarantee box-office success. Audiences had become more discerning, especially in light of many terrible musicals that were being foisted upon the public. The studio learned a lesson from this setback and began to develop starring vehicles for their premier comedy team.

CHAPTER 4

# Whistling the Blues Away
## *The Star Treatment*

*Half Shot at Sunrise* (1930) was the first Wheeler and Woolsey film tailored to showcase their characters, making them the primary focus rather than glorified comic relief operating on the periphery of a main plot they did little to motivate. Dorothy's participation in the previous pictures was enough to cement her in the public's mind as "the Wheeler and Woolsey girl," a sobriquet that would stick with her for the remainder of her career. From this point on, she would receive third billing in almost all of the movies she made with Bert and Bob, establishing the team as a bona fide triumvirate.

A musical comedy set during the closing days of World War I, *Half Shot at Sunrise* was photographed on the studio's Encino back lot, recreating Paris in 1918. Tommy Turner (Wheeler) and Gilbert Simpson (Woolsey) are AWOL American soldiers cavorting around the City of Lights. Their mischievous antics frustrate their commanding officer, Colonel Marshall (George MacFarlane), as well as a pair of persistent MPs (Jack Rutherford, Eddie de Lange). The colonel has additional headaches: His nagging wife (Edna May Oliver) is justifiably suspicious about his association with a sultry siren named Olga (Leni Stengel), and his two lovely daughters, Annette (Dorothy) and Eileen (Roberta Robinson), can't conceal their attraction to the opposite sex.

In later years, Dorothy would dismiss most of her movie roles as "yucky-yucky nothing" parts that afforded her little to do other than react to a comedian's punchline and sing an occasional song. But *Half Shot at Sunrise* provided her with the opportunity to play a dyed-in-the-wool (or in this case, dyed-in-the-Woolsey) comedic character. As Annette, a vivacious 16-year-old eager to experience her first big romance, she's effervescent, spunky and headstrong, qualities that mirrored her off-screen personality. Looking like the quintessential '20s flapper, Dorothy basically repeats the role she had played on stage in *Hello Yourself*, and it results in what is arguably her liveliest screen performance.

Her introductory scene sets the tone. Eluding an MP, Tommy hides behind a parked car, which happens to be the colonel's vehicle. Annette pops out of the equipment

**Bert Wheeler and Dorothy are "Whistling the Blues Away" in** *Half Shot at Sunrise* **(1930).**

trunk — she hid there to sneak a ride into town — and their mutual attraction is quickly established through some playful patter. ("Are you married?" "No, I just naturally look worried.")

By now Bert and Dorothy had a smooth on-screen rapport, and they break into a spirited rendition of "Whistling the Blues Away," where they sing, tap, and whistle to the tune. (Dorothy even gets to incorporate her "snake hips" dance movements.) The entire set piece is not unlike the boy-girl vaudeville routines that Bert and Dorothy had performed on stage with other partners. Dorothy recalled, "We would usually rehearse our numbers at least two weeks straight before doing the picture and learn everything at least a month before that. All of our songs and dances were recorded exactly as we did them. They were never prerecorded as was done years later. I think we did it the best way because it was easier since we already knew what we were doing. And that whistling in *Half Shot at Sunrise* was my real whistling. Bert could not whistle but I could, so we worked it into the routine." (Bert's inability to whistle is a running gag throughout the number. He only succeeds after sucking on a lemon.)

During a reprise of "Whistling the Blues Away," Bob joins in and the trio engages in a very funny mock ballet.

## 4. Whistling the Blues Away

For the grand finish, Bert and Bob place Dorothy atop the roof of the car and she prepares to leap into their waiting arms. Just as she makes the dive, however, the boys dash off after spotting an MP and Dorothy plummets to the ground, landing flat on her behind. As she did on many occasions, Dorothy performed the stunt herself, without the use of a double. She commented: "I was some daredevil! I always insisted on doing all of my own stunts, and they usually let me. In that scene where I jump off the car and land on the ground, a hole was dug and netting was laid down. Grass was then placed on top of the netting where I had to land after the fall. It was supposed to break my fall but it didn't. I did do it without getting hurt, though."

According to a studio press release, it took forty-seven rehearsals and three takes for the camera to get this number right. (A second Bert-Dorothy duet, "Kiss Me, Cherie," was cut from the final-release version.)

The bulk of *Half Shot at Sunrise* has Bert and Bob on the run, cavorting around Paris. Though clearly in support, Dorothy is afforded the rare opportunity to be as uninhibited as the footloose duo. At one point, she petulantly dismisses them, as she snaps her fingers in Bert's face and adds a caustic, "This for you!" She snaps her fingers in Bob's face and states, "And that for you!" Then she lifts the back of her coat and adds, "And this for your papa!," indicating her posterior. Bob dryly notes, "Papa gets the best of everything." Dorothy remembered this exchange vividly: "We never thought they would leave that bit in the picture. Even after we filmed it, we said, 'They'll never use that!' A lot of the humor in those early films was risqué, but we thought we had really crossed the line that time. I'm still surprised we got away with it."

*Half Shot at Sunrise* benefits from a supporting cast of able comic foils, most notably Edna May Oliver (1883–1942), one of the screen's finest character comediennes. Her dry delivery and dour facial expressions provided the perfect counterpoint to the frantic antics. She would co-star with Bert, Bob, and Dorothy again in *Cracked Nuts* (1931), then with Dorothy in *Laugh and Get Rich* (1931) and with Bert and Bob in *Hold 'Em Jail* (1932). She starred in an entertaining series of "Hildegarde Withers" mysteries for RKO (*Penguin Pool Murder*, *Murder on the Blackboard*, *Murder on a Honeymoon*); her film credits also include *Cimarron* (1931), *Little Women* (1933), *David Copperfield* (1935), *A Tale of Two Cities* (1935), *Romeo and Juliet* (1936), *Drums Along the Mohawk* (1939) and *Pride and Prejudice* (1940).

"Edna was a very sweet woman," Dorothy said. "She invited me to her home several times, and she would come to my home too. We had quiet little tea parties. I sensed a loneliness about her and an insecurity about her appearance. She would make self-deprecating remarks about her looks, but I think this was a defense mechanism, as though she was going to make fun of herself before anybody else did. She was always kind and motherly to me, and I have nothing but good memories about her."

There's a half-hearted attempt at a serious romantic subplot involving Eileen Marshall (Roberta Robinson), the colonel's older daughter, and Lt. Jim Reed (Hugh Trevor, from *The Cuckoos*), yet these characters disappear from view early on, and are only seen fleetingly afterwards.

As Olga, the colonel's mistress, Leni Stengel also makes a good foil for the boys, and she and Woolsey perform a duet, "Nothing But Love," in which they merrily prance around an outdoor fountain. Dorothy had a special memory involving Miss Stengel: "One day Bert came to me and said, 'Oh boy, have I got it made! Leni invited me to her place tonight and I think she's got more than dinner on her mind. I can't believe it. Things like this never happen to me.' So the next day I asked Bert, 'Well, how did it go last night?' And Bert grumbled, 'Don't talk to me! I'm mad at you!' I said, 'What happened?' and he said, 'She spent the whole evening pumping me for information about *you*. She's not interested in me — she's interested in *you*!' I was floored. I mean, I wasn't shocked by the idea of lesbianism or bisexuality, not after being in show business for several years, but I was surprised that someone as classy as Leni would be interested in anyone as unsophisticated as me. I wasn't interested in women, not in that way, but I have to admit I was flattered. Bert said, 'I should have known it was too good to be true,' and we shared a laugh over it."

Annette, Dorothy's character, steals an important military communiqué from her father and gives it to Tommy and Gilbert, so they can deliver it to the general at the front lines. (Annette figures that this act of heroism will square things between the boys and her disapproving father.) Arriving at the battlefield, Gilbert callously volunteers Tommy's services for a dangerous mission. Tommy gets caught in an explosion, and a gravely concerned Gilbert rushes to his rescue. In sharp contrast to the wacky tone of the rest of the film, most of this sequence is presented as straight drama, and Bert and Bob play the scene with utter sincerity.

*Half Shot at Sunrise* was one of the few Wheeler and Woolsey pictures Bert would speak favorably about in later years. Bert credited its success to Roscoe "Fatty" Arbuckle, who worked as consultant and contributed additional material, gags and even directorial assistance. Arbuckle's influence is particularly evident in the mock ballet routine and later when Bert and Bob masquerade as waiters in a fancy French restaurant (only to have the bad luck of getting assigned to the table where Colonel Marshall and his wife are seated). Both sequences contain the sort of physical horseplay that was a trademark of Arbuckle's silent comedies; the mock ballet resembles the sort of rough-housing that Arbuckle, Buster Keaton and Alice Lake would have done in one of Arbuckle's silent comedies. Sadly, Arbuckle received no screen credit for his input, due to the scandal that derailed his career several years earlier.[1]

The freewheeling military farce was a box-office hit and earned the team their most enthusiastic reviews to date. In the November 1930 issue of *Photoplay*, an unaccredited reviewer raved: "Peevish after a tough day? Anything wrong? Well then, park the grouch and toddle over to wherever they're showing *Half Shot at Sunrise*. It's one of the most absurdly ridiculous, nonsensical messpots of assorted comedy that ever was cooked up from celluloid. It's virtually all Wheeler and Woolsey.... Leni Stengel as the Paris vamp, cuddlesome Dorothy Lee as the colonel's daughter, and George MacFarlane as the colonel take whatever honors Wheeler and Woolsey don't gobble up."

With plans for more Wheeler and Woolsey vehicles, the studio increased Dorothy's salary to $1,000 a week—a far cry from the $30 a week she was making during her struggling vaudeville days. Dorothy told a *Silver Screen Magazine* journalist, "I don't believe the new contract will change my style of living to any great extent," but the publication noted that within a few months, she traded in her Ford roadster for a high-powered, eight-cylinder coupe and gave up her plain serge coat for an ermine wrap trimmed with sable.

She said that she was also generous with her circle of friends: "Money never meant much to me because I never believed I would ever have a great deal of it. When I started getting big pay checks, I spent a lot of it on my friends. Some of my closest friends were the ones I associated with before I became well known. One of these friends was the first one in our group to have a baby and we were all excited. Her child was born with a birth defect, a problem with his mouth, so I paid to have corrective surgery done. To me, that's what the extra money was good for."

One of Dorothy's new friends was singer-actress Dixie Lee, who shared a similar name and appearance. Dixie was under contract to Fox Studio (which would become 20th Century–Fox) and, like Dorothy, was one of the new stars of the talkie boom. Fox had groomed Dixie for stardom, which is why the studio became concerned about the company she kept. Dorothy explained:

"Dixie was a movie star when she started dating Bing Crosby, who was then a singer [one of the Rhythm Boys] with Paul Whiteman's band. The general attitude among her friends was, 'What is she doing with that nobody? She can do much better than him.' Many people tried to convince her to break off the relationship. Even her studio tried. I liked Bing and I never passed judgment on him. Why would I? Who the hell was I? I always treated him nicely and he appreciated it because he knew the things that were being said about him. Eventually Dixie and Bing got married. Dixie retired and Bing went on to become one of the biggest stars in the world. Bing always remembered that I never looked down my nose at him and we remained friends for the rest of his life."

Dorothy's best friend in show business was actress June Clyde, her co-star in *The Cuckoos*. They were often spotted at various parties and the press had a field day when the pair showed up wearing the same outfit: "We were both invited to this big Hollywood gathering. June and I were not fancy dressers, but this time we decided to get a real fancy expensive dress. So we individually went to Bullocks Wilshire department store and I bought the most beautiful gold lamé dress with pastel colors. I called June and said, 'I've found the most beautiful dress' and she said, 'I did too!' So I arrived at her house and we were wearing the exact same dress! I said that I would go home and change but she said, 'No, don't worry about it. Let's just go like this.' We went to the party dressed the same and sat at the same table. Everyone kept coming up to us and taking our picture. We got quite a write-up in the society columns."

Dorothy was now getting more coverage in fan magazines than Bert and Bob combined, as she provided good "copy" for the publications. Richard Ray, a writer for *Photoplay*, described the day he spent with the indefatigable starlet in his October 1930 article "Miss Midget: A close-up of the little girl — Dorothy Lee to you — who's known to most of Hollywood as Midge":

> I had looked forward to interviewing Dorothy Lee. Ah — a quiet two hours in a tranquil tea room, tête-à-tête, I asking the questions and she answering them with a dreamy look in those big brown eyes. As a matter of fact: "I hate tea rooms," said Dorothy Lee. "Besides, I had a late breakfast and I'm not hungry. Do you play golf?" From that moment on I became tired and footsore. I chased Dorothy all over Southern California. The route included 18 holes of golf at the Lakeside Club, two sets of tennis at the Lakeside Tennis Club, a swim at the beach where Miss Lee has a summer home, and several sets of ping pong in the game room of her house. At the end of the session, I was hoping an ambulance would pass and rush me to my home and bed. She was ready to visit the beach and take on the pleasure of rides and side shows. She is equally proficient of horseback riding. Never in one girl have I seen so much animation and pep.

Fan magazines often made reference to her collection of toy dogs, which numbered up to 150. It began when her mother gave her a woolly toy dog; Dorothy loved it so much that she wound up purchasing additional toy dogs while on tour with Fred Waring. Then Waring got into the act and bought her an assortment of toy dogs, ranging in price from 50¢ to $300. In no time, Dorothy had a collection of 674 stuffed, carved and porcelain canines worth over $6,000.

Nearly every studio produced variety revues showcasing their roster of stars, such as MGM's *The Hollywood Revue of 1929*, Warner Brothers' *The Show of Shows* (1929), Fox's *Fox Movietone Follies* (1929) and *Happy Days* (1930), and Paramount's *Paramount on Parade* (1930). In September 1929, RKO announced they would follow suit with *Radio Revels of 1929*, a "song and musical spectacle comparable to anything on stage or screen" featuring various contract players strutting their stuff. Nothing came of this, but in October 1930 RKO unveiled plans for *Radio Revels of 1930*, an "all-dancing, all-singing, all-star, all-novelty extravaganza" that would recruit Bert, Bob, Dorothy and just about everyone else on the lot. Like some of the other studio revues, it was intended to be an annual event. Unlike some of the other studio revues, the project never materialized.

Instead, the next Wheeler and Woolsey outing was the pleasant — and less expensive — *Hook Line and Sinker* (1930). Bert and Bob are Wilbur Boswell and J. Addington Ganzy, a pair of fast-talking insurance salesmen. On the road, they meet Mary Marsh (Dorothy), a runaway heiress heading to claim her inheritance, a deteriorating Victorian hotel called the Ritz de la Riviera, complete with a mysterious house detective (Hugh Herbert) and an ancient bellboy (George Marion, Sr.). Addington and a smitten Wilbur help Mary refurbish the place. The hotel becomes a success after they advertise it as an elegant playground for the rich; even Mary's wealthy mother (Jobyna Howland) checks in. However, the newfound notoriety also attracts undesirable clientele: an assortment of mobsters, including Buffalo Blackie (Ralf Harolde), intent on robbing the hotel safe where the guests' valuables are stored. But the boys foil the robbery and emerge as heroes during a shoot-out in the hotel lobby.

Though not a cheap-looking film, *Hook Line and Sinker* was produced for a fraction

## 4. Whistling the Blues Away

**Dorothy poses with a portion of her toy dog collection (1930). In time she would own more than 600 stuffed canines.**

of the budget allocated for *Half Shot at Sunrise*. There is a heavier emphasis on dialogue, rather than elaborate sight gags, and the camaraderie between Bert, Bob and Dorothy makes the slight material seem funnier than it actually is.

After her sprightly comedic performance in *Half Shot at Sunrise*, it is disappointing to see Dorothy saddled with a nondescript ingénue role here. Nevertheless, her interplay with the boys remains effective, even though she's basically around to set up their punchlines.

There's a charming scene with Bert and Dorothy sitting on the registration desk with a cash register between them. Bert playfully speculates how many children they'll have after they're married and hits the "10" key on the register. Frowning, Dorothy immediately strikes "NO SALE." Then Bert presses "4" and Dorothy responds with "1," and so on. This provides a perfect set-up for a duet but, alas, there is none. In fact, there are no song and/or dance numbers in the film, except for a ballroom scene where the hotel band plays renditions of "Three Little Words" (which would have made a cute duet for Bert and Dorothy) and "Whistling the Blues Away" (which *did* make a cute duet for Bert and Dorothy).

*Hook Line and Sinker* was made at a time when moviegoers, fed up with the recent glut of inferior product, had declared a moratorium on musicals. Talking pictures were no longer enough of a novelty to make weak product salable. Audiences that had flocked to see quality efforts like *Rio Rita*, *The Broadway Melody*, *Sunnyside Up* and *The Love Parade* now avoided these talkies (or "singies," as fan magazines dubbed them) like the plague. And who could blame them, especially after such wretched endeavors as *Say It with Songs*, *Puttin' on the Ritz*, *The Desert Song* and *The Vagabond Lover* poisoned the market. The situation became so dire that some theater marquees had "THIS IS NOT A MUSICAL" right below the title of the featured attraction, to reassure wary patrons.

By the end of 1930, studios scrapped most of their musical projects, and in some instances songs were deleted from completed productions while other properties were filmed *sans* the intended musical scores. (*The March of Time*, Metro-Goldwyn-Mayer's elaborate musical revue, was completed, then permanently shelved. Warner Brothers filmed the Broadway hit *50 Million Frenchman* without utilizing the Cole Porter score that helped make the play a success.) As a result, *Hook Line and Sinker* provided no musical numbers for its three tried-and-true musical-comedy stars and the film is poorer because of it.

"We called it *Hook Line and Stinker*," Dorothy remarked, dismissing it as a total dud. Yet on its own modest terms, it is a very enjoyable picture. The team works well with reliable comic heavies like Ralf Harolde (from *Dixiana*) and Stanley Fields (who would later co-star with Bert, Bob and Dorothy in *Cracked Nuts*). As she was in *The Cuckoos*, Jobyna Howland is Woolsey's matronly love interest, and Hugh Herbert (who would later co-star with Dorothy in *Laugh and Get Rich* and with Bert and Bob in *Diplomaniacs*) contributes his share of laughs. Director Edward F. Cline, a veteran of silent comedies, keeps everything moving along at a comfortable pace. The prolific Cline would direct Wheeler and Woolsey again in *Cracked Nuts*, *So This Is Africa* (1933), *On Again-Off Again* (1937) and *High Flyers* (1937). (Dorothy did not appear in the last three titles.)

*Hook Line and Sinker* was amusing enough to please the team's devout followers, although critical reception was mixed. *Variety* found it to be a "carelessly made picture.... Both Wheeler and Woolsey are too experienced to hold any brief for their efforts in this one. Dorothy Lee is no help and cannot show to advantage with the experienced Jobyna Howland on one side and Natalie Moorhead on the other."

Regardless, *Hook Line and Sinker* and the distressingly unfunny Amos 'n' Andy comedy *Check and Double Check* were RKO's highest-grossing films for 1930.

Elizabeth Chaney passed away at the age of 75 after a long illness, and Dorothy took comfort in knowing that her grandmother had lived to see her success. Dorothy told the *Los Angeles Times*, "My mother is all alone now — my grandmother died just a few weeks ago. They had each lived for each other, and for me. So I want to stay close to mother until the pain of that experience is softened."

Life as a contract player guaranteed a steady paycheck, a luxury unknown to many during the years of the Great Depression. In return, the studio system exacted obedience

## 4. Whistling the Blues Away

from their employees, as Dorothy recalled: "When the studio said jump, we jumped. We had to do what they wanted because we were under contract and those were the terms. They ran our lives and we had to do whatever they wanted us to do, such as attending premieres, openings, you name it. I loved the work that I was doing, and when you do what you love, you're happy. I just didn't like having to do everything that the studio told me to do. I became a blonde for a while just because some director looked at me and said, 'I wish you were blonde.'

"It sounds glamorous, but for us, working on a picture was just our job. When we were done, we went home just as someone would after leaving the office. It was the same for Bert and Bob. We each went our separate ways after a day's shoot. As soon as I was finished at the studio —*zoom*— I wanted to go some place. I was never the dress-up type, the fancy type, or the sexy type. When I was away from the studio, I hardly even wore makeup, but at the studio, they would pile it on. Back in my day the makeup that was used was greasepaint for when I was on the stage, and in the movies they would use what was called pancake makeup. It didn't take long to be applied. All they did was dip a wet sponge into the pancake, apply it, and it was done. I never wore fake eyelashes either. I tried them once for a party and they were so heavy — I couldn't take them. My eyelashes are very long so every time I'd curl them the curler would hit my eye. The studio wanted us to have a very dramatic and glamorous look but I preferred everything to be as casual as possible."

Away from the studio, Dorothy maintained her active if not exhaustive lifestyle, winning trophies for tennis (her favorite sport) and golf. She was such a whiz at ping-ping that she handily defeated Hollywood newcomer Cary Grant, who was no slouch at ping-pong himself, several times. Dorothy's dainty feminine exterior masked her boundless athleticism, and she would surprise onlookers by doing seventeen chin-ups with ease.

Attending Hollywood premieres was one of the requirements expected of studio contract players, regardless of whether they had any involvement with the specific film in question. For Dorothy, it was not one of the perks of her job:

"I would attend movie premieres for publicity purposes. They wouldn't necessarily be only for a Wheeler and Woolsey picture, but premieres that the studio wanted us to attend nevertheless. I really didn't like to go to those damn things. I felt they cut into my free time. Appearing in the films was my job, but when I was through at the studio, I wanted to work in my garden, play tennis or golf or go sailing. I never realized I was popular or had become some sort of semi-star, so these functions didn't mean anything to me. I could have cared less. The studio dictated who you went with to the premiere. At first RKO would pair me with a male actor they also had under contract but as I became known as the 'Wheeler and Woolsey girl,' I went with Bert and Bob to those things.

"A couple of times, RKO paired me up with Joel McCrea and tried to make it look like we were dating, which was ridiculous. Joel and I were good friends, and he looked upon me as a kid sister. Besides, he was crazy about Joyce Compton, a pretty blonde actress. Joel idolized [humorist and actor] Will Rogers, and for some reason Will took a dislike to Joyce. I don't know why, she seemed to be a nice gal. Will used to say, 'I never met a man I didn't like.' I guess that didn't apply to women. Will told Joel, 'She's not the kind of girl you ought to marry,' so Joel dumped Joyce. Later Joel wound up marrying [actress] Frances Dee. Maybe Will knew what he was talking about because Frances and Joel's marriage lasted longer than all of mine put together."

Dorothy's relationship with Fred Waring became strained as it was up in the air whether they would marry or not. He refused to be pinned down. There were periods of separation and Waring's reputation as a womanizer didn't help matters. Still regarded as Waring's fiancée, Dorothy waited patiently until Jimmie Fidler, a successful publicist, laid eyes on her at a party. Dorothy recalled, "He wanted to meet me, so a girlfriend of mine introduced us. He wouldn't leave me alone...."

Fidler sent her letters, flowers, and telegrams every single day to either say good morning or good night. He wined and dined her but she professed her love for Waring, who got wind of Fidler's public wooing of his long-distance fiancée. Allowing his pride to get the better of him, Waring called Dorothy and broke off their relationship: "I'm through, it's all over between us!" A heartbroken Dorothy accepted Fidler's marriage proposal. "Marrying Fidler was the biggest mistake I ever made. We were better off just being friends. I was still in love with Fred and I married Fidler on the rebound. Take it from me, when you have a fight with your boyfriend, and someone else asks you to marry him, *don't do it!*"

The couple announced their engagement at Dorothy's Malibu Beach home and a month later, preparations were made for their wedding. On November 7, 1930, Dorothy married Jimmie Fidler in the First Christian Church with Ralfe Harolde (Dorothy's co-star in *Dixiana* and *Hook Line and Sinker*) as Best Man and Margaret Brown (Dorothy's cousin) as Maid of Honor. Among the guests were Dorothy's parents, Fidler's mother, actress Sue Carol (who later became a successful talent agent) and screenwriter Anne Caldwell (who scripted *Dixiana*). After the wedding dinner, the newlyweds left for an extended honeymoon at Lake Arrowhead in the San Bernadino Mountains. The trip was cut short because Dorothy was due to begin work on the next Wheeler and Woolsey picture, *Assorted Nuts*.

On the day of the wedding, just before Dorothy was about to walk down the aisle, she received a call from the regretful Fred Waring: "He said, 'Please call off the wedding. I still love you.' Well, here I was, everyone was ready for the ceremony. I told him, 'I'm sorry, but all my guests are here. I can't. I have to go. I'm going to get married. Goodbye.'"

The newlyweds purchased land in Toluca Lake and Dorothy embarked on designing her dream home. The Spanish house was built to Dorothy's specifications, and she made sure it had a tennis court, ping-pong court, swimming pool and a playroom with enough space for dancing. She even selected the furniture, china, glassware and silverware. To keep everything running smoothly, the couple hired a chauffeur, maid and gardener.

## 4. Whistling the Blues Away

During a weekend trip to Big Bear, Jimmie Fidler shot an off-the-cuff 16mm home movie he christened *The Cherry Hunt*, with a cast of four: himself, Dorothy (who received star billing) and Dorothy's friends Honey and Bill "Razz" Razzore. In this five-minute epic "Produced by Carry-Em-Out Co.," Dorothy is kidnapped from her cabin in the woods by an amorous stranger (Razz), to the delight of her unfaithful husband, One-Finger Pete (Fidler), who is now able to spend time with his lover (Honey). Dorothy subdues her captor and rushes back to the cabin, only to discover the cheating couple in the throes of (off-screen) ecstasy — all of which is conveyed by Dorothy's melodramatic gesturing and a shot of Fidler and Honey emerging from the cabin, hastily pulling up their "britches." Dorothy decides she's better off with an interested abductor than an uninterested spouse. (*The Cherry Hunt* was one of the few mementoes from her marriage to Fidler that Dorothy saved.)

Bert, Bob and Dorothy completed the political farce *Assorted Nuts* just before Christmas 1930; it was released under the title *Cracked Nuts* in 1931. It turned out to be a better-than-average Wheeler and Woolsey endeavor in which parts were greater than the whole. Wendell Graham (Bert) is in love with Betty Harrington (Dorothy), but her Aunt Minnie (Edna May Oliver) strongly disapproves of the match. "He'll never make good," Minnie snarls as she forbids Wendell from seeing Betty again. Betty and Minnie set sail for the postage stamp–sized country of El Dorania where Minnie is the largest property owner. Coincidentally, Wendell happens to be on the same ship. He invested $100,000 in the country's revolution, with assurances that he will assume the king's throne — but he is unaware that all of the kings before

**After a fight with Fred Waring, Dorothy married Jimmie Fidler on the rebound, November 7, 1930.**

him were assassinated after making a similar investment. Upon his arrival, Wendell discovers his old buddy Zander Ulysses Parker (Bob) has already won the crown in a crap game with the previous king, who deliberately lost the gamble in order to escape execution.

As Wendell and King "Zup" argue over which head should rightfully wear the crown, General Bogardus (Stanley Fields) and a leading revolutionary (Boris Karloff) plot to take cover El Dorania themselves, even if it means eliminating both pretenders to the throne. Zup becomes the unwitting target of an outdoor public assassination, sitting on his throne as a cross-eyed bombardier (silent-screen great Ben Turpin) tries to zero in on him. (And all the while, the citizens of El Dorania are seated in an oversized bleacher section, cheering the assassination attempt as if it were a college football game.) Luckily, Zup survives; he and Wendell thwart the revolutionaries and join together to make El Dorania a Republic.

*Cracked Nuts* is a mixed bag, but it succeeds in delivering some solid laughs. For a change, Bert and Bob's characters don't even meet until midway through the picture, but once they do, their by-play is as sharp as ever. Particularly effective is a convoluted cross-talk sequence that predates Abbott and Costello's classic "Who's on First?" routine, in which the boys examine a map of two neighboring towns named What and Which:

During the construction of Dorothy's Toluca Lake dream home, RKO had her pose for a series of gag photographs.

Zup: What town is next to What?
Wendell: Which.
Zup: Next to What.
Wendell: Which.
Zup: Which is next to What?
Wendell: Yes.

As always, Edna May Oliver is an ideal comic foil for the boys, and Leni Stengel provides some pleasing eye candy for Bob (as she did in *Half Shot at Sunrise*). Stanley Fields makes for a blustery comic heavy — his

## 4. Whistling the Blues Away

Dorothy's masquerade as a male soldier was a plot element dropped from the final version of *Cracked Nuts* (1931). Left to right: Bert Wheeler, Dorothy and Robert Woolsey.

specialty — and it's fun to see Boris Karloff in a supporting role, though his restrained performance is a disappointment for those expecting juicier histrionics. (Karloff would become a movie immortal for his role in *Frankenstein*, which was released by Universal Pictures some seven months after *Cracked Nuts*.)

As Wheeler's love interest, Dorothy is given relatively little to do. Most of her footage consists of her looking dreamy-eyed at Wendell and defending him to Aunt Minnie. The comedy set pieces involve Bert and Bob's interaction with each other and the rest of the supporting cast, leaving Dorothy with only a few fleeting moments. One of those moments is a charming duet by Bert and Dorothy, "Dance and Let the World Dance with You." The number begins slowly, as they bemoan the obstacles in the path of their romance, and then start to sing, as a way of comforting each other. They find themselves in each other's arms, dancing the tango, until Aunt Minnie arrives on the scene. As he twirls around, Wendell winds up embracing Minnie. Oblivious to the fact that he now has a different dancing partner, Wendell stomps his foot with joy — smashing Minnie's foot in the process. Minnie stomps his foot in retaliation, and all three wind up stepping on each other's toes.

As originally scripted, Dorothy had more to do in the proceedings. Scenes of Betty fighting off the lustful advances of General Bogardus and later masquerading as a male soldier so she can run off with Wendell were filmed but deleted from the final cut.

Although it was a marked improvement over *Hook Line and Sinker*, *Cracked Nuts* also divided the critics. *Variety* remarked: "As a two-reeler, *Cracked Nuts* would be fair entertainment ... but [it is] too wearisome as a full-length feature. Long dissertations about nothing at all will fear down any fan." Mordaunt Hall of the *New York Times* offered an opposing opinion: "This production skips along so merrily that it actually seems too short. It is all wild nonsense, but it is funny."

*Cracked Nuts* was another box-office success for the team, earning plenty of Depression-era dollars that kept RKO solvent. "It was another picture where I was given little to do," Dorothy recalled. "It was another nothing role, though I did enjoy making the film and I did get to perform 'Dance and Let the World Dance with You' with Bert. I've always felt it was one of our best duets."

Also released to theaters around the same time as *Cracked Nuts* was *The Stolen Jools*, a two-reel promotional short (running 18 minutes in length) used for fundraising purposes for the National Variety Artists tuberculosis sanitarium in Saranac Lake, New York — though, ironically, the production was co-sponsored by the Chesterfield cigarette company! (One of the opening titles read "This is Chesterfield's contribution to the fine relief work of the N.V.A." Evidently no one thought to question how much Chesterfield's product "contributed" to respiratory ailments.)

To help support this worthy cause, an impressive array of Hollywood stars appeared in the film free of charge, among them: Stan Laurel and Oliver Hardy, Buster Keaton, Norma Shearer, Joan Crawford, Edward G. Robinson, Maurice Chevalier, Our Gang, Irene Dunne, Joe E. Brown, Wallace Beery, Barbara Stanwyck, Gary Cooper, Loretta Young, Jack Oakie, Bebe Daniels, Fay Wray, Richard Dix, Douglas Fairbanks, Jr., and Mitzi Green. The plot — or what passes for one — revolves around the theft of Norma Shearer's jewelry at the Screen Stars Annual Ball. A police inspector (Eddie Kane) is assigned to contact all the "suspects," thereby providing an excuse for a parade of celebrities.

Most of the cameo appearances are presented in a casual, look-who-that-is sort of way, with material that seems to have been improvised on the spot. Only the Laurel and Hardy bit, an elaborate sight gag involving a collapsing automobile, indicates any real pre-planning. Bert and Bob have an amusing set piece at a lunch counter where Inspector Kane, disguised as the counter man, interrogates the pair, leading to an abbreviated reprise of their slapping routine from *Rio Rita*. Appearing separately, Dorothy has a seconds-long cameo in which she sings a snippet of "I Love You So Much" from *The Cuckoos*, then mistakes Kane for an autograph seeker.

Dorothy had developed an irritated appendix and her physician ordered her to slow down. To avoid having to undergo an appendectomy, Dorothy took a short vacation. Upon her return, *Silver Screen Magazine* writer John Byron asked her if she had a nice rest. Dorothy shot back, "Oh, it was all right. I rode horseback, and played tennis and golf for four days. It was pretty dull, though, so I came home!" But an appendectomy was unavoidable and the surgery was performed, without complications, on January 27.

RKO made plans to showcase Dorothy in her own starring vehicle. She had previously declined offers of making a film without Bert and Bob, stating that she wanted to gain more acting experience before assuming the responsibility of carrying a picture on her own. She suggested that a remake of *The Campus Flirt* (1926), a college-themed comedy that starred Bebe Daniels, would serve as an ideal vehicle for her and give her the opportunity to display her athletic abilities (running, pole-vaulting, high-jumping) within the context of the story. The studio announced Dorothy's first starring film would be *Off Side*, from a Douglas MacLean story presumably based on her suggestion. The title was then changed to *Turned Loose in College*. Shortly thereafter, a press release alleged that Dorothy turned down the role, claiming she didn't feel she was ready to carry a film on her own.

With that project sidelined, Dorothy was cast opposite Edna May Oliver and Hugh Herbert in *Room and Board*, directed and co-written by Gregory LaCava (*My Man Godfrey*, *Stage Door*). The film, released as *Laugh and Get Rich*, dealt with the seriocomic events in a boarding house run by Sarah Cranston Austin (Oliver). Sarah's husband, Joe (Herbert), is a daydreaming idler who passes the time spinning tall tales. Their daughter Alice (Dorothy) is having trouble in the romance department with her boyfriend, Larry Owens (Russell Gleason). And the house is filled with genial eccentrics like Mr. Biddle (Charles Sellon) and Mr. Vincentini (George Davis), a struggling artist who only paints pictures of cows. Joe becomes business partners with Larry, a young inventor who has created the Whistling Valve, which alerts motorists to leaking tires. Joe secretly dips into Sarah's savings and invests in an oil stock that pays off in a big way. After years of financial strife, Sarah relishes the opportunity to associate with the stuffy high-society elite. But the Austins soon learn a basic life lesson: Financial solvency doesn't guarantee personal happiness or a sense of self-worth.

*Laugh and Get Rich* was promoted as a human story contrasting small town and big city life, but it was merely another in a line of unremarkable pictures RKO churned out that year. Oliver and Herbert turn in performances good enough to make the viewer wish they had better material to work with. (If Herbert's downtrodden husband role echoes W.C. Fields, it's no coincidence; director LaCava worked with Fields during the silent era.) By contrast, Dorothy comes across stilted and ill at ease; her character has little depth and she seems to have received no coaching or guidance from LaCava. The film's biggest flaw, however, is the script by LaCava and Ralph Spence (from a story by Douglas MacLean). It wavers from genial comedy to heavy melodramatics, then back again, and the indecisive tone undermines the overall effectiveness.

It was a curious vehicle for RKO to saddle Dorothy with. The studio had initially been gung-ho about showcasing her in her own picture, then they gave her an innocuous supporting role in a mundane project. Nevertheless, Dorothy was relieved not to have the responsibility of carrying the ball herself. She was quoted in studio press material:

**Dorothy, Edna May Oliver, Hugh Herbert and George Davis experience good fortune in *Laugh and Get Rich* (1931).**

"Miss Oliver and Mr. Herbert are wonderful teachers for me, so I'm awfully glad I didn't venture into a picture that rested all on my own shoulders."

Despite her relatively limited footage, RKO promoted *Laugh and Get Rich* as a full-fledged Dorothy Lee movie, awarding her top billing in the promotional materials and on the advertising posters. (On-screen she receives third billing.) Dorothy discovered her status the day she drove her new Studebaker, that had free wheeling, to the studio: "RKO had these huge billboards above the entrance advertising their latest movies. I looked up and will never forget my shock. There was a great big billboard of me, advertising 'Dorothy Lee in *Laugh and Get Rich*.' I took my foot off the gas pedal and the car just sped away!"

*Laugh and Get Rich* received a deservedly lukewarm reception from critics. *Variety* snarled, "The film is slow, hardly gathering any momentum until nearly the three-quarter mark.... But if it lacks speed, it also lacks action.... [T]here is no suspense to speak of. That means no punch." Yet Dorothy retained fond memories of this particular production: "Getting to star in a film of my own meant a lot to me at the time. I even got Fred Waring to eat his own words. Back when I was with Fred's band, I would tell him that one day I would get top billing, like he did, on a theater marquee. He would scoff and tell me to stop daydreaming. I'd say, 'You'll see! Just you wait!' So years later Fred is in New York, walking down the street, and passes by a movie theater marquee that reads 'DOROTHY LEE IN *LAUGH AND GET RICH*.' He called me and said, 'Wow! You were right!'"

The studio also decided to showcase Bert and Bob in solo vehicles. Woolsey starred in *Everything's Rosie* (1931), an uneasy blend of corny comedy and drippy sentiment. In this unofficial reworking of W.C. Fields' 1920s stage hit *Poppy*, Woolsey is Dr. J. Dockweiler Droop, a carnival huckster who adopts an orphan girl named Rosie (played in adulthood by Anita Louise). Woolsey had proven himself to be a very funny comedian, and he strove mightily to breathe life into the maudlin plot, often producing a hearty chuckle and a genuine tug at the heartstrings. But without Wheeler to counterbalance his aggressive personality, Woolsey's antics wore thin with some patrons, including a *Variety* reviewer who noted: "The difference between [Wheeler and Woolsey] is that Woolsey is a wisecracking comedian who must have wisecracks besides his cigar and prop laugh. Wheeler is a comedian who works for his points by gag in dialog or stunts, but with a natural comedy sense that fits a situation besides having the looks to create a love interest equivalent to a light comedian's. Alone, Woolsey's laugh becomes monotonous; his cigar becomes familiar and Woolsey becomes tiresome."

Wheeler didn't fare much better with his solo effort, *Too Many Cooks* (1931), which paired him with Dorothy in their only joint movie without Woolsey. Based on a stage play by Frank Craven, it told the story of Albert Bennett (Bert) and his fiancée Alice Cook (Dorothy), whose plans of building their dream house are nearly ruined by the constant meddling of her relatives. Giving Bert and Dorothy the opportunity to play realistic characters was a noble experiment, but they didn't stand a chance saddled with a monotonous screenplay. The direction by William A. Seiter (*Sons of the Desert*, *Roberta*) was competent, but there was only so much he could do with a losing proposition. Seiter would go on to direct, with better results, four Wheeler and Woolsey pictures (three of them with Dorothy).

Of these solo efforts, Dorothy commented: "The reason the studio split up Bert and Bob was because they used to fight and argue about whatever film they were working on at the moment, but that was to be expected. Otherwise they got along. Bert was usually easy-going but he did have a temper and you could only push him so far, and Bob could be stubborn and arrogant. When RKO first signed Bert, he was already a big Broadway star, so he was considered to be a more valuable property and got paid more. Bob was never as great a star on stage and he resented that Bert made more than he did. Even though they were paid equally later on, I don't think Bob ever completely got over that resentment and every so often he would try to pull rank on Bert.

"During a scene, Bob would upstage you by taking a step back, so when you turned to talk to him, the back of your head would be facing the camera. I was too dumb to know what was going on, but Bert figured out what he was up to and we decided to teach Bob a lesson. So the next time Bob took a step back, Bert and I took *two* steps back. Bob really got upset over that.

**William A. Seiter (in white hat) directs Dorothy and Bert in a scene from *Too Many Cooks* (1931).**

"When Bert and I did *Too Many Cooks* we would look at each other and say, 'Why are we making this movie?' We knew it was a stinker from the get-go. Bert would shrug his shoulders and say, 'I know that it stinks, but they've got to pay us to do something.' So every day we'd say to each other, 'This picture is getting worse by the minute, but at least we're getting paid for it!'"

Upon the film's release, the *New York Times* cut to the chase: "In carving the monument for *Too Many Cooks* even the most hopeful sculptor could only find the words of an elegy. Sad and dreary would be two of them, and down toward the end that mournful one, funereal.... [T]he chief fault of the film seems to be that too much separates the end from the beginning. [Wheeler and Lee] do their best, but there are limits even to the art of acting."

After wrapping up *Too Many Cooks* in late March 1931, Dorothy separated from Jimmie Fidler. Unlike her character in the film, who wound up in a dream home at the conclusion, Dorothy moved out of her custom-built dream home and rented a Malibu Beach cottage.

## 4. Whistling the Blues Away

*Too Many Cooks* was a particularly bitter pill for Dorothy to swallow because her contractual obligation to this misguided production meant that she was not allowed to accept an assignment she really desired: the lead role in director Frank Borzage's Fox film *Bad Girl*. Borzage, a specialist in romantic melodramas, had won the very first Best Director Oscar for his lyrical *Seventh Heaven* (1927). He decided to adapt Viña Delmar's novel and play *Bad Girl* for the screen, and Dorothy was his first choice for the role of Dorothy Haley, the female half of a young couple facing daily struggles in Depression-era New York. (Despite the title, there is no real "bad girl" in the story.)

Dorothy was excited about what promised to be her breakout role. RKO did not share her enthusiasm, however, and refused to loan her out to Fox. "It absolutely broke my heart to lose that part," Dorothy later remarked, her disappointment still evident decades after the fact. "Frank Borzage had no choice but to give it to someone else, which turned out to be Sally Eilers, who won a lot of acclaim for the role. I don't think I realized it at the time, but as I look back on it now, I think that's when I pretty much gave up any hope of becoming a serious actress. I considered nearly every role after that just another job."

*Bad Girl* was released in July 1931, the same time as *Too Many Cooks*, and the reception that greeted each picture was a study in contrasts. *Too Many Cooks* garnered poor reviews and sank without a trace. *Bad Girl* was a critical and box-office success. For his efforts, Borzage won his second Best Director Oscar; scenarist Edwin J. Burke also won for Best Screenplay.

What would have happened if Dorothy had been allowed to accept the role? Would it have had a career-altering impact? Playing the "what if?" game is an ultimately pointless exercise since it mixes a little bit of fact with large doses of speculation. We do know that Dorothy was able to put a lot of her own spunky personality into her musical-comedy roles. We also know that in dramatic parts, her performances were entirely dependent upon guidance she received from directors; lackluster direction resulted in a lackluster portrayal. It's safe to assume that a director of Borzage's caliber would have made a considerable effort to coax a first-rate performance out of Dorothy, despite her inexperience in the dramatic arena. Whether the public would have accepted her in a change-of-pace role is another matter of conjecture. The success of *Bad Girl* didn't result in major stardom for Sally Eilers; although she continued to work steadily for years, Eilers never again had such a prominent showcase.

Audiences that expected to see the usual antics from Bert, Bob and Dorothy were sorely disappointed by *Laugh and Get Rich*, *Everything's Rosie* and *Too Many Cooks*. The public and critics concurred they were more effective as a unit, and RKO agreed. Plans for another Wheeler-Lee vehicle, *If I Was Rich* (based on a play by William Anthony McGuire), were scrapped and the studio went back to the business of making Wheeler and Woolsey movies.

# Chapter 5

# You've Got What Gets Me
## *Parting Company*

Bert, Bob and Dorothy went back to basics with *Caught Plastered* (working title: *Full of Notions*; 1931), which took the premise of *Hook Line and Sinker* and switched the hotel setting for a drug store. Small-time vaudevillians Tommy Tanner (Bert) and Egbert G. Higginbottom (Bob) come to the aid of Mrs. Talley (Lucy Beaumont), the kindly owner of a dilapidated drug store. Harry Waters (Jason Robards), the oily villain of the piece, wants to buy the property from Mrs. Talley because the real estate is worth more than the store—a key bit of information he has not passed along to the elderly woman.

Peggy Norton (Dorothy), the daughter of the police chief (DeWitt Jennings), is suspicious of the boys at first, but Tommy's playful charm wins her over. Waters, however, becomes agitated; not only are these drifters turning the store into a thriving business, complete with live radio broadcasts, but one of the interlopers has stolen Peggy's affections as well. Waters hires a bootlegger to spike a supply of lemon syrup with liquor and sell it to them without their knowledge of it being tainted. (This being Prohibition, any sale of alcohol was illegal.) Before long, customers are clamoring for their special brand of "soda" as the store takes on the atmosphere of a saloon. Even Peggy samples the drink and becomes thoroughly intoxicated.

Waters alerts Chief Morton, who arrests Tommy and Egbert for selling liquor. But the plan backfires when they all catch Waters and his friend in the act of manufacturing the bootleg brew. Mrs. Talley keeps her drugstore, Tommy keeps Peggy, and Egbert keeps out of jail.

*Caught Plastered* isn't so much a feature film as it is a series of enjoyable vignettes. One highlight is a sequence in which Tommy and Egbert try to cheer up a despondent Mrs. Talley by performing their vaudeville act, which consists of a series of wheezy one-liners followed by a quick rendition of "While Strolling Through the Park." This routine is delivered in an easy, off-the-cuff manner, and Bert and Bob's touching attempt to raise Mrs. Talley's spirits gives their characters a humanity that is often lacking in their other films. *Caught Plastered* may not be the funniest Wheeler and Woolsey comedy, but it's one of the sweetest.

**Dorothy samples Bob and Bert's special brand of liquor-laced "soda" in *Caught Plastered* (1931).**

Dorothy, who was underutilized in *Cracked Nuts*, gets to interact with the team to a greater extent. In most of the Wheeler and Woolsey films, Bert and Dorothy's characters are attracted to each other immediately, if they're not already romantically involved. But in *Caught Plastered*, Bert has to win her over. In one of their best scenes, a resistant Dorothy storms into a telephone booth to notify her police chief father about the two suspicious strangers she's met. As she prepares to make the call, Bert draws a face on the soaped-up window of the phone booth, using his finger to form an exaggerated pair of eyes, then an oversized mouth. Dorothy smiles coyly and quickly concludes that he's not so bad after all. This sequence is beautifully acted by Bert and Dorothy, giving their onscreen relationship an added warmth.

Dorothy takes a swig of spiked soda and behaves with a giddiness unseen since *Half Shot at Sunrise*. Bert and a tipsy Dorothy sing a bouncy duet, "I'm That Way About You, After All," written by composer Victor Schertzinger, who was also a director (*Road to Singapore, Road to Zanzibar, One Night of Love, The Mikado*).

The film's opening credits feature animation by the Van Beuren Corporation, whose cartoon shorts were being distributed through RKO. An animated train, with the wheels caricaturing Bob's eyeglasses, is depicted merrily rolling along roller coaster–like tracks, giving the impression that a wacky, no-holds-barred comedy is about to unfold. Instead, *Caught Plastered* is a leisurely paced (and structured) outing filled with amusing set pieces.

Andre Sennwald of the *New York Times* found the whole endeavor uneven: "*Caught Plastered* has its moments — bad, good and medium, with the first and the last predominating. Dorothy Lee makes a sunny ingénue." Other reviewers skewered Dorothy's acting ability, criticizing her voice and her dialogue delivery. While some of her early performances reveal her lack of acting experience, she comes across far less stilted here than she had in *Hook Line and Sinker* and *Cracked Nuts*.

Dorothy grew increasingly unhappy in her marriage to Jimmie Fidler. They lived different lifestyles and he wanted her to cut back on her film assignments. The main source of their incompatibility, however, was the fact that Dorothy was still in love with Fred Waring. Dorothy and Waring remained in steady contact, and she would tearfully phone him whenever she had a fight with Fidler. "I had stupidly married Jimmie Fidler on the rebound from Fred and it was taking an emotional toll on me. We simply didn't get along and it didn't help that I was so obviously in love with Fred. I would call Fred and tell him what a big mistake I had made and how I never should have married Fidler. What I didn't know was that Fidler had tapped my phone and was recording all of these conversations."

When Dorothy filed for a divorce in July 1931, Fidler used the recorded conversations to get what he wanted: "Fidler threatened to blackmail me and Fred, saying that he would ruin both of our careers. I was more concerned about Fred than myself. What Fidler wanted was my dream house in Toluca Lake. He wanted it out of spite because he knew how much it meant to me. My father handled my divorce and he told me to just give Fidler whatever he wanted because he held the upper hand with those recordings. If I decided to fight him in court, I might have wound up losing a whole lot more. So I gave in, but it broke my heart just the same."

In her divorce decree, Dorothy petitioned that Fidler was "exceedingly jealous" and cited mental cruelty, noting he was unsupportive of her career. The divorce would not be finalized until the following year.

Dorothy was loaned out to Warner Brothers to appear opposite Joe E. Brown, their resident comedy star, in *Local Boy Makes Good* (1931). The cavern-mouthed, rubber-limbed Brown was an accomplished physical clown who emerged as one of the biggest box office draws of the 1930s.

In *Local Boy Makes Good*, John Augustus Miller (Brown), a meek botany student, passes himself off as a collegiate track star in order to impress beauty contest winner Julia Winters (Dorothy), whom he has developed a crush on. Julia, a student of psychology, discovers he's a fraud but still convinces the insecure John to participate in a big relay race. Complicating matters are Spike Hoyt (Edward Woods), Julia's jealous boyfriend, and Marjorie Blake (Ruth Hall), a pretty coed who has fallen for John. In the end, Marjorie's love — plus a shot of rubbing alcohol — transforms John into a winner.

**Dorothy had a change-of-pace role opposite Joe E. Brown in *Local Boy Makes Good* (1931).**

This milquetoast-ultimately-triumphs premise provided a sturdy foundation for numerous collegiate comedies, most notably Harold Lloyd's *The Freshman* (1925) and Buster Keaton's *College* (1927). (Like Lloyd and Keaton, Brown was a superb athlete in real life, hardly the weakling he portrays.) And yet *Local Boy Makes Good* stumbles badly where it should have been sure-footed.

Brown was always an appealing performer; his engaging personality could win over an audience right from his first scene. But the screenplay piles on the pathos with such a heavy hand that Brown's character becomes pathetic rather than sympathetic. At one point, he glumly observes, "I'm guess I'm not the kind of fellow people wave at. They just point at me." Brown delivers this and other lines of dialogue with utter sincerity, which, ironically, becomes a detriment. We truly feel sorry for him, so we're not inclined to laugh at (or with) the predicaments that ensue.

Mervyn LeRoy's direction is uncharacteristically slack for a filmmaker responsible for the assured efforts *Little Caesar* (1930), *I Am a Fugitive from a Chain Gang* (1932), *Gold Diggers of 1933* (1933), *They Won't Forget* (1937), *Waterloo Bridge* (1940), *Random Harvest* (1942) and *The Bad Seed* (1956). (LeRoy also directed two other Joe E. Brown pictures, *Broadminded* [1931] and *Elmer the Great* [1933].) Many of the dialogue scenes seem to drag on, hardly in keeping with Warners' brisk house style, making this 67-minute feature seem longer than it actually is. (For a film about a track runner, *Local Boy Makes Good* moves at a snail's pace.) Some reaction shots are awkwardly edited and the comic potential of the climactic relay race is undermined by the obvious—and often unnecessary—use of rear-screen projection.

Although she receives second billing, Dorothy has only a handful of scenes. Her character is oddly conceived: It's neither a leading lady role nor a star turn. Instead, it's a glorified supporting role. Perhaps it's appropriate that, as a student of psychology, the character is more than a bit schizophrenic herself. She initially urges the timid John to become involved in athletics by using a psychiatric approach: "First you must tell me all your sexual problems." Brown reacts like a scared rabbit, but she wrestles him to the floor while spouting advice about taking his inner libido and bringing it to the surface (she has her foot firmly on his chest while offering her views). This sequence would be bizarre in any '30s movie, but it comes across even more so in the context of a Joe E. Brown comedy.

Later, when things look the bleakest for our hero, her demeanor turns from concern to cold-hearted bitchiness as she turns her back on him in his hour of need. Why the sudden mood swing? Simply for plot contrivance: With Julia out of the way, the ever-faithful Marjorie can come to the forefront and cheer John on to victory.

Despite the erratic nature of her limited role, Dorothy gives a well-modulated performance, displaying more range than was required in any of her previous films. Her character here is unlike the ones she essayed in the Wheeler and Woolsey pictures. Julia Winters is a mature and frankly sexual woman, not a girlish kewpie-doll; she openly flaunts her physical charms, and uses her feminine wiles to pursue the skittish bookworm.

*Local Boy Makes Good* is an intriguing but ultimately unsatisfying effort, an opinion echoed by Andre Sennwald of the *New York Times*: "Mathematically speaking, *Local Boy Makes Good* spreads a half hour's worth of amusement through an hour and a quarter…. The cast, in roles that are necessarily minor, provide fair enough foils for Mr. Brown."

For Dorothy, working with the affable comedian was a career highlight: "Joe E. Brown was wonderful. He was such a sweet and kind man. He would often go out of his way to help me do a scene, and it was a lot of fun working with him."

Back at RKO, Dorothy co-starred in Wheeler and Woolsey's best comedy to date, *Peach-O-Reno* (1932)[1], a jazzy, energetic effort that ranks among the team's all-time funniest efforts. After a harmless remark escalates into a battle royale at their 25th wedding anniversary, Joe and Aggie Bruno (Joseph Cawthorn, Cora Witherspoon) head to Reno, Nevada, divorce capital of America. Wattles (Bert) and Swift (Bob) are the most successful attorneys in town (their shuttle bus service picks up customers directly from the train station), handling legal cases by day and turning their law office into a casino at night. Wattles and Swift wind up with both Brunos as clients, while the Brunos' daughters Prudence (Dorothy) and Pansy (Zelma O'Neal) try to stop all divorce proceedings by appealing to the lawyers.

**Zelma O'Neal, Dorothy, Bob and Joseph Cawthorn encounter a femme fatale bearing a strange resemblance to Bert in *Peach-O-Reno* (1932).**

This 63-minute farce is a rapid-fire collection of sight gags, puns, and one-liners, many of them quite risqué. In order to provide Joe Bruno with a co-respondent (which the law defines as a person charged with having committed adultery with the husband or wife from whom a divorce is sought), Wattles disguises himself as the man-hungry "Widow Hanover." Much of Bert's footage is devoted to this extended drag routine, and he milks it for all its worth, playing the randy widow as a road company version of Mae West.

Wattles' masquerade is eventually exposed and Aggie angrily switches her allegiance to a rival law firm, leading to the climactic courtroom sequence, which plays like an extended vaudeville sketch. Bert and Bob's entrance into the courtroom is met with loud cheers from the gathered crowd, as though they are boxing champions. To further the comparison to a fight arena, a radio announcer (Eddie Kane) for station GIN ("The Breath of Reno") gives a blow-by-blow description of the legal proceedings while a vendor (Monty Collins) hawks peanuts, popcorn, chewing gum and candy. Wattles and Swift turn on their unorthodox charm to win over the judge, jury, and the Bruno daughters, as Joe and Aggie tearfully call off the divorce proceedings.

## 5. You've Got What Gets Me

Musical numbers were usually highlights of the Wheeler and Woolsey pictures, and *Peach-O-Reno* showcases two of their liveliest. In the first, Bert (in drag) and Bob entertain the casino crowd with a ballroom dance that becomes, by turns, an Apache dance, an ice-skating exhibition, and a vaudeville buck-and-wing, culminating in Bert tossing Bob clear across the room. This energetic routine captures Wheeler and Woolsey in their prime, proving how their respective performing talents could mesh perfectly.

"Niagara Falls to Reno" is an exuberant Bert-Dorothy duet in which they reveal that the two cities, once far apart, are now just a step away from each other. The number begins in an off-the-cuff manner as Bert sits down at the piano while Dorothy joins in. As a jazz band (the "10 Alimony Jumpers") gathers and starts to play behind them, Bert and Dottie begin a soft-shoe shuffle. Then Dorothy removes her skirt to reveal shorts underneath, and the pair launch into an energetic dance routine. Though it's a bit difficult to convey in words just how charming this interlude is, the easy rapport between Bert and Dorothy is clearly evident, and it allows both to display their effervescent personalities and adept hoofing skills.

Unfortunately, this is the only sequence in which Dorothy is given the opportunity to shine. If there's any complaint to lodge against *Peach-O-Reno*, it's that Dorothy's role is a surprisingly limited one, despite the fact that she receives her usual third billing. Yet comedienne Zelma O'Neal is given a greater share of dialogue. O'Neal had scored a hit on Broadway in the original 1927 production of *Good News* (she introduced the "Varsity Drag" number) and was prominently featured in early movie musicals such as *Paramount on Parade* and *Follow Thru* (both 1930 releases). Yet her movie career never took off. *Peach-O-Reno* was one of the few films Zelma made before her retirement in 1938, and she proves to be a lively foil for Woolsey.

"Zelma was great on stage, but like a lot of stage performers, something was lost when she stepped in front of the camera," said Dorothy. "It's strange. She sure had talent but it didn't always register on film. I got a lesson in humility because of Zelma, though she never knew it. When we were making *Peach-O-Reno*, I remember thinking that the vogue for the type of character she specialized in was on the way out and so was Zelma. Well, I was too full of myself to realize that I was in the same boat as Zelma, because her type of personality wasn't too far removed from mine. I had no self-awareness."

The overabundance of supporting players and their involvement in the plot further pushed Dorothy off to the sidelines. After Bert and Bob, Joseph Cawthorn (*Dixiana, White Zombie, Love Me Tonight, The Great Ziegfeld*) and Cora Witherspoon (*The Bank Dick, The Women, Charlie Chan's Murder Cruise*) dominate the story as the bickering Brunos.

*Peach-O-Reno* was completed on October 14, 1931. It received generally favorable reviews. *Photoplay* observed: "Those nut comedians — Bert Wheeler and Robert Woolsey — are at it again.... It's an absurd plot concoction and although the story is weak on romance it's long on laughs. Peppy Zelma O'Neal comes close to stealing the picture from right under Woolsey's cigar. Dorothy Lee is as cute and pretty as ever."

In November 1931, David O. Selznick took over the reins from William LeBaron as RKO's head of production. The son of pioneer silent film studio distributor Lewis J. Selznick, David followed in his father's footsteps by becoming his apprentice. After the elder Selznick went into bankruptcy in the early 1920s, David secured a position in the story department at Metro-Goldwyn-Mayer in 1926. From there he moved on to Paramount Pictures in 1928. At Paramount, under the command of B.P. Schulberg, David was unable to make creative decisions freely, so he accepted an offer from RKO when they came calling.

RKO had acquired the Pathé organization in January 1931, resulting in a separate entity, RKO Pathé. The merger placed the studio in dire straits financially and in less than a year, the studio was on the verge of bankruptcy. David Sarnoff, chairman of the RKO board of directors, recruited Selznick to revitalize the failing studio.

Selznick, who was promised complete creative control, was not pleased with the way RKO was being run and began implementing a radical makeover. His plan included plenty of cutbacks and putting numerous employees on a sixty-day probation to evaluate their importance to the studio.

Bert, Bob and Dorothy found themselves in the line of fire when Selznick began reviewing their worth. Though the Wheeler and Woolsey films were profitable, Selznick, who had more prestigious fare in mind, had no tolerance for mindless fodder featuring what he considered to be "low-brow comics." With this mindset, Selznick set about to "fix" the team's latest production, *Girl Crazy*.

*Girl Crazy* had been a smash hit on Broadway in 1930, with a lovely score written by George and Ira Gershwin (including "I Got Rhythm," "Embraceable You," "I'm Bidin' My Time" and "But Not for Me"). The show also helped launch the careers of Ginger Rogers and Ethel Merman. The movie rights were purchased by RKO specifically as a property for Wheeler and Woolsey, with the adaptation written by Herman J. Mankiewicz (*Citizen Kane*, *Dinner at Eight*). This promising beginning was upended during the team's first encounter with their new executive producer, as Dorothy recounted:

"Selznick did not feel like having his time wasted with people he did not consider important, and he hated Wheeler and Woolsey. He couldn't stand their kind of humor. It didn't matter to him that their films consistently made money for RKO. His very first day on the set when he met the boys, he said right to their faces, 'Which one is Wheeler and which one is Woolsey?' Can you imagine? He let us know in no uncertain terms that our days were numbered. The atmosphere at RKO had been much more congenial before he arrived at the studio, and it wasn't just the three of us that felt this way about it. He was disliked by almost everyone."

Under the direction of William A. Seiter—who had helmed *Cracked Nuts, Too Many Cooks, Caught Plastered* and *Peach-O-Reno*—production on *Girl Crazy* began on December 15, 1931, and wrapped on January 12, 1932. Dorothy was particularly pleased that she got to sing two of the show's best tunes, "I Got Rhythm" and "But Not for Me."

## 5. You've Got What Gets Me

**Left to right: Kitty Kelly, Mitzi Green, Bob, Dorothy, Bert, Stanley Fields, Chris-Pin Martin, Arline Judge and Eddie Quillan flash smiles that belie the behind-the-scenes turmoil on the ill-fated *Girl Crazy* (1932).**

Then, at Selznick's insistence, the cast of *Girl Crazy* was summoned back to RKO in mid–February to shoot two weeks' worth of retakes, under the direction of comedy veteran Norman Taurog (who would direct the next Wheeler and Woolsey picture, *Hold 'Em Jail*). In the process, most of Dorothy's scenes, including her prized songs, were stripped from the picture. Over six decades later, Dorothy recalled the turn of events with anger and disdain: "*Girl Crazy* turned out to be a dog and it was all Selznick's fault. He took what would have been a good movie and ruined everything. He wound up giving the 'I Got Rhythm' number to Kitty Kelly, who was sleeping with William LeBaron, and Arline Judge [who had a minor supporting role in *Laugh and Get Rich*] got the 'But Not for Me' number because she was sleeping with Selznick. I know I don't have the greatest singing voice in the world, but those gals butchered those songs. My problem was that I wasn't sleeping with anyone connected with the picture, although that creep Selznick did come on to me and I rebuffed him. That may be why he edited out so many of my scenes. It really hurt me that I had originally had a starring role alongside Bert and Bob and my part was reduced to practically a walk-on.

"When this happened, I didn't want to do the picture any more and tried to get out of it, but Bert talked sense into me. 'Lee,' he said, 'you're crazy. You're getting a thousand dollars a week and Selznick is going to throw us all out after this, so what do you care what you do? Just do it!' Bert was right, of course."

The final version of *Girl Crazy* is a disappointing, jumbled hodgepodge that fritters away the memorable Gershwin score.[2] Yet some of the comedy set pieces are top-notch, indicating how good the original cut must have been. Manhattan playboy Danny Churchill (Eddie Quillan) is dispatched to the rural western town of Custerville, Arizona, where his father hopes his eager-for-romance son will have little opportunity to be tempted by the opposite sex. But Danny decides to invigorate his new surroundings by erecting a dude-ranch casino and recruits glamorous showgirls to attract the local yokels. Danny hires Slick Foster (Bob) and his brash wife Kate (Kelly) to handle the casinos gambling element. The penniless Slick manages to con naïve taxi driver Jimmy Deegan (Bert) into driving the couple all the way from Chicago to Arizona, with Jimmy's bratty little sister Tessie (Mitzi Green) tagging along for the ride.

In Custerville, Danny has fallen for local postmaster Molly Gray (Arline Judge), while a pretty cowgirl named Patsy (Dorothy) rescues Jimmy from a lynch mob. Danny's casino and the women employed there draw customers away from a rival gambling hall run by outlaw Lank Sanders (Stanley Fields), who decides to run for sheriff so he can shut down Danny's business. Jimmy, egged on by Slick and Danny, runs against Lank and wins the election, thanks to Tessie's chicanery.

Molly becomes jealous over Danny's interaction with some of the showgirls and she heads to Mexico with George Mason (Brooks Benedict), a city slicker with less-than-honorable designs on Molly. Danny follows Molly, as do Slick, Jimmy, Kate, Patsy and Tessie — and Lank and his henchman Pete (Chris-Pin Martin), who intend to make sure the new sheriff doesn't live to fulfill his term. Danny and Molly are reunited, the villains are defeated and all ends happily. Except for Wheeler and Woolsey fans, who deserved a better movie.

Wheeler and Woolsey's comedic timing is as sharp as ever, even when saddled with substandard material. (Their masquerade as a pair of Indians, a sequence added during the retakes, is particularly uninspired.) With most of her footage relegated to the cutting room floor, Dorothy was given one duet with Bert, "You've Got What Gets Me," a song supposedly written for the film. Actually, Ira Gershwin simply wrote new lyrics for "Your Eyes! Your Smile!," a song intended for but jettisoned from the Broadway show *Funny Face* (1927), which had starred Fred Astaire and his sister Adele. The tune is pleasant, though not in the same league as the rest of the score. Bert and Dorothy's rapport is still intact and after vocalizing, they break into a dance routine, with Mitzi Green joining in. The presentation might have been first-rate if it had been staged and shot properly. Instead, there are unnecessary cutaways while Dorothy is singing, and during the dance number she's obscured by an awkwardly placed pillar. Selznick's sabotage couldn't have been more blatant.

The critical reception to *Girl Crazy* was just as contradictory as the film itself,

## 5. You've Got What Gets Me

with Quinn Martin of the *New York World* claiming, "[Wheeler and Woolsey] attain a pitch and hilarity comparable to that of the Marx Brothers." *Variety* summed it up more accurately: "Wheeler and Woolsey's comedy antics save this one.... [S]ome laffs but weak and below par in sum total. Wheeler and Woolsey are the natural bright spots throughout."

The original movie adaptation of *Girl Crazy* was eventually eclipsed by the 1943 remake starring Mickey Rooney and Judy Garland. In the 1980s, when prints of the Wheeler and Woolsey version became available for rental (it was never included in TV syndication packages), Dorothy was offered the opportunity to see it but declined. "That was one of the few pictures I made that I looked forward to seeing because of the great Gershwin numbers I did. But after Selznick ruined it, I ended up never wanting to see it. I saw it once and that was enough for me. I never wanted to look it again."

During his RKO tenure, Selznick scored some impressive successes — including *A Bill of Divorcement* (1932), *What Price Hollywood?* (1932), *The Most Dangerous Game* (1932) and *King Kong* (1933) — but the ambitious producer could not rescue the studio from its downward financial spiral. The extra two weeks of shooting for *Girl Crazy* cost the studio an extra $200,000, putting the budget over $500,000. In trying to cut corners, Selznick had produced the most expensive of all the Wheeler and Woolsey films. (The next Selznick-produced W&W comedy, *Hold 'Em Jail*, also ran way over budget.)

Today, Selznick is deservedly hailed as the mastermind behind the Oscar-winning movie adaptation of Margaret Mitchell's *Gone with the Wind* (1939). But in 1932, he was an executive producer whose counterproductive decision-making was not sitting well with Merlin Aylesworth, the new president of RKO. Before Selznick departed from RKO in 1933, Bert and Bob would defect to another studio and Dorothy would be scrambling for employment elsewhere.

# Chapter 6

# Niagara Falls to Reno
## *A Star Without a Studio*

Production on the next Wheeler and Woolsey film, *Hold 'Em Jail*, began on April 4, 1932, with up-and-coming starlet Betty Grable in the role that would have normally been assigned to Dorothy Lee. Seven days later, RKO announced that Dorothy had been dropped from the studio's roster. The reason for her dismissal was unclear; years later, Dorothy would elaborate:

"I was trying to break my contract with RKO. I forced their hand because my contract stipulated that I was to receive third billing in every Wheeler and Woolsey picture I appeared in. I didn't get third billing in *Girl Crazy*[1] and I used that as leverage to get out of my contract. I figured the handwriting was on the wall anyway, that I was on the way out. So I raised a stink about it and RKO cut me loose, to make it look as though it was their decision to dump me. But I had already decided to dump them. It was like deciding to divorce a husband who beats you to the punch and files divorce papers on you first."

After parting company with RKO, Dorothy headed to New York for what was intended as a leisurely vacation but turned into a long rest. Having been a contract player may not have always been rewarding, but it did afford her the security of steady and guaranteed employment. Now, as a free agent for the first time in almost four years, Dorothy had to decide what her next career step would be. The stage had always been a comfort zone for her, so she embarked on a series of vaudeville gigs with her friend, comedian Billy Taft. Her association with Wheeler and Woolsey had made her a familiar and marketable name, and she was able to command $2,000 a week for her song-and-comedy act. When reporters inquired about future movie roles, she told them she would welcome the opportunity to play the lead in a film adaptation of Sir James Barrie's *Peter Pan*.

She was once again linked to Fred Waring, as rumors circulated that the couple had not only rekindled their romance but finally planned on tying the knot. While she would neither confirm nor deny the hearsay, she privately held out hope that she and Fred could pick up where they left off. Yet it became increasingly apparent that his continued unwillingness to commit and her impetuous mistakes, primarily the Jimmie Fidler fiasco, had taken its toll on their relationship. A reporter for the *Los Angeles Herald* caught Dorothy in a reflective mood when he asked about the status of her on-again, off-again relationship with Waring: "I shall always *love* Fred, but he has his work and I have mine. He is traveling most of the time and I'm out in California, and well, I guess it can *never* be...."

On May 17, 1932, the *New York Mirror* ran a curious article bearing this headline:

WHEELER AND WOOLSEY PART OVER GIRL
DOROTHY LEE NAMED IN RIFT BETWEEN HILARIOUS COMEDIANS

The brief, inconclusive piece did not explain how Dorothy supposedly caused the rift, aside from noting that "according to studio whispers" Bert and Bob were ending their partnership and Dorothy, the "third member of the team," was the reason behind it.

In truth, Dorothy had nothing to do with the rift. Bert and Bob, enticed by a profit-participation deal, jumped ship from RKO over to Columbia Pictures to make a film titled *Bottoms Up*. Before production began, Bert suddenly decided he would be better off as a solo act and accepted several stage engagements, walking out on Bob and their Columbia contract. The team would reconcile two months later, when Bert discovered that, due to the Depression, the top-price bookings he had hoped for were few and far between.

With Wheeler and Woolsey's departure, RKO's remaining comedy team was Bobby Clark and Paul McCullough, who starred in a series of two-reel shorts from 1931 to 1935. Clark and McCullough were Broadway favorites but their appeal did not transfer to the screen easily and the studio chose not to graduate them to feature films. Instead, RKO announced they had signed the wacky team of Ole Olsen and Chic Johnson for a series of two-reelers, which the studio may have intended to use to test the market for possible full-length features with Ole and Chic. (The team had previously starred in three features for Warner Brothers, none of which established them as viable movie stars.) But Olsen and Johnson never did make a single film for RKO; a few years later the duo would make it big not in motion pictures but on stage with their signature *Hellzapoppin'* revue.

Dorothy signed to appear in *Footlites*, and she was promoted as its main attraction:

A 4 STAR STAGE REVUE
IN PERSON:
THE POPULAR HOLLYWOOD COMEDIENNE, DOROTHY LEE,
FEMININE STAR OF WHEELER AND WOOLSEY COMEDIES

*Footlites* was based on *Speak Easily*, a Clarence Buddington Kelland story about a timid professor who inherits a fortune and decides to back a Broadway show. (The story served as the basis for the film *Speak Easily*, starring Buster Keaton and Jimmy Durante, released that same year.) The cast included Dorothy's vaudeville partner Billy Taft, along with Reginald Sheffield (as the professor), Claudia Dell, Pietro Gentile and Ruth Matteson, and the premise allowed for several musical numbers to be woven into the production.

*Footlites* opened on July 20, 1932, at the Mayan Theatre in Los Angeles. (The Mayan, a historic landmark, still serves as a fully functional stage.) The reviews were mixed, though Dorothy's performance earned praise. Harrison Carroll of the *L.A. Record* noted:

> Except for the vivacious Dorothy Lee and some rather nice tunes, *Footlites* has little to recommend it.... Unfortunately, the professor's adventures emerge here as spiritless, flat and repetitious proceedings. Miss Lee, assisted by Billy Taft, is indisputably the star of the show. The two of them contributed almost every moment of life in the entire production.... Unless heroic measures are adopted, *Footlites* is due for a brief life.

The *Los Angeles Times* was more charitable:

> Staging of the numbers in the second part is highly attractive, and numbers with sparkle capture considerable applause. Individual numbers garnered applause, and plenty of it. Miss Lee and Taft early won those present with their "Haven't Got Music" which was amusingly and eccentrically danced by them. This was one of the brightest moments in the opening act.

The *L.A. Herald* noted that one of Dorothy's *Footlites* songs poked fun at her much-publicized romances, incorporating the names Marsh, Jim and Fred. "Marsh" was a reference to Marshall Duffield, the latest man in Dorothy's life. Everyone knew Duffield for his exploits on the football field. He was the University of Southern California's star quarterback during their 1930-31 season, and had been named All-American Quarterback of 1929. Dorothy first met him at a dinner dance held for the USC and Notre Dame football teams. She reminisced, "When we shared a dance, he told me, 'You're my favorite movie star. Someday I'm going to marry you!' I was still married to Jimmie Fidler at the time, so my chin almost hit the floor. Then he said he had been in love with me ever since he first saw me on the screen."

Dorothy confessed she was attracted to the handsome gridiron hero, but dismissed his remarks as the declarations of a naïve, star-struck young man. After her divorce from Fidler, however, Dorothy and Marsh became inseparable. Dorothy attended every one of his football games, as newspapers and magazines covered their high-profile romance. They shared a love for athletics, and although his goal was to attend law school, he made no secret of his aspirations to work in the film industry.

Dorothy appeared in court on August 10, 1932, seeking the return of $250 advance rent for a Malibu Beach cottage she had rented from February to June of 1931. In a cross-complaint, Mrs. Charles Cooley, the owner of the house, sued Dorothy for $375 as restitution for furniture allegedly damaged during Dorothy's occupancy. Dorothy remembered, "Mrs. Cooley did nothing but complain during the entire time I was renting the cottage. She said I was ruining the place. I had a number of parties there, but all we did was socialize. There was none of the wild goings-on that she kept accusing me of. She finally asked me to leave, which was fine with me because I already had

**Dorothy and new beau Marshall Duffield at the Pacific Southwest Tennis Championship (1933).**

enough of her false accusations. But when I moved out, she refused to return my $250 [one-month] deposit. She threatened to go to the press and tell them about all the wild parties I held there and about how we damaged all of her furniture. She thought that because I was an actress, I would be afraid of any negative publicity and just let her keep the money. Well, I wasn't going to roll over and play dead. I told her I was going to take her to court, and I did. So she decided to get back at me and countersued for all of the furniture that I allegedly destroyed." (The court took the case under advisement and eventually ruled in Dorothy's favor.) "It wasn't the money, it was the principle. I felt I was being blackmailed and I wouldn't stand for it."

Dorothy's divorce from Fidler was decreed final on August 15, 1932, and immediately rumors of an impending Lee–Duffield marriage began to circulate. The couple was quick to deny them — for the time being, at least.

After the short-lived run of *Footlites*, Dorothy accepted an offer from the fledgling Plymouth Pictures Corporation for what would turn out to be her most obscure movie credit, *Mazie*. At the Metropolitan Studios in Fort Lee, New Jersey, production began September 1932, with Dallas M. Fitzgerald, the president of Plymouth, handling the directorial chores — probably out of economic necessity rather than a desire for artistic expression. (Fitzgerald, who had directed over two dozen films during the silent era, hadn't helmed a picture in four years.)

In the title role, Dorothy plays a café waitress who befriends Edith (Kay Ellis), a young woman seemingly down on her luck. Edith turns out to be an heiress who has gone into hiding to protect her sweetheart (LeRoy Mason) from a scandal involving her father. Mazie and Edith take off to a high-society resort where Mazie reunites the separated couple, and even finds romance herself.

*Mazie* was a low-budget production, but its use of real locations made it more intriguing than most of Dorothy's later Poverty Row efforts. The café scenes were filmed at an actual restaurant, and while the camerawork during these sequences may seem static (or even non-existent), the authenticity provides a fascinating time capsule of the era. Likewise the resort beachfront scenes, which are like a living picture postcard.

Adding to the verisimilitude is Dorothy's apparel. She goes through more wardrobe changes than you would expect for a shoestring production such as this, and we suspect the outfits (day dress, evening dress, bathing suit) came from her own closet. One outfit that Dorothy certainly didn't own was the waitress outfit she wore, which, from a perspective several decades removed, gives the café scenes a quaint charm that would have been taken for granted at the time.

While *Mazie* may not rank among Dorothy's best movies, it's a better showcase than *Laugh and Get Rich* had been. As in her other independently made efforts, many of the scenes have a "first take" feel about them, as though the first (and perhaps only) take was used, making passages seem like rehearsals rather than finalized performances. Her character is a welcome throwback to the spirited roles she played in *Rio Rita* and *Half Shot at Sunrise*, making her more engaging here than she was in perfunctory girlfriend or daughter roles that were blandly conceived and acted.

*Mazie* received scant distribution. Like other independent motion picture companies of the era, Plymouth Pictures lacked the distribution set-up of major studios and would have instead marketed *Mazie* on a "States' Rights" basis, which meant it was sold on a territorial basis to independent film exchanges. (In late March 1933, fleeting announcements in trade journals claimed that the film would be released shortly, but we were unable to uncover an exact release date.)

At the end of production, Dorothy had been given a promissory note for $450 back salary that was due by December 1, 1932. When she failed to receive payment by that date, Dorothy sued Plymouth Pictures and Fitzgerald, and won a settlement that included an additional $31 for interest and legal costs.

A motion picture company that couldn't afford to pay its lead actress was obviously not an outfit destined for survival; *Mazie* was the first and last film produced by Plymouth Pictures Corporation. "I never saw the completed picture," Dorothy commented. "I don't think anybody did."

Though she was no longer affiliated with a major studio, Dorothy enjoyed the life of a Hollywood star, hobnobbing with some of Tinseltown's biggest luminaries. Her prowess as a tennis player guaranteed invitations to many social gatherings, including parties at the Harold Lloyd Estate, known as Greenacres:

"Harold was a sweet, charming man, just like the character he played in his movies, and I was a frequent guest in his home, which was an absolutely magnificent mansion.[2] It was a real showplace, but it was never intimidating because Harold was such a warm and gracious host. He kept the mood unpretentious.

"When it came to athletics, Harold was a fierce competitor and so was I, so we shared that connection. I played tennis at Greenacres many times, and Harold and I were usually on the same side in games of mixed doubles because Harold didn't want to square off against me. And I was a little wary of him too, because he was a terrific tennis player. We figured it would be a real bloodbath if we ever played against each other one on one."

Dorothy was also a guest at Hearst Castle, the sprawling estate owned by newspaper magnate William Randolph Hearst.[3] At the Castle, Hearst and actress Marion Davies lived together, a relationship widely known throughout the industry though kept secret from the public at large. Over the years, invitations to the Hearst Castle (often referred to as "San Simeon," which is actually the name of the area adjacent to the estate) were extended to such high-profile guests as Franklin D. Roosevelt, Winston Churchill, Charles Lindbergh, Charlie Chaplin and the Marx Brothers, so Dorothy was in heady company:

"I was invited to the Hearst estate a few times because I was friends with Marion Davies, not because I was such a big celebrity or a member of the elite. Marion was one of the biggest stars in Hollywood yet she was so down-to-earth. She wanted everyone to have a good time. Hearst ran the place like a boot camp. Activities were scheduled throughout the day and at night there was a formal dinner. It was sort of *regimented* fun and sometimes it felt like we were having a party in a museum. But Marion kept things lively, made sure all the guests were comfortable and we certainly did enjoy ourselves.

"I always played tennis while I was a guest at the estate. I once squared off against Ginger Rogers, who would tell anyone who would listen that she was the best female tennis player in Hollywood. She was very good, actually, so when she challenged me, she figured she would trounce me in no time flat. I could never compete with her as an actress or a dancer, but I knew I was at least her equal on the tennis court. She didn't know that [world-champion tennis player] May Sutton Bundy taught me how to play. I still remember the look on Ginger's face when she realized that I was much better than she expected. I wound up beating her — it was a pretty lopsided victory, as I recall — and she never bragged about tennis when I was around."

Away from the tennis court, Dorothy indulged in her other sports passion, golf. A frequent golf partner was Ruby Keeler, whose role in *42nd Street* (1933) made her a movie star overnight: "Ruby and I were crazy about golf. Ruby was married to Al Jolson but he couldn't play golf at the Lakeside Country Club, where we went, because it was restricted, meaning they didn't allow Jewish people there. It's amazing what we all just accepted and took in stride in those days. Prejudice is always wrong, and the anti-Semitism was especially appalling in Hollywood, given how nearly everyone who ran the studios was Jewish and how they were responsible for giving Hollywood all of its glamour and success. But back then this was an accepted way of life, and I'm embarrassed to admit that it took me years to realize how disgusting it was.

"So Jolson played at Hillcrest, which was a Jewish country club. Since she was Mrs. Jolson, Ruby could have gone there and played golf but she didn't, not because she was prejudiced, of course, but because she didn't care to be around Jolson any more than she needed to be. Jolson was a mean-spirited guy and it irked him that Ruby had become a big star while his career was slipping [in the mid–1930s]. He would say nasty things to her, in front of everyone, telling her she was stupid and had no talent. I know that Jolson was a great entertainer, but I could never look past what a louse he was. Sometimes he'd try to present himself as a sweet, lovable man, like Eddie Cantor, but no one who knew Jolson bought that act. Eddie Cantor really was a sweet, lovable man, but Jolson was just a fake. I couldn't stand him."

Meanwhile, over at Columbia Pictures, Wheeler and Woolsey completed *Bottoms Up*, which was retitled *That's Africa*, then finally *So This Is Africa* when it was released in 1933. The film's rampant double-entendre humor ran afoul with the censorship guidelines of the MPPDA (Motion Picture Producers and Distributors of America) and the final cut was shorn of much of the original footage. Dorothy was not involved with this production, though admittedly she would have not been suited for either one of the prominent female roles (a wildlife expert played by Esther Muir and a jungle girl played by Raquel Torres).

Due to Columbia's creative bookkeeping, Wheeler and Woolsey never saw a dime from their profit-participation arrangement. This made it easier for RKO president Merlin Aylesworth to woo the team back to his studio with an irresistible deal that included a raise in their weekly salaries and 20 percent of all of the gross profits over half a million dollars, with the opportunity to negotiate a favorable long-term contract.

Bert and Bob returned to RKO in January 1933, just as David O. Selznick handed in his resignation and Merian C. Cooper took his place as head of production. *Diplomaniacs*, a free-wheeling, atypical political satire (it was more in the spirit of Olsen and Johnson than Wheeler and Woolsey), was the first picture under their new contract. The role of Bert's leading lady was given to Marjorie White, an effervescent singer-comedienne whose powerhouse vivacity predated Martha Raye and Betty Hutton. White had appeared in *Sunnyside Up* (1929) and *Just Imagine* (1930), two of the most popular early movie musicals, and is best remembered for her role in the Three Stooges short *Woman Haters* (1934).

To sweeten their new contract, Wheeler and Woolsey were sent on an all-expense-paid world tour. Bert and Bob asked Dorothy to join them, but she declined, preferring to pursue other opportunities. One of those opportunities was appearing as the headline attraction at the Cocoanut Grove, the famed Hollywood night club, in March 1933, singing with Phil Harris and his orchestra. Regular Grove performers Leah Ray, Arthur Jarrett, and Xavier Cugat and his band took a backseat to Dorothy for the occasion. Bert and Bob, who were preparing to leave on their world tour the following month, were in attendance and stepped on stage to wish her success. Also present were Clark Gable, Howard Hughes, Jean Harlow, Sid Grauman of Grauman's Chinese Theater, Johnny Weissmuller, and William LeBaron. "I really enjoyed that engagement. I wound up working there for a couple months. It was a kick for me because the Cocoanut Grove was in the Ambassador Hotel and I was raised about ten blocks from there. Everyone at the Cocoanut Grove was so kind to me, they couldn't have been nicer. During rehearsals, Xavier Cugat would draw sketches of me and he was quite an artist. Phil Harris was one of the most charming and naturally funny men I've ever known. He would say things that sounded egocentric, but he was actually poking fun at that sort of behavior through his own personality. He would walk into a room and say, 'Well, don't just sit there. Start making a fuss over me!' He could get away with this because people knew he was only kidding. I loved working with him."

Dorothy unexpectedly found herself embroiled in industry politics with the formation of the Screen Actors Guild, founded by a core group of six actors (Ralph Morgan, Alden Gay, Kenneth Thomson, Grant Mitchell, Berton Churchill, Charles Miller). The Guild sought to fight for the rights of motion picture actors who were being exploited by studio contracts that forced them to endure long hours and other restrictive work conditions. In June 1933, three months after its foundation, the Guild appointed its president officers and board of directors (which included Morgan, Alan Mowbray, Eddie Cantor, Boris Karloff, Ann Harding, Lyle Talbot, James Gleason, Noel Madison, Charles Starrett, Tyler Brooke, C. Aubrey Smith and Leon Ames).

SAG received support from such prominent actors as James Cagney, Fredric March, Humphrey Bogart, Edward G. Robinson, Bela Lugosi, Gary Cooper, Dick Powell, Spencer Tracy, Paul Muni, Warren William, Robert Young, Adolphe Menjou, Gloria Stuart, Ralph Bellamy, Robert Montgomery, Chester Morris, Jean Hersholt and Gene Lockhart, yet others refused to join the group. The resistance stemmed from a concern that arbitration between SAG and the studios would only benefit established, higher-profile stars instead of every actor in the industry.

As the membership of the Screen Actors Guild increased, Frank Gillmore, the president of the Actors Equity Association, issued a warning to twenty-four actors who had refused to join SAG, an Equity affiliate. However, the actors in question remained adamant. AEA placed them under suspension and urged Equity members "in good standing" not to work with any of these individuals. Dorothy was part of this suspended group, which also included Lionel Barrymore, Jack Oakie, Rosalind Russell, Alice Brady, Nat Pendleton, Frank Sully and Ian Keith. In time, all of the twenty-four holdouts became SAG members, though their misgivings would last for a few years until the studios agreed to negotiate with the Guild.

In the summer of 1933, RKO extended an olive branch to Dorothy by casting her opposite comic actor Chick Chandler in the political farce *A Preferred List*, a musical-comedy short that was intended to be the first entry in a series of Lee-Chandler two-reelers. *A Preferred List* was released on October 6 and was so well-received it was nominated for Best Short Subject (Comedy) at the 1934 Academy Awards. The Lee-Chandler series never materialized, but Dorothy had reconnected with RKO and plans were made to reunite her with Wheeler and Woolsey.

In July, Wheeler took a trip to Washington, D.C. On July 11, at the Shoreham Hotel, while Bert danced with current girlfriend Patricia Parker, band leader Barney Briskin tipped off a newspaper reporter that Bert was dancing with Dorothy Lee. Bert told the reporter that Dorothy was scheduled to appear in the next Wheeler and Woolsey picture, and

**Dorothy and Chick Chandler at the Santa Monica Pleasure Pier in this publicity shot promoting *A Preferred List* (1933), which was intended to be the first in a series of Lee-Chandler comedy shorts.**

left it at that. The resultant news article, however, claimed that Bert and Dorothy (who wasn't even in town) danced the night away, celebrating their engagement. Bert would spend the next six months telling the press about the overzealous reporter's inaccurate account. Dorothy chose a more expedient method of straightening things out by announcing her engagement to Marshall Duffield. On July 19, Dorothy told a reporter for the *L.A. Record*, "[We] are just waiting until he finishes law school and gets established in practice before we get married."

Dorothy headed east to play a supporting role in *Take a Chance* (1933), Paramount Pictures' adaptation of the Broadway hit. Despite a promising cast (James Dunn, June Knight, Lillian Roth, Cliff "Ukulele Ike" Edwards, Charles "Buddy" Rogers) and a musical score that included "It's Only a Paper Moon," it was a disappointingly hit-and-miss affair.

**Charles Richman (third from left), Lilian Bond, Lillian Roth and Charles "Buddy" Rogers watch Dorothy perform her snake-hips dance in *Take a Chance* (1933).**

Although the film didn't follow the play to the letter, it retained the same basic plot: Carnival barkers Duke Stanley (Dunn) and Louie Webb (Edwards) get involved with the legitimate theater when singer Toni Ray (Knight, repeating her original stage role), their carny cohort, falls for Kenneth Raleigh (Rogers), a millionaire's son who is writing and directing his first play, a Broadway-bound stage revue titled *Humpty Dumpty*. Duke and Louie's attempts to go straight are complicated by their inability to curb their larcenous tendencies and Duke's contentious relationship with his on-again, off-again girlfriend Wanda Brill (Roth, in a role played on Broadway by Ethel Merman).

Filmed largely at the Eastern Service Studios in Astoria, New York, *Take a Chance* had two directors, Monte Brice and Laurence Schwab, which may account for the unevenness of the results. (The theater-trained Schwab had little experience as a movie director.) The assembled players, as appealing as they are, seem to have been directed as though they were delivering their lines from a stage, and their performances often come across stilted or over-emphatic. The handling of the musical numbers is wildly uneven. Edwards' novelty tune "I Did It with My Little Ukulele" is executed in a breezy and imaginative manner, and is one of the few highlights. Roth does a nice rendition of "Eadie Was a Lady," which also features a young Vivian Vance, years before her TV stardom as Ethel Mertz on *I Love Lucy*. On the other hand, "It's Only a Paper Moon" is presented in such a clumsy fashion (it is interrupted midway through by a ponderous fantasy sequence) that it spoils what should have been a surefire number.

Dorothy was cast as Consuelo Raleigh, Kenneth's ditzy, hot-to-trot little sister, a role played onstage by Mitzi Mayfair. Dorothy's participation is mostly limited to fleeting scenes where she tries to convince everyone she's worthy of a part in the play by displaying her snake-hips dance gyrations.

Oddly, Dorothy is not involved in any of the musical numbers, but she gets the opportunity to undulate as an Indian maiden during the revue's climactic comedy sketch, "Daniel Boone's Defense," which employs the time-honored premise of last-minute cast replacements (in this case, Dunn, Edwards and Dorothy) whose disruptive antics are construed as inspired lunacy by the audience and critics. This contrived set-up rarely succeeds — the humor generally comes off as forced and hollow — and here the rapturous response the sketch receives is particularly unconvincing.

Modern viewers are often shocked to see symbols that appear to be Nazi swastikas on Dorothy's Indian costume. These are actually *swatisks*, or "Rolling Logs," which stand for "peace" (in Hinduism and Buddhism the symbol means "health"), and they are common in Native American art and culture. When Adolf Hitler rose to power, the Nazis corrupted the image and its meaning, turning it into what was referred to as a swastika. Those who see a swastik today usually confuse it for the Nazi symbol.

Dorothy was scheduled to work for two weeks on *Take a Chance*, but it was extended to over a month due to production delays created by two lead stars. "I liked Jimmy Dunne and Lillian Roth very much. They were both darling people ... when they were sober. When they began drinking heavily, they couldn't work at all. As soon as Jimmy sobered up, Lillian would go on a bender, and vice versa. They shot around them as much as they could, but they had scenes together and it was difficult to get them on the set at the same time. So I wound up staying in New York longer than I expected." (Dunn continued to star in films throughout the decade and went on to win an Academy Award for Best Supporting Actor for his performance — ironically, as an alcoholic — in *A Tree Grows in Brooklyn* [1945]. Roth, once one of Broadway's brightest stars, detailed her battle with alcoholism in her 1954 autobiography *I'll Cry Tomorrow*.)

Given the flat-footed results, *Take a Chance* garnered better reviews than one would have expected. *Variety* called it "[s]ufficiently entertaining.... [It] stacks up favorably against the more elaborate Hollywood musicals whose much higher costs naturally permit a lavish grade of production which *Take a Chance* doesn't enjoy.... [It has] the most ambitious name line-up captured for any eastern indie production in recent years." Mordaunt Hall of the *New York Times* was reserved but charitable: "*Take a Chance* has several good ideas, but it is quite obvious that they are not set forth as well in the film as they were on the stage. There is no denying, however, that this screen work has speed and a certain rhythm.... It is a passable affair of its type and some of the participants succeed in being quite entertaining in their respective roles."

While in New York, Dorothy starred in *Plane Crazy* (1933), a two-reel musical filmed at Warner Brothers' Vitaphone Studio in Brooklyn. In this charming short, she aligns herself with a pair of small-time aviators (Arthur and Morton Havel) who stage a bogus around-the-world flight. The charade is a stunning success and at a reception held in their honor, the trio spins tall tales about their exciting, tune-filled adventures in foreign lands.

The speculation over Dorothy and Marsh Duffield ended when they were married on September 3, 1933. Dorothy remembered, "Marsh graduated USC with honors. He was also awarded the Rhodes Scholarship which was quite an event, but he turned it down so we could get married instead." The ceremony was performed at the Agua Caliente Hotel in Tijuana, Mexico, with Ferris B. Webster, also of USC, as best man and June Clyde as maid of honor. It was reported that after the couple exchanged their "I do"s, the minister turned to Duffield and ordered, in jest, "Now tackle her!" Fred Waring sent Dorothy the following telegram:

DARLING POOCH[4]

JUST RECOVERED MY EQUILIBRIUM AFTER THE SUDDEN SURPRISE. WOW AND A COUPLE OF WOW WOWS. I DIDN'T KNOW YOU NEEDED A VICTROLA THAT BADLY. NO KIDDING PLEASE GIVE MY CONGRATULATIONS TO MARSH AND TELL HIM I THINK YOU ARE LUCKY TOO. WILL SHOP FOR BEST BARGAIN IN MUSIC BOX UNLESS YOU'D LIKE TO DOUBLE THE BET ON A JUNIOR BEFORE FEBRUARY. YOU KNOW YOU HAVE ALL MY BEST WISHES ALWAYS IN ALL WAYS SO BE GOOD AND I'M PROUD OF YOU.

FRED

The newlyweds enjoyed a short honeymoon in Agua Caliente before returning to Hollywood. It was an eventful occasion, says Dorothy: "June Clyde, T. Freeland [June's husband], Marsh and I went out to a restaurant, but we had to wait for a table to become free, so the only place you could go was to a bar and wait until they had a table ready. Marsh was on one side of me talking and John Wayne recognized Marsh because anybody interested in football would know who Marsh was, and I think that they had known each other from USC. Marsh pointed towards me and said to John, 'I think you know....' He answered, kind of kidding me, 'Yes, I know, you're Dorothy Lee, aren't you? Marsh's girlfriend.' I had known John Wayne casually enough to say hello. I never worked with him, but we would see each other on adjoining sets. We liked to visit each other's sets and watch each other work.

"Anyhow, we were down in this little Mexican town now and John was standing next to me at the bar. The men were talking among themselves and us gals were talking with each other. The men were drinking and June and I didn't drink very much, nothing stronger than a gin and tonic. John says, 'I bet I can drink you under the table.' I never turned down a dare, so he began pouring tequila and it is very strong. Heck, I never even drank tequila before. If you've never drank tequila, well, don't, it's a waste of time. So as the men started drinking, so did I, but I didn't drink as fast as they did. It had to be over an hour [before] I began to really get a little woozy, and John was doing all right too. Then he really started to get bombed and while I was still standing he was the one who ended up under the table! I held on and left with Marsh and my friends who were feeling the effects of the alcohol, but we still wound up having dinner. Next morning, I found out John surely got bombed because he was still hung over!"

Dorothy had another celebrity encounter during the honeymoon vacation: "While we were out having a good time and talking, I felt someone tap me on the side. I said, 'Pardon me,' and turned to see it was Tallulah Bankhead. She was always saying outrageous things and she tried to shock me by asking, 'Are you a lesbian?' She caught me off-guard and I answered, 'No, should I be?' I thought Tallulah would just collapse because she thought it was so funny. Here I am a dainty little thing and I look so innocent. The last thing in the world she expected was for me to answer that way. The boys almost fell over too, because they knew how many boyfriends I had had. Throughout the years when Tallulah and I would run into each other, we would put our arms around each other and laugh about it. Tallulah loved telling that story. She'd say, 'Do you know what this little lady said to me?' She was a riot."

Back in Hollywood, Marsh Duffield secured a job as an assistant director for Paramount Pictures while attending law school at night. He worked on the film *Eight Girls in a Boat* and Dorothy often drove to the San Francisco shooting location to visit him. Marsh's sister Harriett and Dorothy became good friends; Harriett would accompany Dorothy to a number of her film sets. Marsh also took an interest in politics and ran as a mayoral candidate in his home town of Santa Monica.

As Marsh maintained a busy schedule, Dorothy was prepared to reunite with the other men in her life, Bert Wheeler and Robert Woolsey.

## CHAPTER 7

# Keep on Doin' What You're Doin'
## *Back with the Boys*

Beginning on October 17, 1933, Dorothy was once again part of RKO's Wheeler and Woolsey unit, at the request of Bert and Bob and with the wholehearted approval of producer Merian C. Cooper. Serendipitously, her reunion film, *Hips, Hips, Hooray!*, was the team's best effort to date.

Dorothy reflected on her homecoming: "It was so wonderful to be back at RKO. We didn't have anything like a party to celebrate reuniting, but I can tell you that we were so happy to be back together, and everyone on the set of *Hips, Hips, Hooray!* was great. It turned out to be my personal favorite among all the movies I made with Bert and Bob."

*Hips, Hips, Hooray!* is a glossy, highly entertaining Wheeler and Woolsey vehicle, with a bright script and score by songwriters Bert Kalmar and Harry Ruby, who had contributed to the scripts for two outstanding Marx Brothers comedies, *Horse Feathers* (1932) and *Duck Soup* (1933). (Kalmar and Ruby also co-wrote the Marx Brothers play *Animal Crackers* and the Clark and McCullough play *The Ramblers*, which served as the basis for the Wheeler and Woolsey film *The Cuckoos*.) In the director's chair was Mark Sandrich, a comedy-shorts veteran whose previous RKO feature, *Melody Cruise* (1933), was brimming with imaginative visual effects.

"Mark Sandrich was one of the nicest men I ever met," Dorothy said. "He cared about our opinions. He'd discuss the script with us and was always open to suggestions. He loved to use a lot of visual gags. Other directors, like Luther Reed [*Rio Rita, Dixiana*], wanted you to do the script exactly as written and didn't want you to stray from your lines at all. It was different with Mark. When we were rehearsing a scene and we thought it would come across better in another way, we would go to Mark and ask, 'We like this better, could we do it this way?' He would watch and listen, then see how it was written, and he would agree by saying, 'It gets the same point across so that will be fine.' That was especially good for Wheeler and Woolsey because as comedians they knew how a joke or gag would come off best and the way it would look most natural for them. Mark was a genius. He listened and cared about how we felt and

**Bob, Bert and Dorothy with Thelma Todd (right), one of the screen's finest comediennes, in *Hips, Hips, Hooray!* (1934).**

allowed us to use our ideas. That really made you care more about the work that you were doing.

"Kalmar and Ruby were wonderful. They weren't always on the set but they would write these songs and they would play them for us. They had a great partnership."

In *Hips, Hips, Hooray!*, Andy Williams (Bert) and Dr. Dudley (Bob) are fast-talking street peddlers — specializing in flavored lipsticks — who manage to convince cosmetics model Daisy Maxwell (Dorothy) that they're successful businessmen. Amelia Frisby (Thelma Todd), owner of the Maiden America Beauty Products (and Daisy's boss), is impressed by the boys' apparent business acumen and merges with them in an effort to revive her faltering company. Andy and Dudley inadvertently come into possession of stolen investment securities and before long two private detectives (Matt Briggs, James Burtis) are hot on their trail. Armand Beauchamp (George Meeker), Miss Frisby's corrupt sales manager, complicates matters by feeding company secrets to competitor Madam Irene (Phyllis Barry) and plotting to take off with the securities himself. Before they clear themselves with the law, Andy and Dudley take the wheel of a race car and wind up winning a cross-country competition representing Maiden America.

## 7. Keep on Doin' What You're Doin'

The film offers plenty of saucy, pre–Code fun, with scantily clad girls, double entendres and wild sight gags set against '30s art-deco design and slick production values. As always, Bert, Bob and Dorothy share an effortless chemistry and Thelma Todd makes it a perfect foursome. Dorothy fondly remembered, "Thelma was a great gal and I just loved her. She was so warm and so funny, and she had the kind of personality that made you gravitate to her immediately. She had no ego whatsoever. She only wanted to do what was best for the picture. And as beautiful as she was on screen, she was even more beautiful in person, if you can believe that."

Though assigned her usual ingénue role opposite Bert, Dorothy is afforded the opportunity to be funny and spirited, and nowhere is this more evident than in the production number "Keep on Doin' What You're Doin'" (often referred to as "Just Keep on Doin' What You're Doin'"). The Kalmar-Ruby tune was originally composed for the Marx Brothers film *Duck Soup*, but when a romantic subplot involving Zeppo Marx and Raquel Torres was dropped, so was the song.[1] In *Hips, Hips, Hooray!*, the number is staged as a mock ballet, with Bert, Bob, Dorothy and Thelma merrily prancing around (and trashing) an office. At one point, Dorothy leaps off of a desk and into Bert and Bob's waiting arms, reminiscent of a similar leap she took off a military car during the mock ballet in *Half Shot at Sunrise*.

While performing one of the stunts, Dorothy sustained a back injury that would last a lifetime: "Bert and Bob caught me after I jumped off a desk and they began to swing me back and forth as they held on to my arms and legs. A mannequin was used where they are swinging me around and around, then they let go and the mannequin flew up in the air. In the next shot, you see me hanging from a chandelier. What happened was, it was really me hanging about twelve feet off the ground. When I let go, Bert, Bob and Thelma were supposed to break my fall by catching me in a [tiger-skin] rug, using it like a fireman's net. They broke my fall but the rug slipped out of their hands and I hit the ground, landing right on my spine. [This shot is in the film.] I hid the pain the best I could and danced off with a big smile on my face. I knew I had to perform. I must have been in shock because after that I was stiff and couldn't move. I had to take a couple of weeks off from work. For a while, I walked with a cane and had to see an osteopath."

Vocalist Ruth Etting—who popularized "Love Me or Leave Me," "Ten Cents a Dance" and similar torch songs—received third billing, after Bert and Bob, but only appeared in the film long enough to warble the opening tune, "Keep Romance Alive." Etting was slated to perform another song, "Tired of It All," but it was scrapped after her husband, gangster Marty "Moe the Gimp" Snyder, demanded more money for the additional number. (She was already receiving $10,000 for her services.) As Dorothy remembered, it was all for the best: "Ruth was a sweet woman but her husband Marty was impossible to deal with. He would tell Mark Sandrich how to direct Ruth's number. [Marty] was a pushy, intimidating guy and we were glad to get him off the set."

Production on *Hips, Hips, Hooray!* was completed on November 6; one week before wrapping, Bert and Bob spent a day shooting *Signing 'Em Up*, a four-minute short promoting the newly-established National Recovery Administration. Bert, Bob and Dorothy (who has no dialogue) appear as themselves, as do RKO contract players Bruce Cabot, Pert Kelton and Roscoe Ates.

In January 1934, as RKO prepared the next Wheeler and Woolsey project — *Frat Heads*, a musical-comedy about college fraternities — Bert, Bob and Dorothy embarked upon a three-week vaudeville tour, in part to promote *Hips, Hips, Hooray!* which was scheduled for a February release. The tour began in Washington D.C., where on January 15 the trio visited the House of Assembly and the proceedings stopped to acknowledge their presence. (Bob drew laughs when he quipped, "We got a tip there might be some good joke material here.") From Washington it was on to New York and finally Baltimore, performing five shows a day. The act was a hodgepodge of old and new material, with Bert and Bob incorporating bits of old stage routines that predated their partnership. Bert would introduce himself as "Bert Wheeler of Wheeler and Woolsey" and Bob would introduce himself as "Robert Woolsey of Woolsey and Wheeler," and they had audiences eating out of the palms of their hands.

Dorothy would look back fondly on the personal-appearance tour: "The reception we got from audiences was amazing. They went crazy over everything we did, and we could do no wrong. Now, we had some solid, funny material — singing, dancing, joking around — but a lot of the response was because of the good will that carried over from our movies. Plus, the crowd was excited just to see us in person. We really weren't sure what to do at the beginning, so we relied mainly on things we had done before, separately. Bert and Bob did some vaudeville routines and I used some material I had done when I was first starting out with Homer Dickinson. I also sang a song called 'I'm a Pepper-Upper' and did my snake-hips dance. We were doing whatever we could think of, and all of it went over gangbusters.

"I always knew Bert and Bob were funny, but I don't think I realized just how funny they could be until I saw them work in front of a live audience. They were so much funnier on stage than they were in most of their movies, and it really hit home how many of the scripts didn't do them justice. Bert and Bob really came to life on stage, doing tried-and-true routines and not bogged down by some of the half-assed scripts the studio stuck them with. I've seen that happen with other comedians who were also funnier in person than they were in the movies. The Ritz Brothers were a riot if you saw them live but I don't think their films captured that. Same thing with Olsen and Johnson. *Hellzapoppin'* was the funniest play I ever saw, but Olsen and Johnson's movies were dogs."

On the trip back to Hollywood, their plane was grounded in Omaha due to mechanical difficulties. Faced with a four-hour layover, Dorothy passed the time by going to the movies with another passenger. When reporters asked Woolsey if Dorothy was romantically involved with the gentleman, Bob quipped, "Naw, she's really in love with me." The joke backfired when the reporters took the remark seriously. Dorothy said, "We both had a terrible time living that down."

*Hips, Hips, Hooray!* opened on February 2, 1934, to mixed reviews, typical for a

## 7. Keep on Doin' What You're Doin'

Wheeler and Woolsey picture but unfair for one that was a considerable cut above the others. *Variety* observed, "Not too exacting lovers of stale jokes may forgive this one's transgressions, but they'll probably be the minority. For general appeal it has little else besides a generous display of hotcha femininity in various forms of peek a boo dress or undress.... [T]he production all around is much better than the material provided." The *New York Times* noted, "There are three reasonably hilarious gags and perhaps fifty more that depend on whether you are for or against the ex-vaudeville clowns to begin with."

Nevertheless, *Hips, Hips, Hooray!* scored a hit at the box office, making it one of the team's most profitable vehicles. It even pleased Dorothy, always a harsh critic of these pictures, and Bert, who declared to Nelson B. Bell of *The Washington Post* that the film was "the best thing we've done since *The Cuckoos*."

Beginning on February 17, Dorothy headlined a Fanchon-Marco stage show for a one-week stint at L.A.'s Orpheum Theater, in conjunction with the featured attraction *Hips, Hips, Hooray!*

During Dorothy's time away from RKO, other stars had emerged, most notably the team of Fred Astaire and Ginger Rogers, and a classically trained actress from the New York theater, Katharine Hepburn. Dorothy recalled Hepburn for us: "Hepburn was, next to David O. Selznick, the biggest snob I ever met in Hollywood. When you were on the RKO lot, everyone said hello to everyone else. You'd see Irene Dunne or Ginger Rogers or Ann Harding, and they were all friendly. Not Hepburn. She looked down her nose at everybody. Some of us tried to engage her in conversation, but she wouldn't even make eye contact.

"I never understood snobbism, especially when it came from another actor. None of us are better than anyone else. I never deliberately hung around so-called big stars just for the sake of being seen with them. It was really about the type of person they were. Some of my friends were what you would call 'character actors,' people like Chick Chandler, Jimmy Flavin and George E. Stone. I didn't care if they were character actors or lead stars or whatever. Things like that didn't matter to me. As long as they were nice people, that's all that counted."

RKO shelved the college farce *Frat Heads* in favor of a costume farce, *Cockeyed Cavaliers*, resulting in what is generally considered to be the best of all Wheeler and Woolsey comedies. And though Dorothy would make two more films with Bert and Bob, it marked her last notable role with the team.

Production began on March 29, reuniting the triumvirate with director Mark Sandrich and co-star Thelma Todd. Where *Hips, Hips, Hooray!* and other previous Wheeler and Woolsey pictures had loosely structured storylines serving to accommodate comedic set pieces and musical numbers, *Cockeyed Cavaliers* features the shapeliest and sturdiest plot of any of their vehicles.

In 17th century England, two itinerant peasants (Bert and Bob, whose characters are unnamed) are rescued from the pillory by a plucky young lad. Unbeknownst to the pair, the young lad is actually a young lady named Mary Ann (Dorothy), who has disguised herself as a boy to avoid marrying the undesirable Duke of Weskit (Robert Grieg), a union arranged to settle a family debt. Through a series of mishaps, further complicated by Bert's kleptomania, the trio winds up at the duke's home, where Bert and Bob pass themselves off as the king's physicians. Bert discovers Mary Ann's true identity and promptly falls in love with her, and Bob romances the duke's niece, Lady Genevieve (Thelma Todd), who is stuck in an unhappy marriage to a brutish, ill-tempered baron (Noah Beery). When Mary Ann forgoes her masquerade to marry the duke and save her father from punishment, it's the boys' turn to come to her rescue. They capture a killer boar — in a thoroughly unorthodox manner — and the reward money allows Bert to buy Mary Ann's freedom while Bob makes a similar deal for Lady Genevieve.

*Cockeyed Cavaliers* is a delight from start to finish, showcasing Bert, Bob and Dorothy in peak form, aided and abetted by a sterling supporting cast, including an impressive lineup of seasoned comics: Franklin Pangborn, Billy Gilbert, Jack Norton, Snub Pollard, Kewpie Morgan and Charlie Hall. Sandrich keeps the action moving at a merry pace, and for a change, the gags and tunes spring organically from the plot, rather than having the storyline come to a halt for a comic routine or musical interlude. "(I Went Hunting) And the Big Bad Wolf Was Dead," a lively novelty number set in a tavern, allows Bert and Bob to exhibit their skills as eccentric hoofers, while Dorothy, Noah Beery, and other cast members raise their voices in song.

Dorothy's gender masquerade provides her and Bert with one of their most memorable comedic set pieces. Bert, unaware that Dorothy is a girl, treats her like a lackey. Dorothy, attracted to Bert, gives him a quick kiss. Startled and indignant, Bert becomes irate, then has a sudden change of heart after she reveals her true identity. Bob, still under the impression Dorothy is a boy, enters the room, discovers Bert and Dorothy in a romantic lip-lock and lets loose with his trademark "Whoa-ohhhh!"

The musical highlight is "Dilly Dally," which starts off as a charming duet between Bert and Dorothy, who harmonize beautifully.[2] Bob and Thelma Todd join in, and the resulting dance, with slow-motion photography accentuating the grace of Bert and Bob's movements, is clever and amusing. Dorothy recalled, "That number was done normally by us while they ran the camera at a faster speed. As Bert and Bob danced, Thelma and I were waiting for them on a bench. They finished their dance, in slow-motion, then jumped up on the bench with us. It was a riot." Hermes Pan, who helped choreograph the Fred Astaire–Ginger Rogers musicals, was the unaccredited assistant dance director. Pan would repeat the slow-motion dance technique for Astaire's "Stepping Out with My Baby" number in *Easter Parade* (1948).

Playing a tomboy came naturally to Dorothy, who relished the opportunity to perform her own stunts: "I jumped out of a window and right onto the back of a horse and rode off. That was so natural for me because I rode bareback from the time I was old enough to ride a horse, so it was a lot of fun. The studio didn't want me to do this stunt but I wanted to jump. I always loved doing my own stunts when I could. I had that fight in the street with a boy. You saw us rolling around and he ended up getting the worst of it."

But the back injury she sustained while working on *Hips, Hips, Hooray!* was evident during the making of this film: "When I jumped out the window and landed on the horse, I felt a sharp pain in my back that reminded me I hadn't fully recovered from my injury. Then during the 'Dilly Dally' number, Bert and I are sitting in a tree and we fall out when Bob shakes tree. But the stunt went wrong because when we fell down, Bert fell right on top of me. Boy, did that hurt! I wound up with two slipped discs and many years later had to have a severe back operation. It's a wonder I've lasted this long."

*Cockeyed Cavaliers* is a handsomely mounted production, with lovely costumes by Walter Plunkett, who was the costume designer on *Rio Rita*, *Dixiana* and *Hips, Hips, Hooray!* (He would later design costumes for *Gone with the Wind*, *An American in Paris*, *Singin' in the Rain* and *Forbidden Planet*.) Plunkett's wardrobe remained a vivid memory for Dorothy: "It's a pity [*Cockeyed Cavaliers*] wasn't shot in color because Walter's costumes were magnificent. That dress I wore at the end of the picture was the most beautiful thing I ever put on. It was a lovely pink color and just so incredibly detailed. I don't think the black-and-white photography did justice to it or to any of the other costumes in that picture. Walter also designed that dress I wore in *Dixiana*, in the number I did with Bert ["My One Ambition Is You"]. Everything he created was wonderful."

**Dorothy, flanked by Bert and Bob, wore a gown created by acclaimed costume designer Walter Plunkett in *Cockeyed Cavaliers* (1934).**

*Cockeyed Cavaliers* is a high-spirited romp that even appealed to the unconverted. One such non-convert, Richard Watts, Jr. of the *New York Herald Tribune*, confessed:

> The important news of the new Wheeler and Woolsey comedy is, to this prejudiced observer, that it is fairly funny. It has always seemed to me that the chance for these decidedly minor-league comedians to achieve hilarity lay in the possibility that some day they would become so bad that they would seem almost festive, somewhat in the manner of a fabulously bad pun. That, I think, is what happened in *Cockeyed Cavaliers*.... [T]he film possesses a properly insane mood and is aided by the presence of such lively young women as Miss Dorothy Lee and Miss Thelma Todd in the cast.

While *Cockeyed Cavaliers* was still in production, Dorothy was also in rehearsals for the West Coast production of *She Loves Me Not*, which had been a smash hit on the Broadway and London stage.[3] Dorothy had seen the play in New York and when the West Coast edition was announced in March, she auditioned for producer Homer Curran and won the lead role of Curley Flagg, beating out dozens of other applicants.

For the play, Dorothy learned thirty-five pages of dialogue in one day; at the same time, she was memorizing her lines for *Cockeyed Cavaliers*. Dorothy was required to be on the movie set from 9 A.M. to 6 P.M. Then, with only time to grab a bite to eat between productions, she would make a mad dash to the theater, where she would be in rehearsals for *She Loves Me Not* from 7 on. Of this frantic period Dorothy would remember, "It was crazy! I never had one day off, but boy, I just loved it."

Adapted by Howard Lindsay from a novel by Edward Hope, *She Loves Me Not* deals with the exploits of nightclub dancer Curley Flagg, who flees from mobsters after witnessing a gangland murder. Pursued by the underworld and the police, and hounded by newsreel cameramen and reporters, Curley is befriended by a group of Princeton University students. She hides out in the men's dormitory, where she masquerades as a college boy.

Dorothy headed a cast of thirty, which included June Clyde as the dean's daughter (at Dorothy's insistence, Homer Curran auditioned June for the role), Laura Treadwell, Elizabeth Young, and Russell Hopton. Phillip Faversham and John Arledge played a pair of hapless frat boys who get into hot water through their association with Curley. The play consisted of nineteen scenes that were enacted on an elaborate double-deck, six-cubicle stage set (three cubicles per level), allowing the action to unfold simultaneously in several rooms of the same house and giving the proceedings a cinema-like continuity. (It was the first Sextuple Flexible Stage to receive a U.S. patent.) Another novel aspect of the production was the screening (within the play) of a movie newsreel, projected on a full-sized screen.

Under the direction of Edgar MacGregor, with assist from Lucille Ryman, *She Loves Me Not* opened at the Belasco Theater in Los Angeles on April 26, 1934, two days after *Cockeyed Cavaliers* completed filming. (Bert and Bob attended the opening night performance to show support for their spunky leading lady.) With admission prices ranging from fifty cents to two dollars, the play was an immediate hit.

Whenever she reminisced about her career, Dorothy always singled out *She Loves Me Not* as her favorite and most gratifying experience: "That was a wonderful show and I had a great time doing it. For me, it was a chance to get back on the stage, in front of a live audience, which I loved. What I remember most about it is the elaborate set that we used. We opened at the Belasco because they needed a theater big enough to accommodate that set. It was two stories tall and had several sections to it, so there was something always going on. The action never seemed to stop. It was a good thing I was in shape back then, because it was such a physically demanding role. It was for everyone connected with the show.

"Once my character got to the dormitory, I masquerade as a man. There was a scene where Johnny Arledge cuts my long hair. I actually wore a wig for that. However, dear Johnny liked to have a few drinks before curtain time, so there were some occasions when he actually wound up cutting off some of my own hair as well."

*She Loves Me Not* garnered uniformly excellent reviews. The *Los Angeles Herald* called it "a play you must not fail to see.... You'll be laughing all the way home and for days afterward." The *Los Angeles Examiner* felt it was "cast brilliantly and with taste.... A packed house shrieked its approval."

The production moved to the Curran Theater in San Francisco, where it opened on May 21 and ran through June 2. Lloyd S. Thompson of the *San Francisco Examiner* reported, "Dorothy Lee, famous song and dance gal of filmland, is perfectly cast as Curley Flagg. She exudes a combination of energetic impudence and engaging obtuseness [and] can do an occasional bit of hoofing, of which she offers frequent samples.... If you like to laugh, you really ought to see [*She Loves Me Not*]."

**Dorothy played a nightclub dancer eluding gangsters by masquerading as a boy in *She Loves Me Not* (1934).**

During the San Francisco run, Dorothy told Thompson, "It's nice to have a career, of course. But it's nicer still not to feel you have to depend upon it entirely. That's why, I guess, I don't mind being just a stooge for Bert and Bob in their comedies. If I were terribly ambitious for a career I'd go to New York and see what I could do in a show there. But that would take me too far away from my home and my husband. I guess I'm not really ambitious, am I?"

On closing night, Dorothy thought she was being greeted by some well wishers. Instead, it was much more ominous: "After the closing of the show, Marsh and two other friends of ours were standing a few feet away from me when three men came up and said, 'Miss Lee, could we speak to you for a minute?' I went over in the corner and they circled around me. One of them put a gun to my stomach and demanded that I hand over my paycheck. I was so angry that the thought of dying didn't cross my mind. I said, 'For one thing, I don't get paid today and if I had, I wouldn't give it to you. I work hard for my money!' Somehow they got scared off and after I told Marsh, I called the police. Then it hit me how dangerous that was and I started to cry. The three guys, who were in their twenties, were caught by the police as they tried to escape on a streetcar. The next day I told Bert and Bob what had happened. They got upset and said, 'You know you could have been killed!' I just said to them, 'Well, I wasn't.'"

Dorothy returned to RKO to star in *If This Isn't Love*, a musical-comedy short with Walter Wolfe (later Walter Woolf King) and Keye Luke. She had a per-film contract with the studio, which allowed her to freelance. But she didn't stray too far when she appeared in *School for Girls* a low-budget programmer released in 1935 by Liberty Pictures, a Poverty Row operation that rented sound stages on the RKO lot. The most notable aspect of this women-in-reform-school tale was a cast that included some of the prettiest starlets of the era: Dorothy, Toby Wing, Dorothy Appleby, Lona Andre, and Kathleen Burke (the Panther Woman in *Island of Lost Souls*). Real-life criminal institutions never had such alluring inmates.

She took a pass on the next Wheeler and Woolsey picture, *Kentucky Kernels*, so the role of Bert's leading lady was assigned to Mary Carlisle, a pretty RKO contract player. On August 24 Dorothy began work on Liberty Pictures' *Without Children* (a.k.a. *Penthouse Party*; released in 1935), one of her better Poverty Row efforts. As the spoiled child of an indulgent single parent (played by Marguerite Churchill, who was only six months older than her screen daughter), Dorothy displays the insouciance of her early Wheeler and Woolsey films and even gets to sing a flirty rendition of "Man About Town." After her character is accidentally shot, her errant father (Bruce Cabot) rushes to her bedside and reconciles with the family. During this emotional reunion, Cabot had more than parental concern on his mind, as Dorothy remembered:

"Bruce Cabot was a big jerk who thought he was God's gift to women. Maybe he was, but I never bothered to find out. Toward the end of [*Without Children*], I'm lying in bed, recovering from a gunshot wound. Cabot is leaning over me and he's practically drooling. He looked at me like he wanted to jump on top of me right then and there. I told him, 'Knock it off! You're supposed to be my father, you ass!'"

Dorothy co-starred in *The Curtain Falls*, another programmer for another Poverty Row outfit, Chesterfield Pictures. (Like Liberty, Chesterfield also rented space at RKO.) Dorothy's flat delivery indicates a certain degree of unpreparedness, perhaps due to the haste in which director Charles Lamont, a veteran of slapstick comedies, had to make this unremarkable melodrama.

In October Dorothy traveled to New York to film *In the Spotlight* (released in 1935), a musical short starring tap dancer Hal LeRoy, at Warner Brothers' Vitaphone Studio in Brooklyn. It was announced that she would then begin rehearsals for a new stage production titled *Thumbs Up*, but nothing came of it.

Bert, Bob and Dorothy embarked on another vaudeville tour. Traveling by train this time, they played large theaters in Illinois, Ohio, Pennsylvania and New York, and once again patrons flocked to see them. For their New Year's stage offering in January 1935, the Palace Theater in New York, the nation's oldest vaudeville house, booked

Dorothy for a week-long personal appearance. She shared the bill with an incorrigible young comedian named Milton Berle, whose phenomenal success on television was still more than a decade in the future. Dorothy recalled: "Milton was something else! He was like a mischievous kid brother. While I was doing my song-and-dance act before a live audience, he was hiding behind the curtain where no one could see him, and he would yell obscenities out to me trying to trip me up and make me repeat what he was saying. I don't think the audience heard him, but no matter how hard he tried, I didn't mess up. He tried to get me so mad, but we just laughed about it later on. His mother Sadie would sit in the audience and laugh loudly at everything her son did. She was a wonderful woman and she would cook us delicious Jewish meals."

In mid–February, Dorothy started work on *The Old Homestead*, her final film for Liberty Pictures. She got to play "the other woman," a big-city vixen who comes between an unassuming country boy (Lawrence Gray) and his corn-fed sweetheart (Mary Carlisle). She also sang "Somehow I Knew," which demonstrated a maturity in her vocal range, compared to her higher-pitched singing in the early talkies. Also in the cast was Leonard Slye, who was then a member of the country-western singing group, the Sons of the Pioneers. Three years later Slye changed his name to Roy Rogers and went on to become one of the most popular stars in motion pictures and on television.

When Thornton Freeland, June Clyde's husband, accepted directorial assignments from British film producers, Dorothy and Marsh journeyed to London to join them. Upon her arrival, Dorothy received a movie offer from producer Walter C. Mycroft of British International Pictures. She went in and read for the role, but she was unimpressed by their facilities: "Back then, their technology was at least two years behind the Hollywood studios. It was like the early days of talking pictures, only on a lower scale. Then I got homesick, and I didn't want to stay any longer, although I loved spending time with June and T. As soon as I boarded the ship to sail for home, I received word by telegram that I had secured a part in the picture. But I wasn't about to get off of the ship. I said, 'No way. I'm going home.'"

The role Dorothy walked away from was the female lead in *Dance Band* (1935; released in the U.S. in 1936), a genial musical comedy starring another American actor, Charles "Buddy" Rogers, who played Dorothy's brother in *Take a Chance*. At Dorothy's suggestion, June Clyde was hired for the part. (The Freelands continued to work in the British film industry until the outbreak of World War II.)

In retrospect, it's a shame Dorothy didn't appear in *Dance Band*. The tale of a rivalry between the leader of an all-male dance band and the leader of an all-girls orchestra would have been a good showcase for her (as it was for June) and it was appreciably better than the non–Wheeler and Woolsey films she made during this period. Besides, it's tough to dislike any movie that spotlights a specialty act such as Ho Li Wung and his Chinese Syncopators.

On her return to the States, Dorothy was offered the opportunity to co-star with Jimmy Durante and Paul Whiteman's Orchestra in legendary producer Billy Rose's lavish Broadway musical *Jumbo*. Boasting a script by Charles MacArthur and Ben Hecht

**Dorothy, standing next to Eddie Nugent, sings "Somehow I Knew" in *The Old Homestead* (1935).**

(authors of *The Front Page*), a Richard Rodgers-Lorenz Hart score that included "The Most Beautiful Girl in the World" and a line-up of genuine circus acts (clowns, acrobats, trapeze artists, wild animals), the gargantuan production promised to be the most dazzling spectacle ever seen on the Great White Way, and the producers felt that Dorothy was an ideal choice for the leading lady:

"They thought I'd be perfect for the show because I could sing and dance, plus I was athletic enough to perform real circus routines. ['The Most Beautiful Girl in the World' was to be sung on horseback.] I met with Billy Rose, [director] George Abbott, [dance director] John Murray Anderson and the producers and they were willing to hire me on the spot. I had the job but I got this gut feeling that it just wasn't right. I mean, I should have been overjoyed but I wasn't and to me, that wasn't a good sign. So at the last minute I backed out and decided I'd rather stay in Hollywood. I never had any regrets about it although every time I hear the song 'The Most Beautiful Girl in the World,' I think, 'That could have been me.'"

Dorothy's gut instinct served her well. The Actors Equity Association ruled that *Jumbo* was a circus and not a play, so as per union rules, the performers could not be paid until after opening night. *Jumbo*—its title character played by a live elephant—

spent eleven weeks in rehearsals, as the complicated logistics of the presentation were worked out. During this time, Ella Logan, who was cast in the role Dorothy turned down, left the show and was replaced by Gloria Grafton. The show's scheduled Labor Day debut was pushed back six times and it finally opened on November 16, 1935, at the 4,500-seat Hippodrome Theatre, which was reconfigured to create a circus atmosphere with a revolving stage, grandstands and sideshow arcades. *Jumbo* was a hit with theatergoers but the production costs were so exorbitant (a then-record $340,000) that it wound up losing money.

Dorothy had been unable to appear in Wheeler and Woolsey's latest vehicle, *The Nitwits*, so Betty Grable handled the leading-lady chores (as she had done in *Hold 'Em Jail*). Now Dorothy was set to rejoin her old partners once again, but this time her career and her love life would veer off sharply in two different directions.

# Chapter 8

# Isn't Love the Grandest Thing?
## *Marriage Between Movies*

During Dorothy's excursions abroad and elsewhere, Bert and Bob made two of their most successful comedies, *Kentucky Kernels* and *The Nitwits*. Both were directed by George Stevens, and because of his fine work on these pictures, he graduated to more prestigious RKO productions (*Swing Time, Quality Street, Gunga Din*). Now that she was available again, Dorothy was ready to rejoin Bert and Bob in their next picture, *The Rainmakers* (originally titled *Silver Streak*).

In July 1935, just before shooting began, RKO sent Bert, Bob and Dorothy on a publicity junket to Catalina Island. There they posed for photographs, including several with their friend Jan Garber, a popular orchestra leader. Dorothy recalled, "If there was a plane, I would have left as soon as we were done. But Jan said, 'I'll fix you up on the best date on the island.'" With her marriage to Marsh Duffield on the wane, she went along with it mainly to placate Garber. However, when the so-called best date failed to show up on schedule, she was furious: "I thought I had been stood up and I was so upset I could have killed him. Bert and Bob teased me endlessly about it. But it was all just a misunderstanding. I was under the impression that Mr. Atwater was going to come for dinner and he thought he was to come *after* dinner since he had already eaten at P.K. Wrigley's mansion."

"Mr. Atwater" was Albert Gordon Cox Atwater, senior vice-president of the Chicago-based Wrigley Jr. Company. Atwater's brother-in-law was chewing-gum mogul Philip Knight Wrigley, whose holdings included the Chicago Cubs baseball team and, coincidentally, Catalina Island, and that made A.G. (as Atwater was known to family and friends) an ideal tour guide: "A.G. drove me around Catalina Island, because only someone with money or a connection to Wrigley could drive around the island freely. We had a lot of fun and that night he asked me to marry him! He only kissed my cheek, so that is how romantic it was. We went to dinner the next night and he said, 'I have news for you ... I'm married.' And I said, 'Well, I have news for you ... I'm married too.' It turned out both of our marriages were on the rocks."

Dorothy's attraction to Atwater forced her to admit that her feelings toward Marsh

Duffield were no longer the same. On her return from Catalina, she asked for a trial separation, or a "marital vacation," as she called it. When a reporter from the *L.A. Examiner* inquired about the current status of the union, Dorothy optimistically quipped, "We're taking a separation *vaccination*. I'll take no chance on this marriage going haywire." Duffield, still hoping to salvage the marriage, half-heartedly agreed with Dorothy's decision.

Production on *The Rainmakers* began on July 17, 1935. There was a key difference between this and Dorothy's previous films with Bert and Bob. The Motion Picture Production Code, which went into effect during 1934, was now prohibiting the use of "objectionable" material: sexual double entendres, skimpy wardrobe, implications of nudity, and off-color subject matter. This was censorship masked as "industry guidelines" and the adoption of the Code forced certain filmmakers and performers to sanitize their approach. For Wheeler and Woolsey, it meant they could no longer be as delightfully risqué as they were in such efforts as *Half Shot at Sunrise*, *Peach-O-Reno*, *Hips, Hips, Hooray!* and *Cockeyed Cavaliers* (the last of their pre–Code productions). For Dorothy, it meant no more characters who could act on their sexual impulses or spout saucy wisecracks; she was now a bland third-wheel to watered-down versions of Bert and Bob.

Which is not to infer that Wheeler and Woolsey could not survive without risqué material: *Kentucky Kernels* and *The Nitwits* were bereft of innuendo and turned out to be two of their finest efforts. But these films had solid scripts and a real craftsman (George Stevens) at the helm. *The Rainmakers* did not.

*The Rainmakers* employs a Depression-era Dust Bowl story of starving farmers being taken advantage of by an unscrupulous landowner (Berton Churchill). The community has been hard-hit by a drought, so the local banker (Frederic Roland) enlists the help of Roscoe Horne

Dorothy displays her impressive golf swing at the Catalina Visitors Country Club as Jan Garber's wife, also named Dorothy, looks on (1935).

**Dorothy retrieves the key component to Bert and Bob's cloudburst-producing machine in *The Rainmakers* (1935).**

(Woolsey) and his assistant Billy (Wheeler), professional "rainmakers" who save the day.

Director Fred Guiol was a veteran of silent-comedy shorts but he seemed to be at a loss as to how to pace a feature-length film, and several scenes lack the momentum required to give the action the necessary comedic spark. Nevertheless, the climax involving two runaway locomotives contains some impressive and genuinely funny visual gags, making one wish the rest of the picture had been on the same level of inventiveness.

As Margie, the banker's daughter, Dorothy has little to do, although she and Bert perform one of their most amusing duets, "Isn't Love the Grandest Thing?" Borrowing from an old burlesque routine called "The Tree of Truth," Bert and Dorothy are seated under an orange tree with magical powers: Anyone who tells a lie gets hit on the head by a falling orange. As they assure each other, through verse, that this is the first time they've ever been in love and they'll always remain true, oranges fall on their heads to punctuate each falsehood. The final vow that they'll never fight is too much of a whopper for the tree to bear, and the lovebirds are buried beneath a hailstorm of citrus fruit.

The number made an impression on Dorothy — literally: "It was really cute, one of the most darling things that Bert and I ever did. All of these oranges were held by a wire and as we sang the song there was someone in the tree who would drop the oranges on us on the proper cue. I did wind up getting conked on the head more than once. It was a riot."

As far as the critics were concerned, *The Rainmakers* ran as dry as the Dust Bowl itself, with the *New York Times* remarking: "There isn't anything very funny about the latest contribution to the Wheeler–Woolsey–Lee triumvirate to the gaiety of nations. The material provided the comics is negligible, and struggle as they may to project hilarity, the laughs just aren't there."

Despite its shortcomings, however, *The Rainmakers* does have its share of amusing set pieces and tends to be underrated because of the better Wheeler and Woolsey vehicles that preceded it. For whatever its worth, *The Rainmakers* was more fondly remembered by moviegoers of the era than other, superior W&W endeavors, primarily on the strength of the locomotive finale.

On August 12, Dorothy and Marsh Duffield signed a separation agreement. Shooting on *The Rainmakers* wrapped four days later, and Dorothy departed for Reno to take up the residency required to obtain an expedited divorce. She told the *Los Angeles Times*, "Unfortunately, [our marriage] didn't work out. Please be kind to Marsh, he is a dear and we are good friends. He has wished me luck on my coming marriage and I wouldn't hurt him for the world."

Dorothy and Marsh Duffield filed for a "quickie divorce" on November 8 in a Reno courtroom. Charges of mental cruelty were cited, though Dorothy would always note that it was, for the time, the standard term for "incompatibility." Ten days later, however, the newly divorced couple had reconciled and went on a trip to Palm Springs. Columnists and reporters speculated that they would remarry but nothing came of it. They parted amicably, though mutual friends would attest that it took a few years for Marsh to emotionally recover for what had been, for him, a storybook romance.

At this point, Dorothy had been married and divorced three times in eight years — with additional spouses to follow. She reflected on her relationships some six decades later: "I'll take the blame for the way things turned out with Marsh. I had no business marrying him in the first place. I certainly had feelings for him, but it wasn't the kind of deep love I had for Fred [Waring]. As time went on, I realized I had made a mistake but I hung in there thinking things would change, which was another mistake. Poor Marsh — he really did love me and when we separated, he didn't know what hit him. He honestly didn't see it coming.

"One of the reasons I think I was married and divorced so many times is because back in my day it wasn't acceptable to be going together without being married, and that is how a lot of mistakes were made. I often married without really getting to know the person as well as I could. Today, it is okay to live with someone and see if you really are compatible before committing to marriage, and I think that is great. I wish that was acceptable in my day."

Dorothy renewed her friendship with Buster Keaton, who had fallen on hard times.

## 8. Isn't Love the Grandest Thing?

Buster was one of Hollywood's biggest stars when Dorothy first met him in 1929, and they often ran into each other at various social gatherings. But the loss of creative control over his pictures led to a struggle with alcoholism that in turn led to the collapse of his career and his marriage to Natalie Talmadge. By October 1935, Keaton ended a disastrous second marriage, recovered from a nervous breakdown and was reduced to starring in a series of cheaply produced two-reel comedy shorts for the low-rent Educational Pictures Corporation. Dorothy recalled, "I would host little get-togethers at my place and Charlie Lamont and his wife Estelle [the former Estelle Bradley, who appeared in silent comedies with Lloyd Hamilton] would attend. Charlie directed me in *The Curtain Falls* and he was directing some of those shorts Buster was making for Educational. Buster was going through a rough spell. He had lost his home and his children—I never forgave Natalie for changing their kids' names from Keaton to Talmadge—and he had just gotten divorced from this horrible woman [Mae Scrivens] who he apparently married while he was intoxicated. So I got word to Buster that he was welcome at my home any time, and I was delighted when he began showing up regularly.

"My place was a far cry from the lavish Italian villa that Buster once owned, but he liked our group because we had simple get-togethers. No egos or temperaments, we just had fun and enjoyed each other's company. At first, Buster was quiet, maybe a little too quiet. He would sit there and listen to the rest of us tell stories, usually about our early days starting out in the business. But he began to open up and became more relaxed and talkative. He would bring his ukulele and sing these old songs that he had learned in his childhood, and I would get a kick seeing him strum on his ukulele, as though he didn't have a care in the world.

"Buster had what I would call 'old-school manners' and he would never swear or tell an off-color story if ladies were present. And he would get upset if someone else did. Buster would help co-host my little parties. He would help me prepare the snacks and he would go around and ask the other guests, 'Would you like something to drink?' or 'Would you like some cheese and crackers?' We had been on friendly terms before, but as I got to know Buster even better I discovered how unpretentious and down-to-earth he was. He felt a little out of place at fancy Hollywood events and he was always self-conscious that he never had a formal education, so he had a bit of an inferiority complex, socially speaking. But he had more basic intelligence than most people I've known.

"There was something about Buster that was almost magical. It's hard to explain, but it was like he existed on a different level than the rest of us, and I mean that in a positive way. He had a real affinity for animals and he would make an instant connection with dogs and cats and other living creatures. We would be sitting outside and butterflies would land on him! I'm not kidding you. It was the wildest thing I ever saw."

While her relationship with the now-divorced A.G. Atwater was blossoming, Dorothy returned to RKO on December 5 to begin work on *The Wild West*, her final picture with Wheeler and Woolsey—and the last movie she would make for the next three years. The film, released as *Silly Billies*, is by far the weakest W&W comedy Dorothy appeared in. During the Gold Rush era, traveling dentist Philip "Painless" Pennington (Bob) and his assistant Roy Banks (Bert) meet schoolteacher Mary Blake (Dorothy) on a stagecoach headed to a frontier destination. Unbeknownst to the trio, the citizens of the western town are about to pull up stakes, having been deceived by promises of relocating to a gold-rich territory. Roy and Pennington learn that the townsfolk have been set up for an Indian ambush and ride to the rescue, saving the day and discovering that the gold everyone was searching for was actually back in the town everyone forsook.

Fred Guiol again handled the directorial chores, and the results made *The Rainmakers* look like a comic masterpiece. The pity is that *Silly Billies* is a good-looking picture, with period costumes and location filming which add to the production sheen. The wagon-train attack, with Bert and Bob using slingshots to fire ether-soaked cotton balls at rampaging Indians, should have made for an amusing conclusion, but instead it is as sluggishly paced as all the scenes that preceded it. Even the sole musical number, "Tumble On Tumble Weed," is a letdown. It isn't even a traditional Bert-Dorothy duet. The mediocre tune is first sung by the townsfolk around a campfire, with Bert and Dorothy and later Bob joining in. The sequence, like the rest of the picture, comes off flat and uninspired.

The film was shot in the dead of winter. Dorothy recalled, "I remember it was so cold! We filmed a lot of it on location and we had to report to the studio at four o'clock in the morning to have our makeup put on, our hair done, and so on. Then it was an hour-and-a-half ride out to the location site [the San Fernando Valley] and it was cold. I felt sorry for those poor guys who had to play the Indians. They were all bare-chested and it was freezing.

"There was a terrible accident that occurred while we were filming the picture. Bert, Bob and I were sitting right behind the cameraman. Woolsey's double was right in front of the camera, holding one of those old-fashioned western guns. It was loaded, and when he pulled the trigger, the thing exploded and blew his arm off! It flew straight over the camera! Well, I threw up. Bert and Bob were in a state of shock. As it turned out, the guy was on the RKO payroll for years and even became quite a good tennis player, in spite of his handicap."

Some of the Wheeler and Woolsey films were unfairly dismissed by critics, but the *Motion Picture Herald*'s harsh review of *Silly Billies* was justified — and accurate: "The silliest thing about this one is that RKO chooses to throw away a good comedy team in trash like this. No story value, few really funny incidents, no musical numbers [perhaps the reviewer took a break during "Tumble On Tumble Weed"], no production values. In short, everything's against the stars before they even started. Too bad!"

At the time, no one, including Dorothy, was aware that this would be her final film with Wheeler and Woolsey, so in retrospect, the fadeout is an unexpectedly poignant one. Dorothy is seated between Bert and Bob, who are in disguise as Indians. They simultaneously plant a kiss on her cheek, and she emerges from the clinch blissful and

## 8. Isn't Love the Grandest Thing?

**Wheeler and Woolsey kiss Dorothy good-bye in *Silly Billies* (1936), her final film with the team.**

covered with greasepaint. Though the movie itself leaves a lot to be desired, this last image provides a heartwarming coda to Dorothy's happy and fortuitous seven-year association with the team.

While they were making *Silly Billies*, Bert, Bob and Dorothy would drop by the set of *Follow the Fleet*, a concurrent RKO production, and watch Fred Astaire and Ginger Rogers go through their paces. Dorothy remembered, "We would watch Fred and Ginger film some of their scenes and they would come over and watch us work [on interior scenes]. When Fred was rehearsing his dance numbers, he was a tough taskmaster, a real perfectionist. He was tough on everyone but he was toughest on himself. Hermes Pan was the choreographer who helped Fred with the dances, and he looked so much like Fred that it was hard to believe they weren't related to one another. Hermes was calm and easy-going, a different temperament than Fred's. Maybe that's why they got along so well.

"One day I was watching Fred and Randolph Scott film a scene and someone in the publicity department got the idea of having Randy and me pose for photos that would promote both our movies. So I got dressed up in a sailor suit and they took photos of me with Randy and some by myself on the [ship deck] set. Some people who saw those photos said, 'I didn't know you were in *Follow the Fleet*.' I said, 'I wasn't — I was promoting *Silly Billies* but I guess it was confusing because I wasn't wearing a western costume.'"

Dorothy once got to dance with Fred Astaire, an opportunity most women wished they had: "We were at a party and Fred asked me to dance. I was thrilled, but it turned out he danced like everyone else. It's only in the movies that it's really romanticized, gliding across the floor and dancing all over chairs and tables. But how many women get to say they danced with Fred Astaire?"

On December 16, 1935, twenty-nine-year-old Thelma Todd was found dead under mysterious circumstances. Though her death was ruled a suicide (by carbon monoxide poisoning), many associates expressed serious doubts about that claim and the case remains unresolved to this day. Dorothy offered these observations of her friend and former co-star: "Thelma was so beautiful and outgoing and such a happy person. We were shocked to hear she was found dead, and everyone was sure that she was killed by her ex-husband [Pat DiCiccio]. None of us ever liked him. They owned a restaurant together [Thelma Todd's Roadside Rest Café]. It was just past Santa Monica, close to Malibu, and I used to pass it on my way home from work since I had a house in Malibu and a house next to Lakeside Golf Course. They had put money into the restaurant together, but most of the money was hers.

Dorothy with Randolph Scott on the set of the Fred Astaire–Ginger Rogers musical ***Follow the Fleet*** (1936). This is a posed publicity shot; Dorothy did not appear in the film.

"Her death was labeled a suicide, but if you knew her, you'd know that she would never have committed suicide. We all knew she didn't do it. When they found her, she was in her car and the garage door was down, you had to pull it down, and the motor was still running. They said she died of carbon monoxide poisoning, and as she fell forward she hit the steering wheel and knocked one tooth out. She had capped teeth. They said she fainted or turned the motor on herself. That's nonsense. First of all, she was too sharp to pull the garage door down with the motor still running. There's no way she could have pulled into her garage and not have turned it off. Any person would automatically turn the motor off before they got out of the car to pull down the garage door.

"And then there was a door leading from the garage to the house. I had been a guest in her house many times and that door was always open. But when she died, that door was closed! She wasn't the kind of person who would have committed suicide, and there's no way she would have done it by accident. Me, Bert, Bob — all of us felt that there was no doubt in the world that her ex-husband did it, but it could never be proven."

In the decades since Todd's death, it has been generally agreed that she did not take her own life. Her turbulent relationships with men seem to hold the key to the mystery, and there have been varying (and speculative) accounts of the events leading up to the alleged murder — some of them credible, some of them straight out of tawdry crime novels. Many of Thelma's friends, Dorothy included, blamed ex-husband DiCiccio. Despite Dorothy's claims, however, it was director Roland West (*Alibi*, *The Bat Whispers*) who co-owned the café with Thelma. West is another suspect in this mystery, as is, some say, gangster Charlie "Lucky" Luciano.

The focus on Todd's death unfairly overshadows her real legacy: her marvelous motion picture performances. Even Dorothy was largely unaware of it until years later. Said Dorothy, "I knew Thelma was a busy working actress, but when you're making movies yourself, it's all you can do to keep track of your own stuff, let alone what someone else is doing. So I didn't realize just how many films Thelma made until they started turning up on television. She worked with so many comedians! I saw her with Buster [Keaton], Laurel and Hardy, the Marx Brothers, Joe E. Brown and some of the things she did on her own. And, of course, those pictures we did with Wheeler and Woolsey. She was so lovely and so funny — she looked gorgeous and she could do all that wild physical stuff. What a talent! No wonder all those guys wanted to work with her."

Production on *Silly Billies* wrapped on January 3, 1936, and a short time later, Dorothy accepted A.G. Atwater's marriage proposal. On March 7, the couple eloped to Crown Point, Indiana, and from there they made their home at 3033 Normandy Place in Evanston, a suburb of Chicago. The men in the Atwater and Wrigley families frowned upon their spouses pursuing careers, and Dorothy toed the line. She told the press that she was giving up show business to become a stay-at-home wife. Woolsey made it clear that he, for one, hoped it would be a union that would last, telling her, "Dammit, Lee, will you stop getting married! I'm going broke buying you wedding presents!"

Dorothy's retirement made her unavailable for the next Wheeler and Woolsey picture, *Mummy's Boys* (1936), and the two that followed, *On Again — Off Again* (1937) and *High Flyers* (1937). Despite memorable set pieces (Bert does a terrific impression of Charlie Chaplin in *High Flyers*), these films were below the standards established by earlier efforts and Dorothy's presence was certainly missed.

The new Mrs. Atwater found herself in the same sort of high-society social circles that she had no use for during her days at the Westlake School for Girls. But early in the marriage, Dorothy and A.G. were happy together and did a lot of traveling, so much so that both obtained pilot's licenses and bought their own private plane (called a Stinson) that they used for frequent trips from coast to coast. They flew to the Kentucky Derby with Charles R. Walgreen, Sr., founder of Walgreens drugstores, and in December 1936, Dorothy accepted Buster Keaton's invitation to attend the premiere of 20th Century–Fox's *Lloyd's of London* (a film neither one was directly involved with).

Yet Dorothy was content to be a homemaker and attended all the social soirees as expected of her. She was involved with numerous charities but she requested that her contributions remain anonymous. Instead, society columns commented on her fashion and jewelry, notably a charm necklace, a gift from A.G., that she kept as a memento for the rest of her life. Each charm carried a specific meaning for Dorothy, including her favorite one that denoted "ants in the pants," which is how A.G. described her demeanor.

Dorothy married A.G. Atwater in March 1936 and retired, momentarily, from show business.

Robert Woolsey's health had been deteriorating for years, due to his heavy drinking, and in 1937 during the filming of *High Flyers* it was painfully evident his days as a performer had come to an end. Bert Wheeler, coping with the dissolution of his third marriage (to actress Sally Haines) and facing a career without Woolsey, decided to dust off his stage act for a series of engagements. For the role of his stage partner, Bert called upon Dorothy to step back into the shoes she was so comfortable in. A.G. reminded her of her promise to give up show business, but she shot back, "Too bad, Bert needs me!" For a March 1938 appearance in Philadelphia, advertisements heralded the return of Wheeler and Lee:

## 8. Isn't Love the Grandest Thing?

> 7 GREAT HITS ON THE STAGE!
> DIRECT FROM HOLLYWOOD MEET THE CLOWNING KING OF NITWITS,
> BERT WHEELER, FAMOUS SCREEN COMIC OF
> THE CUCKOO WHEELER AND WOOLSEY TEAM.
> THE DAZZLING FILM BEAUTY WHOM BERT WHEELER
> IS ALWAYS FALLING FOR, DOROTHY LEE,
> GORGEOUS EYEFUL IN HER FIRST PHILADELPHIA APPEARANCE.

Dorothy boosted Bert's enthusiasm for performing, and their stage act was a great success: "We would have probably gone on to be another Bert and Betty Wheeler had we continued as a team, but in the long run, I wanted to leave show business to have a family. But Bert was able to establish himself as a single act and did well on his own." These stage appearances would mark the last time Bert and Dorothy performed together, though they remained close friends for the rest of Bert's life.

Robert Woolsey contracted kidney disease and died at his Malibu Beach home on October 31, 1938, at age 50, with his wife and mother-in-law at his side. Dorothy remembered: "Some newspaper articles quoted me as saying that I lost 'the best friend I ever had,' which was an exaggeration. I got along well with Bob but I was always closer to Bert. I hadn't seen Bob since we made *Silly Billies*. The poor guy drank himself to death. Bert told me he visited Bob often in his final days and that Bob's body had swollen up terribly because of his illness. It was just awful and he really wasn't that old when he died. It was a shame. I know that Bob's passing was tough on Bert."

Dorothy sent a large wreath to Woolsey's funeral and shared her feelings with the *Chicago Tribune*: "It hardly seems more than a couple of weeks ago that we were watching Bob's antics on the lot. This is certainly a shock to me."

As the wife of a wealthy businessman, Dorothy was leading an enviable lifestyle, attending lavish parties, frequenting the Arlington Park Racetrack, and going to nearly every Chicago Cubs baseball game. But she missed performing more than she cared to admit. It hit her during a visit to Hollywood in November 1938. "My mother-in-law and I went out there for a visit. We went to the RKO lot and looked at all the sets like any other tourist, and I met several old friends. One was Lew Landers, the director. I kidded him about giving me a job in pictures and he said, 'Okay.' You could have knocked me over with a feather. So I ran it by A.G., and he said, 'All right.' I took the job more for sentiment's sake than anything else. But I promised to return home as soon as the picture was finished."

Dorothy essayed a minor supporting role in *Twelve Crowded Hours* (released in 1939) starring Richard Dix and a rising star named Lucille Ball. Dorothy played a telephone switchboard operator and her romantic interest was played by John Arledge, her co-star from *She Loves Me Not*. Though she and Lucy had few scenes together, they formed a common bond and would lament over their unfulfilling roles: "Lucy and I would look at each other and say, 'Why are we playing such small parts?' RKO was grooming Lucy for stardom then, and she'd say, 'Well, we're getting paid well for it, so why not?'"

A.G. grew increasingly impatient with his wife's renewed interest in performing and Dorothy became bored with her role as society matron. The marriage was showing signs of stress. Dorothy recalled: "In those days, women in the Wrigley family didn't work. I was at the peak of my career when I married A.G., but he wouldn't let me accept any job offers. I had always been able to be myself, to do what I wanted, to say what I thought. But he wanted me to see older family friends, no one my own age. Performing became a way of reclaiming my identity."

By April 1939, Dorothy let it be known that she was open to any acting offers. Producer-director Charles Reisner pitched an idea to team her and Bert Wheeler for a series of feature-length comedies at RKO, but nothing came of it. The studio evidently had no interest in a Woolsey-less Wheeler[1] and instead tried to fill the void left in their comedy roster with a one-shot Marx Brothers picture, *Room Service* (1938), and an assortment of Joe Penner vehicles (*Go Chase Yourself*, *I'm from the City* and *Mr. Doodle Kicks Off*, among others).

After Bob's death, Bert's movie career never recovered. For Warner Brothers, he starred in *The Cowboy Quarterback* (1939), an inferior low-budget remake of Joe E. Brown's *Elmer the Great* (1933).[2] Contract starlet Marie Wilson co-starred as his leading lady, although if Bert had his way, it would have been Dorothy: "Bert told me that my name came up when they were casting that picture. Well, if my name was brought up, I'm sure Bert was the only one who brought it up. Why would [Warners] be interested in me when they had any number of actresses under contract they could cast in the role? But it was sweet of Bert to keep me in mind, and I appreciated the gesture."

No longer caring what her husband thought, Dorothy accepted a supporting role in *Tidal Wave*, a low-budget Republic Pictures production that relied on stock footage from *Deluge* (RKO, 1933) for its spectacular depiction of New York City submerged by the title disaster. The plot, far-fetched even by Poverty Row standards, involved a racketeer using phony footage of a tidal wave to keep voters away from the polls. Yet in a novel angle, the storyline dealt with commercial television, which would not become commonplace until after World War II.

The film was a quickie in every sense of the word. It was shot in less than two weeks (April 14 to April 26, 1939) and was released to theaters a little over a month later (June 2) under the title *S.O.S. Tidal Wave*. It represented Dorothy's last significant movie role. She adds a welcome note of comic relief as Mabel, the sarcastic, long-suffering girlfriend of newsreel cameraman Peaches Jackson, played by Frank Jenks. Dorothy and gruff comic actor Jenks make an unlikely couple, but they work well together, exchanging wisecracks with a seamless rapport. Their scenes provide a respite from the relentlessly melodramatic plotline, and they even get to share the final fadeout as Peaches proposes to Mabel during a TV broadcast.

Reluctantly, Dorothy accepted an offer from ex-husband Jimmie Fidler to be a guest on his *Hollywood on the Air* radio program. "I was really conflicted about it, but his show was popular and I figured it would be good exposure. At my request, I got to sing 'My One Ambition Is You' [from *Dixiana*]. I sang it because it was my favorite

*8. Isn't Love the Grandest Thing?*

**Dorothy reluctantly agreed to be a guest on ex-husband Jimmie Fidler's radio programs in 1939. Her smile masks her true feelings.**

song from the Wheeler and Woolsey pictures, but Fidler had such a big ego he probably thought I was singing it to *him*."

Dorothy's marriage to A.G. Atwater was falling apart at the seams, a situation underscored in June 1939 when she decided to revive her stage career by accepting a role in the Broadway revue *One for the Money*, which was now playing at the Harris Theatre in Chicago. Director John Murray Anderson, whom Dorothy had impressed during her audition for *Jumbo*, chose her as the replacement for Grace McDonald, who left the show when she was signed by Paramount Pictures.

With twenty-one scenes presented in two acts, *One for the Money* brought Dorothy back to her musical-comedy roots. She appeared in nine scenes, including two specialty numbers, "Syncopated Rhapsody" and "Teeter Totter Tessie," opposite an up-and-coming dancer named Gene Kelly. Dorothy was immediately impressed: "Gene was so wonderful. A darling, handsome and talented man. I think that it was a great compliment that I danced with him. Gene and I went through all the dance routines together since he was also the choreographer. He was a great dancer, a perfectionist, but so patient and very easy to work with. I just loved him, he was such a happy, wonderful guy to be around. We would rehearse day and night and we did a really cute fast tap, jitterbug-type of dance. We worked so hard on it that my legs were so sore that I had to have them rubbed each day. But it was fun.

"I also thought it was nice that Gene knew of my work years earlier because he once remarked to me while we were rehearsing, 'It must have been a lot of fun to work with Bert and Bob.' So he was really delighted to have me work opposite him. He asked me out on a date and I wish I would have taken him up on it, but at that time my marriage to A.G. was practically over and I was so burned out on relationships that I didn't feel like starting a new one. But I can tell you that his Irish charm was hard to resist."

The cast included Alfred Drake, Keenan Wynn, Nell O'Day, George Lloyd and Don Loper, stage veterans who also had or would have careers in Hollywood. As she became involved with the show in mid-run, Dorothy was aware of the tension between some of the players: "This was a big, elaborate revue with a cast of sixteen, and there was a definite feeling of dissatisfaction within the ranks. Quite a few of them felt they weren't getting as much stage time as they deserved. When Grace McDonald was signed to a movie contract, there were those who grumbled, 'Why her and not me?' And when I replaced her, I got a lot of write-ups in the local papers, which didn't sit well with some of the people who had been with the show from the very beginning. It was not a particularly happy group, but none of the backstage drama was evident on stage. Fortunately, I dealt mostly with Gene, who was a doll."

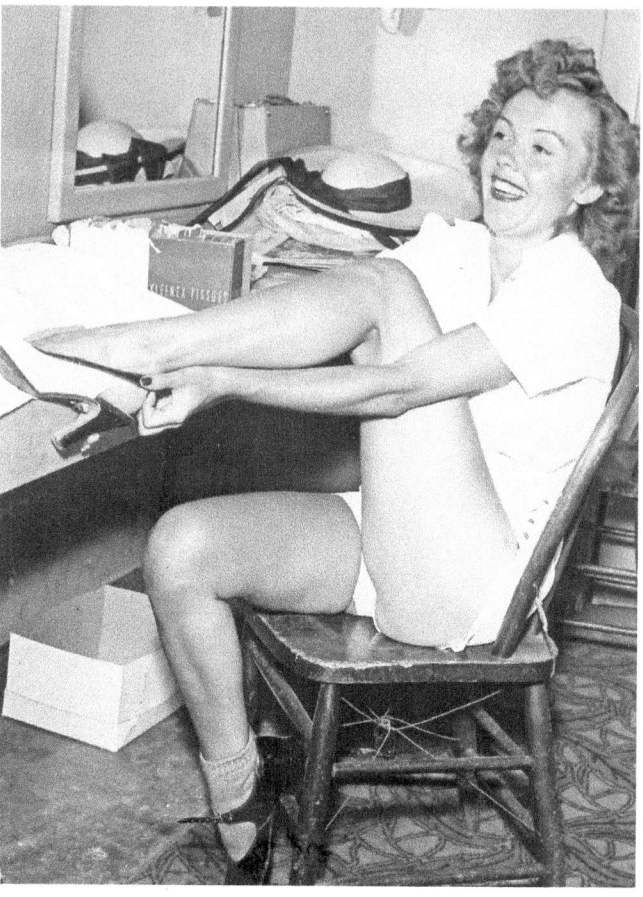

**In 1939, Dorothy donned her dancing shoes and joined the Chicago production of *One for the Money* which marked her return to the legitimate stage.**

While she only appeared in *One for the Money* during its Chicago engagement, Dorothy's brief partnership with Gene Kelly was one of her proudest career achievements and for years she kept a publicity photo of them prominently displayed in her home. Then she loaned the photograph to a friend, in good faith, and she never saw it again.

On the early morning of July 6, 1939, before Superior Judge Williams, Dorothy was granted an uncontested divorce from A.G. Atwater. In her testimony, she cited cruelty, charging that Atwater struck her on two occasions. She waived alimony but received a substantial (and undisclosed) out-of-court settlement along with the return of her maiden name.

When asked about the cruelty charges, Dorothy dismissed it as the sensationalism of the press in those days and claimed that she and Atwater remained friends. She never spoke about A.G. as often as she did ex-husband Marsh Duffield or former flame Fred Waring, perhaps because Atwater eventually cut himself off from the world: "It's a shame that A.G. turned into a recluse and no longer wanted to see anyone. He was so full of life. We stayed in touch for years, but later on when I wanted to go and visit him, I was told that it would not be a good idea so I never did. I eventually got to know all of A.G.'s wives, and I really became close friends with one of them, Donna Atwater. Donna and I would often laugh about how A.G. brought us together."

While Dorothy had a home in Illinois, she retained a residence in California in order to maintain her career. She renewed old acquaintances and made new friends in the Hollywood community, thanks in large part to the hospitality of actress and club owner Grace Hayes: "Grace was a wonderful comedienne and entertainer, one of the funniest people I ever knew. She opened up a club called the Grace Hayes Lodge and just about everyone in the business went there. On any given night, you'd see Errol Flynn, Jimmy Cagney, Alice Faye, Barbara Stanwyck, Loretta Young, Ann Sheridan ... and many of them would get up and perform. Charles Laughton did a dramatic reading, Jane Wyman and Ronald Reagan did a little dance number, and the Ritz Brothers would just go crazy. Judy Garland showed up one night, but she was forbidden by her studio [Metro-Goldwyn-Mayer] from performing in public without their approval.

"Grace's son, Peter Lind Hayes, and I were good friends. He was in love with a very nice gal named Mary Healy, but for some reason, Grace took a dislike to her. She didn't think Mary was good enough for her son, and she would invite me to the lodge, hoping that Peter would drop Mary and hook up with me. Peter and I kept telling Grace that we were just friends, but she was not the kind of person who took 'no' for an answer and she kept trying to push us together. Eventually, Peter and Mary were married [from 1940 until his death in 1998] and the joke is that their marriage lasted longer than any of mine did."

# Chapter 9

# My One Ambition Is You
## *Motherhood, Matrimony and Retirement*

In 1939 Dorothy took on what she felt was the most important role of her life — motherhood — when she adopted a three-year-old boy named Dick. Adoption laws were much more relaxed compared to later rules and regulations, and involved relatively little red tape, even when it was a single-parent arrangement. The process was made easier because Dick was a distant blood relation, through a cousin. Additionally, his parents went to Dorothy and asked her to take care of their son; his birth mother was stricken with cancer and would later succumb to the disease at the age of 23.

Movie roles were scarce for an actress who had been so firmly associated with a bygone era, and her final film appearances were mere bit parts. At RKO, where she had been one of the studio's leading lights a decade earlier, she received no billing for her walk-ons in *Laddie* (1940; as a bridesmaid) and *Repent at Leisure* (1941; as a sales clerk). Monogram Pictures heralded *Roar of the Press* (1941) as Dorothy's comeback, but her fleeting, insignificant role as a jilted paramour was hardly designed to catch anyone's attention.

Dorothy made her final screen appearance in *Too Many Blondes* (1941), one in a string of moderately budgeted mini-musicals cranked out by Universal Pictures. She was offered the role by director Thornton Freeland, an old friend who, with wife June Clyde, had returned to the U.S. after spending the past few years making films in England. Her role (as one of the title blondes pursuing lead player Rudy Vallee) was a glorified bit part, but she accepted the offer simply as a favor to the director:

"T. Freeland basically wanted me around to play a practical joke on Rudy Vallee. Rudy fancied himself a ladies' man. He had a lot of success in that department and he sure liked to brag about it. So before I shot my scenes, T. had me put on a dark wig and then introduced me as a French starlet who was trying to break into American pictures. I started flirting outrageously with Rudy and he fell for it, even though I was speaking with a phony, god-awful French accent. We had met before, but Rudy didn't recognize me, or at least he was so caught up in the idea of making a conquest that it clouded his senses. Rudy thought he was really making progress, feeding me all these hokey romantic lines, and I was swooning all over him. The whole crew was in on the gag, and they were standing off to the side, fighting back laughter. Finally, T. revealed my true identity and everyone got a big laugh out of it. I have to say that Rudy was a pretty good sport about it, although he was awfully disappointed."

Despite her limited footage, Dorothy received surprisingly prominent billing on screen and on the promotional posters. Universal felt her name still had a degree of marquee value and left the door open for future supporting roles in the studio's "B" pictures.

Instead, Dorothy was signed for *New Orleans*, a new Sigmund Romberg–Oscar Hammerstein operetta. (She had auditioned for Romberg at his Beverly Hills home.) With music by Romberg and lyrics by Hammerstein, the show's book (also by Hammerstein) was reminiscent of *Dixiana*, with its 19th-century setting and storyline involving a café singer in love with a Southern aristocrat. It would turn out to be her final stage show.

"I just loved doing the show," Dorothy recalled. "I got along great with both Romberg and Hammerstein. Romberg was a little more difficult to work with when I would go up to him and make suggestions, though, such as with my opinions on a song. I would say, 'This song that I have to sing is a little slow. Do you think that we could pep it up a bit more?' But when I would ask Hammerstein the same thing or really just about anything, he would be absolutely wonderful about it, and it was a lot of fun when he rehearsed with me. He even autographed my little book with the inscription, 'To my favorite troublemaker.'"

Hammerstein directed the show and John Murray Anderson, who had directed Dorothy in *One for the Money*, served as production supervisor. "I enjoyed the whole experience," Dorothy commented. "I played the role of a Southern belle and did a comedic song-and-dance opposite Tommy Ewell [future star of the play and movie *The Seven Year Itch*]. What was really exciting is that it debuted at the St. Louis Municipal Opera House, an open air theater that seated ten thousand. It was really something."

The previews of *New Orleans* were held in June 1941. While Dorothy's lively supporting performance was singled out for praise, the ambitious production was panned by reviewers, who found it trite and old-fashioned. Dorothy remarked, "It was such a crushing blow to Hammerstein. The show had lovely songs and some remarkable, innovative touches and he had worked so tirelessly on the entire production."

The show underwent some retooling and eventually opened on Broadway as *Sunny River* (named after one of the songs Hammerstein had hoped would be a breakout hit) on December 4, 1941. By this time, Dorothy was no longer in the cast: "I was asked to go along and perform with them on Broadway, but I turned it down because I didn't want to move to New York." Despite the revisions, *Sunny River* met with a vicious reception from the critics and the show closed after 36 performances.[1] Yet Hammerstein's approach — intertwining the story and characters with the songs — would be validated two years later when he applied it to his smash hit *Oklahoma!*, co-written with Richard Rodgers.

## 9. My One Ambition Is You

During the *New Orleans* tryouts, Dorothy spent time in Chicago. Despite having gone through four divorces, she had not ruled out the possibility of getting married again, settling down and raising a family, though she was in no hurry to do so.

One of Dorothy's favorite Chicago hangouts was The Pump Room, a restaurant and bar frequented by celebrities and political bigwigs. She became friendly with hotelier Ernie Byfield, its owner and host, and he in turn became quite smitten with Dorothy. "Ernie was an outgoing, gregarious guy who I became very fond of, and we would often go out together. But I didn't realize how serious his feelings towards me were until the day he proposed to me." Byfield, who was twenty-one years Dorothy's senior, laid out his proposal like a business deal: "He told me that he would see that I was well taken care of, and that he would allow me to carry on affairs with other men, just as long as I didn't embarrass him publicly. Well, I was absolutely floored by his proposal and didn't know how to respond, so I told him I'd think about it. Thank goodness I didn't accept because I met John a short time later."

"John" was Frank John Bersbach, a Chicago socialite and business executive. His father, Frank John Bersbach, Sr., was vice-president and general manager of the Manz Engraving Company and John Jr. was an executive with the firm. (Incorporated in 1866, Manz began as a wood-engraving company and later became a successful color-printing press.) In social circles, John Jr. was better known for the rumors that swirled around his ex-wife, Durie Kerr Malcolm, who had allegedly once been the "secret" spouse of future president John F. Kennedy. The speculation prompted a journalist from *Time* magazine to confront Bersbach in search of "the truth." Bersbach stated he had no clue as to the allegations regarding his ex-wife's marital history. (Subsequently, the rumor was debunked.)

"I remember meeting John as if it were yesterday," Dorothy reminisced. "I was sitting in the bar in The Buttery at the Ambassador West Hotel waiting for Ernie Byfield. Instead of my girlfriend sitting next to me as usual, it was John, and I accidentally nudged him. Well, he knew who I was and I made my apologies. Ernie invited him to dinner with us, and that was that. We liked each other right away, and he was very good looking, too. John was also a good friend of my ex-husband, A.G. Atwater, and I was a good friend of John's ex-wife, although I had never met John until then."

It didn't take long for Dorothy to fall in love with John, or for John to propose to her: "I accepted immediately. I knew that this time I was going to give up show business and raise a family. I didn't want someone else to raise my children while I was off working. I wanted to be with my family full time. So I rented my house in California and I took my mother, my darling son and my dog, and drove to Chicago for my marriage. During the trip, the news broke that Pearl Harbor had been attacked on December 7. When we arrived in Chicago, I told John, 'I think it is crazy for us to get married at a time like this.' But he just said, 'Well, why not?' Because John was a young, single guy and the Pearl Harbor attack had just happened, a lot of people thought that the reason we got married was to keep him out of the service, which was not true at all.

"You know, it's funny how things work out sometimes. A good friend of mine named LaSeur who was stationed at Pearl Harbor invited me to visit him and his wife that week but I couldn't because I was getting married. Who knows what could have happened if I went to Hawaii. I would have been right in the middle of everything."

Dorothy married John Bersbach on December 9 (his birthday) in a little church in Winnetka, Illinois, with only the family and a few close friends in attendance. After the ceremony, the reception was held at the Skokie home of Joseph Gries, John's former roommate. The newlyweds spent their honeymoon in Lake Placid, New York, where John participated in the National Bobsled Races.

The couple had little time to settle down before John joined the Navy. John, Dorothy and Dick began living as most military families did, stationed around various parts of the country. John's first stint was training in Jacksonville, Florida. His social connections kept him stateside, but his duties still kept him occupied.

In 1943, Dorothy gave birth to their daughter Betsy in Daytona Beach, Florida, followed by two sons: Brent in Greenwich, Connecticut, in 1945 and Billy in Chicago in 1947. Dorothy would often state that the years she raised her four children were the happiest times of her life.

After John's Navy hitch was over, the Bersbachs settled in Winnetka, roughly 22 miles outside of Chicago. The new home gave them a stability they had lacked in previous years, as they could now enjoy activities as a family unit, from winter sports to swimming in their backyard pool. Dorothy finally had the domestic life she had longed for, although she still maintained an active social life. She kept in contact with many of the friends she made during her show business years, including her RKO pals Bert Wheeler and June Clyde. When Bert came through town in September 1947, touring in a stage production of *Benchwarmer*, he and Dorothy saw each other often during his stay. She would occasionally run into Harold Lloyd and Joe E. Brown when they passed through town: "Harold never seemed to change. He still had the same boyish charm after all those years. Joe was such a down-to-earth guy. He'd smile with that famous ear-to-ear grin of his and say, 'Hey, Lee, remember me?' How could I ever forget him? He was wonderful."

One not-so-wonderful reunion was with ex-husband Jimmie Fidler: "Fidler left word for me at the Pump Room that he was in town and wanted to see me. I had no interest in seeing him but I heard he had just gotten divorced from his second wife [former actress Virginia Roye] and I was dying to know if he still had my old dream house or whether he lost it in the settlement. So I agreed to have lunch with him just to find out. It turned out he still had it. I should have known that bastard was too shrewd to ever let it get away. Once I got my answer, I really didn't have anything more to say to him. He tried to get in touch with me a couple times after that but I just ignored his messages."

During trips to the West Coast, Dorothy would make an effort to get in a couple rounds of golf, and often ran into Bing Crosby and Bob Hope: "Whenever Bing and Bob saw me, they'd yell, 'Hiya, Lee!' and I would join them. They were such devils because they'd always try to throw off my game by making me laugh. I'd tell them, 'Knock it off, guys' but they never stopped. Bob was hilarious — he could ad-lib for hours on end. Bing was just as funny but in a different style. Bob would rattle off a string of jokes then Bing would fire off a one-liner that just devastated Bob. Playing golf with them was like being in one of their movies."

Dorothy kept in contact with Jane Wyman, whom she had befriended when Jane was a young actress just breaking into the movies: "Jane and I looked enough like each other that it would confuse some people. We used to laugh about the fact that when she was just starting out, people would come up to her and ask, 'Are you Dorothy Lee?' Then after she became a big star and I was long forgotten, people would ask me, 'Are you Jane Wyman?'"

A portrait of Dorothy from the mid–1940s.

Jane married Ronald Reagan in 1940, and even in those days Reagan had a keen interest in politics. Dorothy recalled: "Ronnie was a very intelligent man, and if you ever got into a discussion with him, he could talk in-depth about every subject under the sun, especially politics. Jane used to say, 'Don't ask him what time it is — he'll tell you how a watch is made.' And she was right. If I ever had an opposing opinion, Ronnie would smile and say, 'Well, Lee, I can understand where you're coming from but I've done a lot of reading up on that and....' This was his way of telling you that you didn't know what the hell you were talking about. But he did it in such a disarming and diplomatic manner, you could never take offense at his remarks, which were basically lectures. I wish I could tell you that I always knew he would be president one day, but I honestly didn't see it coming. I thought he would have made a great teacher, but a politician? It never entered my mind that he would one day hold the highest office in the land. I didn't even see it coming when he became governor of California, though I knew his interests extended way beyond show business."

The Bersbachs were the first family in the neighborhood to get a television set, and all of the kids on the block were cordially invited to their home to watch *Howdy*

*Doody* every week. Dorothy also enjoyed watching, for obvious reasons, *The Fred Waring Show* on CBS, and in the fall of 1950 (November 13, 1950, to be exact), she tuned in to NBC's *Musical Comedy Time* to see Bert Wheeler[2] in an hour-long adaptation of *Rio Rita*, which also starred Patricia Morison, Hal LeRoy, John Tyres, Henry Calvin, Donald Buka, Treva Frazee and Ray Jacquemot.

Every so often, a performer or celebrity would recognize Mrs. John Bersbach as the former Dorothy Lee. When she attended an Ambassador Hotel cocktail party honoring singer Johnny Johnston, who was appearing at the Chicago Theatre, Johnston spotted her and called to everyone's attention that she was one of his favorite actresses, even though she hadn't made a film in years. In their coverage of the party, the *Chicago Tribune* (May 7, 1952) described her as "not having changed a bit since her career days."

Throughout the 1940s, Buster Keaton had been reduced to minor film roles and serving as an anonymous gag writer at Metro-Goldwyn-Mayer, where he had once been the studio's top box-office star. By the end of the decade, however, Keaton began receiving belated critical recognition as one of the screen's greatest artists, and the advent of television opened up a new career for him. Soon after, Dorothy reconnected with her old friend: "We had fallen out of touch, partly because of my retirement and partly because Buster had been out of the country, making personal appearances in Europe. Then he came back to the States and began making all those appearances on television. Lee Cox, who was married to my dear friend Bill Cox, was the script girl [supervisor] on one of Buster's TV shows, and they became very close to him. So I caught up with Buster again, and even though we hadn't seen each other in a while, we resumed our friendship as if we had just seen each other the day before. By this time, Buster was married to a great gal named Eleanor.[3] She was the best thing that ever happened to him. She was caring and supportive in a way his other wives were not, and she really saved his life. She was a godsend."

Thanks to the television exposure and revivals of his classic silent comedies, Keaton was enjoying the kind of career resurgence that would have seemed impossible a decade earlier. Dorothy reflected: "For those of us who knew and loved Buster, his comeback was very gratifying because he had been forgotten by Hollywood for so many years. It was lovely to see the way he was excited about working again. Buster was never boastful or egotistical, but he took great pride in those wonderful TV commercials he made. And that was because he was allowed creative input, so it was like the way he made movies in the silent days."

The Keaton revival resulted in countless appreciative articles and studies, in addition to an autobiography: "Buster was never comfortable with all the praise he was getting. He thought that people who were analyzing his movies were reading way too much into them and they were missing the point that all he was trying to do was be funny. He'd say, 'Why can't they just watch these movies and laugh? Why do they keep looking for things that aren't there?'

"Buster didn't like it when comedians took themselves too seriously. He hated the 'g' word—*genius*—and he would actually get upset whenever somebody tried to make

**Dorothy with her friends Buster Keaton and Donna Atwater at a party at Dorothy's home in the late 1950s.**

that label stick. He didn't want to be idolized. I remember he complained about a flattering article that referred to him as a genius, and I said, 'But Buster, you *are* a genius.' Boy, did he shoot me a dirty look. He scolded me: 'Cut that out! Don't ever say that again!'

"He wrote an autobiography [*My Wonderful World of Slapstick*, 1960]—actually, it was written by a fellow named Charles Samuels who interviewed Buster at length and based the book on those interviews. For some reason, Buster didn't hit it off with Samuels. I don't know why, but it wasn't the writer's fault. Maybe Buster was uncomfortable about talking so much about past events he didn't care to relive. Whatever the case, he never read the book. When he received his copy, he drove over to Bill Cox's house and handed it to him and said, 'Let me know if this thing is any good.' I asked Buster why he never bothered to read his own book and he said, 'I don't need to. I already know what happens.'"

Career resurgence aside, he was still the same old Buster: "I went to visit him and Eleanor out at their place in the San Fernando Valley. When I first met Buster, he was living in this lavish Italian villa. Now, he had this humble property with chickens running around, and he was happier than he had ever been. There was no pretense about him, and that's what made him such a darling person.

"He never lost his fondness for practical jokes. While we were standing in his house, he slipped and fell flat on his back, right on the hardwood floor. I let out a scream and he stood up and started laughing like crazy. He said, 'I can't believe I can still fool you!' I was worried because he was no longer a young man, but it didn't faze him at all. He got such a kick out of pulling that prank on me. He was the same old Buster who loved to laugh, but he still guarded his trademark image. Whenever he posed for a photo, he wore the same frozen-face expression. I said, 'You have such a beautiful smile. Why don't you let someone take a picture of it?' He told me, 'Smiling in public doesn't work for me. I tried it a few times [in films] and it never felt right. People expect me to be a stone face.'"

When the Orphan Adoption Amendment of the Special Migration Act of 1953 was passed, Dorothy's good friend Jane Russell (*The Outlaw*, *Gentlemen Prefer Blondes*) founded the charitable organization WAIF (World Adoption International Fund) in order to raise money to help facilitate overseas adoptions. The Hollywood chapter of WAIF was so well-received that Jane started chapters in Palm Springs and New York, then others across the U.S. Jane asked Dorothy to help her organize a Chicago WAIF chapter and beginning in 1958 Dorothy served as the president of the local division. WAIF was responsible for assisting in over 50,000 inter-country adoptions, and the Chicago chapter raised a large amount of money for the cause.

Staging charity shows for WAIF allowed Dorothy to tap into her years of showbiz experience as she produced, directed and even wrote some of the material for the variety programs, which were praised for their humor and inventiveness. Dorothy was prouder of these WAIF productions than she was of most of her movies.

At one of the WAIF benefits, Dorothy welcomed special guest Fred Waring (he stopped by to attend after taking time off from one of his cross-country tours). He applauded her work and Dorothy chided, "Don't mind if it sounds like we're quarrelling, it is just that we always rib each other."

To promote the WAIF shows, Dorothy appeared live on the local ABC affiliate WBKB-TV (now WLS-TV) and was talked into serving as pitchwoman for one of the sponsor's products. When Dorothy suggested injecting a little humor into the sales spiel, the director was horrified: "He looked at me like I suggested we commit murder. He said, 'Oh, no ... we don't want to upset the sponsor.' I thought it would just lighten the mood. I wasn't suggesting that we make fun of the actual product — which was a refrigerator, as I recall — but he was having none of it. Nowadays, they use humor to sell practically everything."

Coincidentally, WBKB had some of Dorothy's movies in their station library. In 1957 the United Artists Corporation offered TV stations a package of over 700 feature-length films (and a handful of comedy shorts) that had originally been produced and released theatrically by RKO Radio Pictures from 1929 to 1954. Referred to as the "Movietime USA" package, the films were hastily printed in the then-standard 16mm format, with references to RKO clipped out or omitted optically to accommodate the distributors' new "C & C Television Corporation" identity.

## 9. My One Ambition Is You

The package included several of RKO's most distinguished productions (*Citizen Kane, The Magnificent Ambersons, King Kong, Top Hat, Bringing Up Baby*) and many of their misfires (*Down to Their Last Yacht, Check and Double Check*). Among the RKO titles were eleven of the thirteen Wheeler and Woolsey features Dorothy had appeared in, along with her solo efforts *Laugh and Get Rich, Too Many Cooks,* and *Twelve Crowded Hours*. WBKB was one of the very first TV stations to purchase the Movietime package. (Today, they still have broadcast rights to these films.)

Dorothy didn't go out of her way to watch any of her old movies when they turned up on television; she had closed that chapter of her life. But some friends didn't hesitate to notify her when one of her films was broadcast, most notably old pal Wayne Morris[4]:

"Wayne was a dear friend and he told me on several occasions that I was the worst actress he had ever seen, which I thought was hilarious. One day he's watching TV at his home in California and *Too Many Cooks* comes on. So he picks up the phone and calls me. When I answered, he didn't identify himself or say hello, he just yelled, 'Marjorie Millsap, you stink!' and slammed down the receiver. I called him right back and said, 'Okay, you son of a bitch, which one of my movies are you watching?' He said, 'How did you know it was me?' and I said, 'Who else could it be?' We both got a big laugh out of it."

Dorothy still enjoyed playing an occasional game of tennis and avidly followed news of the sport. She had become increasingly critical of the racial discrimination practiced in professional sports and private establishments; when Jackie Robinson broke baseball's color barrier in 1947, Dorothy hoped for a similar breakthrough in tennis. She was ecstatic when Althea Gibson became the first African-American woman to win the prestigious Wimbledon tennis tournament in 1957, and again the following year when Gibson repeated the victory. (Dorothy was equally thrilled years

**Bert and Dorothy in the backyard of Dorothy's home in July 1958.**

later when African-American tennis player Arthur Ashe won the U.S. Open, the Australian Open and Wimbledon.)

During the years after her retirement, Dorothy kept in close contact with Bert Wheeler: "I saw Bert several times after I left show business. He used to come and stay at our house and it was always a pleasure to see him."

Though his career never regained the momentum of his Broadway and Hollywood days, Bert was a guest on various radio and television shows, and kept busy by appearing in an assortment of touring stage shows.[5] One of these productions brought him back to Dorothy's home in July 1958:

"Bert was playing Captain Andy in a stage production of *Show Boat* starring Allan Jones, out in Highland Park [Illinois]. He stayed with us for the run of the play. I told him, 'Why should you go and pay for a hotel room when you can stay here?' We would sit out in the backyard and I would read his lines to him and we would rehearse his scenes. He would often take naps in the middle of the day and it was the first time I realized how much older he was. When we were making our pictures I didn't pay attention to age, but he and Bob were about 20 years older than I was. It was really great having him over and he just adored my kids. They would call him Uncle Bert, and he made a recording of one of his comedy routines ['Mousie'] for them. It was cute. He was the same sweet man he had always been."

# CHAPTER 10

# I Love You So Much
## *Kindred Spirits in the Autumn Years*

By the late 1950s, says Dorothy, she and her husband John Bersbach had "drifted apart ... it happens. We no longer had the same interests. We both loved our children, of course, but the relationship between me and John became strained. We were incompatible."

Dorothy liked to socialize and play tennis and golf, while John increasingly preferred quiet evenings at home. To compensate for being a "party pooper," he encouraged Dorothy to pursue those activities with one of their neighbors, the recently widowed Charles Calderini. Dorothy recalled:

"Charlie and Eleanor Calderini lived two blocks down the street from us. I really didn't know them that well, although I would see them at parties and other functions. After Eleanor died [in the fall of 1957] we saw Charlie more often because everyone in the neighborhood sort of looked after him. He was going through a rough spell."

Charles J. Calderini was born in Chicago on August 14, 1905. His grandparents were Italian immigrants who, like so many others, came to America hoping for a better life. The family faced financial hardships, but Charles worked hard to get an education and save money to pursue a legal career. Earning his law degree at DePaul University, he took advanced studies at the University of Michigan Law School. By the 1930s, he was a member of the American Bar Association and had earned a reputation for being one of the sharpest legal minds in the country. His rags-to-riches success story culminated with him becoming a senior partner at Winston and Strawn, a prestigious Chicago-based law firm.

Dorothy enjoyed keeping company with the affable, easy-going Calderini, and over the course of two years, they developed deep feelings for each other. In 1960 Dorothy divorced John Bersbach, citing irreconcilable differences, and on August 9 of that year she married Calderini. The ceremony was held in a suite at Chicago's Drake Hotel, with their children in attendance. After honeymooning in Hawaii, they returned to live in Calderini's home in Winnetka.

The union turned out to be the longest and happiest of Dorothy's marriages: "I'm finally at a point in my life where I think I've got this marriage thing figured out, and it only took me 30 years and six husbands. Charlie and I share mutual interests, but we respect each other's privacy. I give him his space and he gives me mine. It works out beautifully."

Dorothy and Charlie shared a passion for golf. And when Charlie was off on one of his hunting or fishing trips, Dorothy would play tennis (she was still good enough to win local tournaments), swim and tend to her garden and her pets (a steady stream of dogs and cats). To relieve the hassle of having to commute from the suburbs into the city, Charles purchased a condo at 1212 North Lake Shore Drive (in an area known as Chicago's "Gold Coast"), which enabled the couple to see more of their inner-city friends.

Dorothy remained active as the president of the local chapter of WAIF. For a sold-out, black-tie dinner dance held at the Guildhall of the Ambassador West Hotel in November 1961, she devised a theme based on the evolution of fashion, song and dance trends from the 1920s to the 1960s. The charity show opened with a rousing rendition of "If You Knew Susie," and among the chorines were Dorothy's Hollywood pals Martha O'Driscoll and June Travis, who were now married to Chicago businessmen, and Mary Hartline, the star of the local children's programs *Super Circus* and *Princess Mary's Castle*. Longtime friend June Clyde came to town to participate, as did WAIF founder Jane Russell, who was present at all of the events. The show, which included an all-male fashion show, raised a considerable amount for the WAIF organization and earned accolades in the local papers. Under Dorothy's supervision, they would become even more elaborate affairs.

For the December 1963 WAIF show, Dorothy conceived "The Millionaire Ball" in which she parodied well-known millionaires and decked out the Ambassador Hotel ballroom with a white and gold candelabra and an eight-foot money tree adorned with gilded branches, jewels and gold coins.

In November 1967, Dorothy opened the WAIF festivities as "Glitter McPearl," singing "Take Me to the Jewelry Store," spoofing everything from television commercials ("Take Me to the Jewelry Store" was a riff on "Take Me Along," the theme of a then-current United Airlines advertisement) to the Miss America Pageant. In the latter, Dorothy emerged as "Miss Gold Nugget of 1968," wearing a pink tutu, ballet slippers, and fighting to keep her crown from being yanked off of her head by fellow contestants as she yelled, "It's mine! It's mine! Get my lawyer!"

Dorothy and Charlie divided their time between the Midwest and the West Coast. Dorothy's daughter Betsy had relocated to San Diego; in 1965 Betsy gave birth to Todd Schneider, Dorothy's first grandchild.

Although Dorothy preferred tennis to golf, the latter would become her sport of choice when arthritis began taking its toll. Despite health setbacks, Dorothy tried to hit the golf course as often as possible: "Charlie and I were in Palm Springs and I wanted to get out and play golf even though I was in a back cast and couldn't bend over. This was after my big back operation that I had done in La Jolla [California]. So

Actresses June Travis, Martha O'Driscoll, June Clyde and Jane Russell join Dorothy (right) for a WAIF charity show in November 1961.

I was out on the golf course, and a familiar-looking guy walked past me. I thought to myself, 'That looks like Marsh Duffield.' Marshall Duffield was my favorite ex-husband and I hadn't seen him in at least 30 years. I walked up to him when he was hitting the golf balls and I asked, 'What's your name?' He answered, 'Marsh Duffield.' I said, 'I'm Dorothy!' He dropped his club and we put our arms around each other. By the time Charlie and our house guest got there, Marsh and I were kissing each other. I said, 'Charlie, who do you think this is?' And he says, 'Without a doubt, it's Marsh Duffield.' He had seen photographs of Marsh. That night we were all at this big fancy party and Marsh came over to introduce us to his wife Betty, who was much younger than he was. She was young enough to be my daughter! After Charlie came over to meet Betty, he said to me and Marsh, 'Shouldn't you two dance sometime?'

"I was stuck in this back cast and could hardly move but I knew that we had to dance. I went up to the orchestra leader and said to him, 'When I dance with Mr. Duffield, will you play this song which was our theme song from when we were married? It went like this: 'Beside a shady nook, among the brook, we take the time for love.' So Marsh and I were dancing and he said, 'Dorothy, do you remember this tune?' I said, 'Yes, darling. I asked them to play it for us.' I thought that was pretty cute. Later on, Charlie said, 'I want to say this to you two. I think the greatest mistake that you ever made was divorcing each other.' Marsh said, 'Well, she *made* me divorce her.' Charlie answered, 'I'm sure she did!'"

Though Charlie harbored no feelings of jealousy toward Duffield, it was a different story when Fred Waring asked Dorothy to make a guest appearance at a March 1968 concert in Dubuque, Iowa. (At the time, Dorothy's son, Bill Berbasch, was a sophomore at the University of Dubuque.) Charlie knew that Fred still held a special place in Dorothy's heart — she hung a framed 1920s-era photograph of her and Fred on the bedroom wall of their Galena home — and he became quite vocal about his reluctance to attend the event. After repeated assurances from Dorothy (she told him to stop acting so foolish), he begrudgingly went along for what turned out to be a pleasant evening. At the Loras College fieldhouse, Waring presented a show titled "The Next 50 Years" and announced to the audience that "a very special lady, my first girl singer, is here tonight." He dedicated a number to her and asked Dorothy to stand and take a bow, which she did, smiling with appreciation. Later, at a post-show dinner, Charlie looked on in amusement as Dorothy and Fred got into a heated argument, just like old times. "It was over nothing, really," Dorothy later explained. "We just fell into our old pattern of fighting and arguing." The incident only served to prove that, despite their love for each other, Dorothy and Fred would have never made it as a long-term couple. Charlie had nothing to worry about.

On February 1, 1966, Dorothy's old friend Buster Keaton died of lung cancer. In a life and career filled with peaks and valleys, Keaton had lived long enough to see his once-battered reputation restored and to be embraced by a new generation of ardent fans. Dorothy reminisced: "I have nothing but fond memories of Buster. He may not have been the most demonstrative person I've ever met but he wasn't the cold fish some biographers claim he was, either. If you were his friend, you knew it because he made sure you knew it. He was caring and very loyal. It didn't matter what anyone else said about you; if he liked you and you became his friend, you were his friend for life. Toward the end, we didn't see each other that much and he didn't like to talk on the telephone because he had hearing problems, but our friendship always remained strong. We had plenty of mutual friends and we would always trade 'hellos' through them.

"If I have one regret concerning Buster, it's that I never got the chance to be a leading lady in one of his movies. Not that I'm such a great comedienne or anything like that, but I was athletic enough to have done some of the physical comedy, and under Buster's guidance, I think I could have performed whatever stunts would have been required. To have worked with Buster would have been a highlight of my career."

Dorothy harkened back to her flapper days at the November 1964 WAIF show.

Bert Wheeler, whose fortune and health had declined over the years, reconnected with Dorothy one last time. Dorothy recalled: "Around Christmas of 1967, Charlie and I decided to have Bert come stay with us [in Winnetka] for the holidays. He was staying at the Lambs Clubs in New York. We called the Lambs and were shocked when they told us he was up at Saranac, where they sent those [club members] who needed a lot of medical attention. So we called him there and said, 'Bert, we'd love to have you come and spend Christmas with us.' He said, 'I'd love to.' He mentioned that the Lambs had given him a car. I said, 'Now Bert, we don't want you to drive, so we'll send you a round-trip plane ticket.' 'Okay,' he said, 'but first I'll have to get out of here.' A few weeks later, he was dead."

Bert died of emphysema on January 18, 1968, and Dorothy mourned the passing of a dear friend who had been a pivotal figure in her life: "It was so sad. Bert had been one of the biggest stars on Broadway and died alone and broke. I would check in on

**Dorothy, as Glitter McPearl, performs "Take Me to the Jewelry Store" in the November 1967 WAIF show. The other players are unidentified.**

him and ask if he needed anything, but he rarely accepted any of my offers to help him out. He didn't want people to think of him as a charity case, and he would rather earn his keep than accept what he felt were handouts. And he didn't want to be a bother to anyone, which he never, ever was.

"I owe Bert so much, I can't fully express it. He allowed me to ride his coattails so when he and Woolsey became big movie stars, I was able to share in the glory. He was a true friend in every sense of the word, always supportive and always watching out for me. To say that I'm eternally grateful to him doesn't even begin to cover how appreciative I am. He was the sweetest, most darling man and there isn't a day that goes by that I don't think of him and smile."

After Charlie retired, the Calderinis sold their Winnetka property and had a beautiful home built on 275 acres of land in scenic Galena, overlooking the Mississippi River. Dubbed "Little Ponderosa," the customized residence on Rocky Hill Road was two stories high, with five bedrooms, four baths, two kitchens and four fireplaces. A four-acre man-made pond served as their swimming pool since they had concerns about leaving a real swimming pool unattended during their travels. In order to maintain the property, live-in caretakers were employed. Of the five homes Dorothy owned over the years, this was her favorite, even surpassing the dream house she lost to Jimmie Fidler

## 10. I Love You So Much

in their divorce settlement. Of this period, she would later remark: "That was the time of my life. It was paradise, and being with Charlie was wonderful. I loved him."

Galena is known for its history (Ulysses S. Grant had been one of the city's residents) and architecture, as well as its golf and ski resorts. None of the locals were aware of Dorothy's showbiz past and that's the way she preferred it. Ironically, it was Charlie who would become a local celebrity. Inspired by the success of the 1969 Woodstock Festival, a coterie of rock music promoters set their sights on the wide open spaces of Galena, which they felt would serve as an ideal setting for a similar outdoor music festival. The citizens of Galena, justifiably concerned about the chaos that would ensue, became panic-stricken. Then Charlie interceded, assessed the situation and suggested enough legal roadblocks to prevent the plans from going forward.

Charlie was hailed as the city's savior and for years after that, people would stop him on the street or come up to him in restaurants to thank him profusely for coming to their rescue. Dorothy was perfectly content to be known as Mrs. Calderini, the Great Man's wife, and they quickly became a prominent and well-liked couple in the community. Little Ponderosa became a popular destination for friends old and new, and the Calderinis' open-door policy (visitors often dropped in without phoning in advance) seems astonishing in this era of heightened security issues and escalating crime rates. Actually, their open-door policy was astonishing back then too.

Traveling was something Dorothy had missed during her years with John Bersbach, so she and Charlie took trips to various locales around the world. She loved visiting Italy and Greece, and spent her 60th birthday (May 23, 1971) in Turkey.

Dorothy relinquished her participation as writer-producer-director of the WAIF benefit shows ("Thirteen years, that's enough!" she quipped), although she continued to support the charity wholeheartedly. For the November 1971 WAIF benefit, Dorothy turned the performing chores over to six student artists from Northwestern University's Waa-Muu Show.

That same year, a revival of Vincent Youman's 1925 musical comedy *No, No, Nanette* became one of the hottest tickets on Broadway. Ruby Keeler, the tap-dancing sweetheart of numerous '30s movie musicals (and Dorothy's old golfing buddy), headlined the feel-good, nostalgic show, with veteran comedienne Patsy Kelly in a prominent supporting role. (The producers also hired legendary choreographer Busby Berkeley in an advisory capacity, though the move was primarily intended to exploit his name for marquee value.) When the subject of a touring company arose, Dorothy's name came up as a possible candidate for the lead role. "Somebody who was familiar with my WAIF shows suggested me to the producers to star in a Midwest road company version of the show. At first, I turned them down flat but then I thought maybe I should check out the show first before I made my final decision. So I went to New York and saw the Broadway production. It was entertaining, though I realized it was too strenuous for me to do night after night, even on a short-term basis. I wouldn't have been able to handle it, physically. But I had a great time getting together with Ruby Keeler again, and Patsy Kelly was the same warm, funny doll she had always been."

**Dorothy and Charles Calderini in Venice in the spring of 1971.**

## 10. I Love You So Much

The revival of *No, No, Nanette* was the byproduct of a renewed interest in movies from Hollywood's Golden Age. Berkeley's lavish musicals, particularly the ones featuring Keeler, had captured the fancy of a new generation, along with those who were old enough to have seen them on their initial release. These and other vintage films made the rounds on television and were showcased in special screenings at colleges, museums and art-house theaters.

Forgotten by all but the staunchest film buffs and historians were the Wheeler and Woolsey pictures that had once been RKO's chief breadwinners. None of this mattered to Dorothy, who couldn't have cared less if her own work remained mired in obscurity. Besides, she thought, were these old movies even worth remembering?

# Chapter 11

# Dilly Dally
## *An Unexpected Rediscovery*

The nostalgia boom of the 1960s and '70s resulted in books and film festivals celebrating the works of Laurel and Hardy, W.C. Fields and the Marx Brothers, among others. Yet Wheeler and Woolsey received only scant references (if that) in surveys of other '30s-era screen comedians. Despite being part of the C&C Movietime library, the Wheeler and Woolsey films remained obscure, though limited exposure was not the primary reason for the neglect. In truth, the W&W pictures lacked the timeless quality that made Laurel and Hardy so enduring and the anarchic spirit that made Fields and the Marxes so contemporary.

Ironically, the qualities that held Wheeler and Woolsey back from a major revival are the same qualities that make their best films so appealing today: Their humor and music are so firmly rooted in vaudeville, Broadway theater and '30s Hollywood that they preserve the bygone era better than most movies of the period. Contemporary viewers with little appreciation or comprehension of what they're watching invariably find the W&W movies a chore to sit through — and in all fairness, some of them *are* a chore to sit through. However, when placed in their proper context, the films remain vital and entertaining on their own terms. The best of the Wheeler and Woolsey comedies are delightful and often hilarious time capsules.

Leonard Maltin's *Movie Comedy Teams* (Signet, 1970) was the first book to provide an appreciative career study of Wheeler and Woolsey, in addition to other teams that — at the time, at least — had not received their critical due (the Three Stooges, Abbott and Costello, the Ritz Brothers, Olsen and Johnson, and Martin and Lewis among them). The chapter on Wheeler and Woolsey, expanded from a 1968 article in Maltin's fanzine *Film Fan Monthly*, also acknowledged Dorothy's contributions to their films.

While it didn't trigger a major Wheeler and Woolsey revival, *Movie Comedy Teams* sparked a re-interest within the movie-buff community, as film societies began to screen some of the pictures and appreciative articles appeared in various publications. Chief among the latter was *Classic Film Collector*, an Iowa-based tabloid edited and published by Samuel K. Rubin. Rubin and his editorial staff were devoted to covering every aspect of vintage motion pictures — not only acknowledged classics but ignored, unsung movies that were never mentioned in generic history-of-Hollywood studies. (Rubin's policy continued long after the publication changed its name to *Classic Images*.)

While Bert and Bob were gone, no one was sure what happened to Dorothy Lee. "Retired and moved to Chicago" was the way sketchy biographical info summed up the end of her career. Not much to go on, but it was still a lead.

> Living in Chicago, I had seen some of Dorothy's films when they were broadcast on Channel 7, the local ABC affiliate that had picked by the C&C Movietime package. Since Chicago was given as her last-known whereabouts, I attempted to track her down via telephone directories and actors' unions. In 1974, after failing to uncover any solid leads, I finally wrote to the now-defunct *Chicago Daily News*, which had a local-interest Q&A column called "Beeline." I inquired if anyone knew of Dorothy's current whereabouts. To my surprise — and to Dorothy's, as it turned out — the newspaper identified her as Dorothy Calderini and gave the address to her Lake Shore Drive condominium. Disclosing this kind of private information is a journalistic faux paus. The regular editor had been on vacation, so an assistant just printed the information they had on file. This upset Dorothy, and I can't say that I blamed her. However, this is how our friendship began, so something positive did come out of this potentially messy situation.
>
> — Ted Okuda

Dorothy was completely blindsided by the latter-day interest in her career: "How the hell does anyone remember *me*? I haven't made a movie in years and the ones I did make weren't all that good!" As articles on Wheeler and Woolsey appeared in *Classic Film Collector* and *American Classic Screen,* she began receiving fan mail for the first time in decades: "Isn't this something? I thought I put all this stuff behind me when I retired and here I am signing autographs again." In an interview with Eleanor Page for the *Chicago Tribune,* Dorothy stated she had no regrets about walking away from Hollywood: "I gave up my career to have babies. I did what I wanted — first show business, and then a family, because I knew when I had children I wanted to be with them."

Answering fan letters and doing phone interviews were pleasant and undeniably flattering diversions, but Dorothy turned down requests for personal appearances at film screenings and nostalgia conventions. At the urging of family and friends, she relented when the Flicker Buffs, a Chicago-based social club that ran movies at their get-togethers, invited her to be their guest of honor. On April 27, 1976, the Flicker Buffs hosted a screening of *Hips, Hips, Hooray!* at the Merchants and Manufacturers Club in the Merchandise Mart, with many of Dorothy's friends in attendance. Most of them knew her primarily as Mrs. Charles Calderini, and may have had some inkling that she had once been in show business. The usually unflappable Dorothy was visibly ill at ease when called upon to give an introduction: "I'm in the picture you're about to see, but I don't think I've ever seen it myself, so I couldn't tell you if it's any good. If it isn't, could you please keep the bar open?" *Hips, Hips, Hooray!* received a hearty response from all in attendance; even the ultra-critical Dorothy admitted it was "pretty corny" but enjoyable.

Invitations from other organizations followed, but with the exception of a charity-sponsored screening of *Cockeyed Cavaliers* in Galena a few years later, Dorothy declined the requests. She explained, "At that Flicker Buffs event, I was surrounded by my family and friends. It was like a party or a reunion. But I wouldn't be comfortable in a roomful of strangers. I mean, imagine how disillusioned they'd be. They'll be watching this 20-year-old girl running around on the screen, then when the lights come up, this old bag comes shuffling out. It's better to let them keep that youthful image of me rather than be shocked into reality."

Fans sent her publicity photos — many of which she barely remembered posing for — and movie posters to autograph and these items reminded her of all the memorabilia she had saved and eventually discarded. "At one time, I had a ton of old photos, but every time I moved, I'd wind up tossing some away. I'd fill up a suitcase with them, and whatever didn't fit got thrown out. I never thought that, all these years later, anyone

Dorothy in her eighties, wearing the engagement ring Fred Waring had given her in the late 1920s (courtesy John Cavallo).

would be interested in old photos of me. I'm sorry I don't have them now, because I could send them to people who are nice enough to write to me."

With the advent of the VHS home-video format, Dorothy began collecting copies of her movies, something she had never given a second thought about previously. However, seeing her film work (in some instances, for the first time) was a rude awakening: "When I watch myself — oh, brother! I have no idea how I lasted as long as I did. I guess I got by on whatever charm I might have had. And the movies are pretty bad too. A couple of the Wheeler and Woolsey pictures are cute, but most of them just aren't very good, and it makes me wonder why these films were so popular. I guess the only explanation is that they were good for the time they were made. For instance, I saw *Just Imagine* [1930] when it first came out, and I thought it was the most fantastic movie ever made, with all those futuristic sets and special effects and musical numbers. Sixty years later, someone gave me a video copy of it and I couldn't believe it was the same picture I enjoyed all those years ago. It was so awful that I stopped watching it after the first half-hour. I remember how marvelous I thought it was way back when, and it probably *was* marvelous for that time. But it sure didn't hold up, and I think the same is true with the Wheeler and Woolseys. They don't stand the test of time.

"I like some of the musical numbers or individual routines, but I hardly ever sit through one of my movies all the way through. Not for my own enjoyment. I appreciate that people still get a kick out of them but the appeal of these pictures escapes me. I'll admit, though, that I'm not the best judge when it comes to these things. I mean, I never cared for Laurel and Hardy or Charlie Chaplin, yet a lot of people whose opinions I respect adore them. Buster Keaton and I once watched a Laurel and Hardy movie together and Buster laughed so hard I thought he was going to fall out of his seat. He told me how great these guys were, and Buster knew more about comedy than anyone I've ever known, so if *he* said they're great, then there's no doubt they *are* great. But they never appealed to me, and I realize the problem is with me, not them. Whatever makes them great escapes me, so that's a shortcoming of mine. I've always loved watching Buster and Harold Lloyd, but the other ones never did it for me. So I'm probably not the best person to offer an opinion on the Wheeler and Woolsey pictures, even if I am in so many of them. Some fans have had trouble accepting that I'm not as crazy about the films as they are and they've gotten a little irritated because my opinions seem so harsh."

While Dorothy was not reluctant to talk about the past, she shied away from calling attention to herself. During a 1986 installment of *The Tonight Show*, host Johnny Carson took movie critics Roger Ebert and Gene Siskel to task for not knowing who Wheeler and Woolsey were. (As a youngster, Carson had been an avid W&W fan.) Friends urged Dorothy to write Carson a letter and send it to him along with a publicity photograph from one of the films, but she dismissed the suggestion: "Just because Johnny remembers Bert and Bob doesn't mean he has any idea who the heck I am." Producers of the BBC documentary *The RKO Story* (1987) asked her to appear in the film as one of the interview subjects. She declined.

Belated trips down Memory Lane underscored how many people were no longer in her life. In the mid-1980s, she lost two men who had been closest to her. Fred Waring, who she always referred to as the love of her life, passed away on July 29, 1984. Privately she would admit, "I know it sounds like a corny old cliché, but when Fred died, a piece of me died too. It was the end of a very important chapter in my life."[1]

The following year, she lost Charles Calderini. His health began to fail in the early 1980s. He suffered a series of debilitating strokes and Dorothy acted as his primary caregiver. He died on August 16, 1985, at the age of 80. Their 25-year-marriage had been Dorothy's most durable union. Although she still had her children, grandchildren, and a close-knit circle of friends, her life was never the same without him. Outwardly, she remained cheery and optimistic, but those near to her sensed a lingering melancholy that intensified as time went on.

Dorothy lost her dearest friend when June Clyde passed away on October 1, 1987. (June's husband, Thornton Freeland, died the previous May.) They had been close since their earliest RKO days, and though June's death was not unexpected — she had been in poor health for some time — it was still a devastating blow to Dorothy.

The Calderini home in San Diego now seemed too empty for one person, so Dorothy's half-sister Melissa moved in. After a few years, Melissa moved to New Orleans, and Dorothy spent her quiet time visiting with family and old friends, and answering her ever-increasing volume of fan mail.

## Chapter 12

# Dance and Let the World Dance with You
## *A Final Bow*

*"I'm a collector's item now! Can you believe it?"*— Dorothy Lee

As the American Movie Classics cable channel began devoting much of their program schedule to the RKO library, the Wheeler and Woolsey films were now given wider exposure. (The tradition continues on Turner Classic Movies, where RKO titles are regularly showcased.) Additionally, the release of select W&W titles on VHS and the laserdisc format made these obscure films more accessible. While none of this resulted in a major revival, it served to introduce Bert and Bob — and Dorothy — to a generation of fans who were born long after the team's heyday. Dorothy was dumbstruck: "Why are these kids interested in those old movies? Why aren't they watching something more recent? A lot of the new stuff is better than the things we did." Though she claimed to be confused and embarrassed by the praise-filled letters she received, she was deeply touched by their genuine affection: "I'm astounded that these kids have any interest in me and what I have to say. I try to answer them the best I can, but it was all so long ago that old Granny here can barely remember anything."

> I was a fan of Dorothy's since the first moment I saw one of her movies. My initial contact with her was in 1992, and she was genuinely surprised that a young girl like me would be so enthralled by her work. "Why would you be interested in an old bag like me?" was one of the things she asked me during our first conversation. Her term "old bag" was in complete contrast to the kind of person she really was. People will advise you not to get too close to someone you admire, because you'll be setting yourself up for a big letdown. I'm happy to say that Dottie was everything I expected her to be and more — sharp, witty and vivacious.
> 
> — Jamie Brotherton

John Cavallo, a historian-memorabilia collector residing in San Diego, became one of Dorothy's closest friends and even managed the impossible when he convinced her to attend Cinecon, an annual gathering of film enthusiasts, held in Los Angeles over Labor Day Weekend. At John's urging, Dorothy accepted a guest invitation for the 1991 Cinecon, though when the time came, she was as apprehensive as ever. Appearing at a screening of *Cockeyed Cavaliers*, Dorothy timidly stood up when the lights came on. She fielded questions from the audience, and after answering each inquiry, she quipped, "Is that it? Can I leave now?" The crowd roared with laughter, but John knew she wasn't kidding.

Dorothy was surprised by the number of people in attendance and signed autographs for everyone who requested one. Everything went smoothly, yet afterwards she breathed a sigh of relief and told John, "I love you but I am *never* going to do this again." John commented, "It always amazed me how someone who had spent so many years in front of large audiences and movie crews could be so uncomfortable with a relatively small group of strangers."

True to her word, Dorothy never appeared at another tribute, despite the invitations that were extended. She did, however, continue to reach out to fans and honor interview requests. She was contacted by historian Mark A. Miller for a two-part article on Wheeler and Woolsey in *Filmfax* magazine, and she provided the introduction for Edward Watz's detailed career study *Wheeler and Woolsey: The Vaudeville Comic Duo and Their Films, 1929–1937* (McFarland, 1994). Appreciative articles about Dorothy turned up in such niche-market publications as *Classic Images*, *The Big Reel*, *Cult Movies* and *Movie Collector's World*.

Now in her early eighties, Dorothy was resigned to the fact that her failing eyesight meant she could no longer drive herself around town. Her children and grandchildren would often visit and take her out; granddaughter Carrie took her grocery shopping every week. John Cavallo also checked in on her regularly, offering his services for various errands and tasks, and taking her out for an occasional lunch and dinner. Although she tried to remain a social butterfly, Dorothy gave up long-distance travel. She grew more concerned about her health, with good reason. Repeated bouts of pneumonia left her vulnerable to other types of illness.

Virgie Mills, Dorothy's best friend from this period, suffered from diabetes. Virgie lived in Palm Desert and Dorothy worked out an arrangement whereby she would spend the winters with Virgie, then have Virgie live with her in San Diego during the summer. Dorothy welcomed the change of pace and the fact that Virgie lived right off the golf course. Dorothy had given up playing the links a while ago, but the sight brought back fond memories of her early morning golf games with Charles Calderini. The trips to Palm Desert lasted for a few years, until Virgie required the services of a full-time nurse.

Age was taking its toll on the octogenarian. While family members and friends still looked in on her, Dorothy began receiving assistance from Ann and Pat, two kind caregivers. Ann drove Dorothy wherever she needed to go, and Pat took care of her other important needs.

In 1997, to Dorothy's delight, her great-grandchildren were born: a son to her first grandson Todd (a successful attorney living in Chicago), and a daughter born to her granddaughter Carrie. Since she lived in closer proximity to Carrie, Dorothy enjoyed watching Carrie's daughter Carly grow and learn how to walk and talk. Carly would

## 12. Dance and Let the World Dance with You

refer to her great-grandmother Dorothy as "Gigi" and always bring her a little token of her affection such as a cookie.

A short time later, Dorothy had dinner at her favorite piano bar in San Diego and caught a cold from sitting too close to an air conditioning vent. She developed pneumonia and was hospitalized; her weakened and scarred lungs complicated her recovery. When she was finally released from the hospital, she still needed to be on oxygen. Since she was used to an active lifestyle, she grew frustrated by her situation. She was forced to slow down, literally, unable to walk at the natural pace she was accustomed to. As she grew more frail, she was given heavy doses of morphine to ease her pain. Her once cheerful, alert voice now sounded strained and winded.

Incredibly, Dorothy continued to answer fan letters and honor as many interview requests as her health permitted. She was one of several actresses profiled in William M. Drew's collection of interviews *At the Center of the Frame: Leading Ladies of the Twenties and Thirties* (Vestal Press, 1999). The interaction with fans meant more to her now than ever before. She would become teary-eyed while reading a flattering letter from an enthusiastic fan, then break the sentimental mood by cracking, "I'll bet this kid has no idea that the young lady he thinks he's writing to is actually an 86-year-old bag."

Dorothy was losing weight rapidly and her medication was playing havoc with her alertness. She was physically unable to tend to her flower garden, and little pastimes such as bird watching were no longer as pleasurable as they once had been. Her son Brent and her daughter Betsy were among the family members who were devastated by her fragile condition. For several nights, Brent would lie in her bedroom, watching television with her and holding her hand until she fell asleep.

May 23, 1999, marked Dorothy's eighty-eighth birthday, and she celebrated by having her hair and nails done. She looked far healthier than she actually was. She told family and friends that she knew that the end was near. She even joked, "A lot of my friends are dead now. I have quite a few up there and maybe some of them *down* there. So, I'll have friends no matter where I wind up."

During the following weeks, her health worsened and the pain increased. In the early morning hours of June 24, 1999, she removed her oxygen mask and died of congestive heart failure.

Dorothy was cremated and a memorial ceremony was held at her home with family and friends in attendance. A beautiful portrait from her RKO heyday was placed next to her urn, as everyone shared happy memories. Her ashes were taken to Illinois and interred to a cemetery in Galena, where she now rests next to her sixth husband, Charles Calderini. The time came for her San Diego home to be sold, and when the new residents learned of the former owner, they hung up a youthful photograph of Dorothy from her movie days as a tribute to her.

Shortly after her eightieth birthday, Dorothy touched upon her own mortality ("I don't know if I'll be around much longer"), which prompted the question how she would like to be remembered. Ever the pragmatist, Dorothy responded:

"I'd like to be remembered by family and friends as someone who always had their best interests at heart and always tried to do the best she could. But if you're asking that question the way you probably mean it, in terms of how the world will remember me after I'm gone, then I'll answer it this way: Why would anyone who didn't know me remember me? What legacy am I going to leave behind? I was never in a movie of any lasting value, something like *It's a Wonderful Life* or *The Wizard of Oz*. I never came up with anything to benefit mankind. And Heaven knows I was never a scholar or a deep thinker. I was just a lucky little girl who caught a lot of breaks, had a lot of fun and met a lot of wonderful people. I don't think of my life in terms of how I'm going to be remembered because I never accomplished anything that the world will remember me for. But I would like it if the people I loved would think of me every so often and say, 'The old gal was really something, wasn't she?' That would be a perfect epitaph."

# Afterword

*Jamie Brotherton:*

Dorothy would often tell me, "I may be old, but I think young." How true that was. Over the years we developed a very special connection. A week wouldn't pass without phoning each other even if it was only to say, "I was just thinking of you." She would often say that we had ESP when it came to thinking about one another because regardless of which one of us phoned first, we would share that the other one was just about to pick up the telephone to do the same. She liked to kid me about that by jovially saying, "You beat me to it!" I loved surprising Dottie with various photographs and news clippings I obtained from memorabilia dealers and collectors. She'd tease that I was "crazy" for feeling the way I did and for taking such an interest in her career, but I know that deep inside she was touched and often got a kick out of it. During bleak periods in her final years, she never dwelled on the negative and always remained upbeat whenever we spoke. She continued to give motherly advice to me and my family, always telling us, "You are my family, too, and don't you ever forget that!" I can hear her as if it were yesterday telling me, "You're

**Dorothy enjoys the California sun in the summer of 1930.**

## Afterword

my granddaughter, and I love you." She insisted that I call her Granny and I am honored that she called me her granddaughter.

On the morning that she died I happened to look up at the sky and noticed a strange aura that consisted of a yellowish glow between the misty white clouds that I had never seen before, or have since. I initially shrugged it off, but deep down couldn't shake that ominous feeling. Soon after, I received a phone call notifying me that Dorothy had passed away. I do believe that mystic sky was a sign from Dorothy, her way of telling me goodbye, for that is how connected we were. Not a day goes by that I don't miss Dorothy, or think about her, and the indelible impression she made on me. Whenever I do think about her, I feel her vivacity and the love that she radiated. She was one of a kind in many respects, and I will treasure her forever.

*Ted Okuda:*

When I first met Dorothy, I was just a fan who enjoyed her movies. It didn't take long to realize that she looked upon her show business career as a relatively minor facet of the life she led. She appreciated being remembered but she simply had no desire to live in the past. More than anyone I've ever met, Dottie managed to grow old without becoming old. By that I mean she always maintained a youthful perspective; she had an inquiring mind and remained an astute observer of the world around her.

She was also one of the nicest people I've ever known, and she treated me like a surrogate son. I had the pleasure — make that *honor*— of being her guest countless times at her residences in Chicago, Galena and San Diego. On numerous occasions, I brought along 16mm prints and videotapes of her films; in an age before DVD audio commentary, I sat and listened as Dottie's memory was sparked by the images she saw, some of them for the very first time. She was intrigued by my interest in her and her career, and it sparked a re-interest on her part as well. She would thank me profusely for "rediscovering" her and making her realize that perhaps her work hadn't been so unmemorable after all.

Dorothy in costume for her role in *The Cuckoos* (1930).

For twenty-four years, we spoke to

each other every Christmas Day, and on most of those twenty-four holidays, she'd say, "Well, son, I've had a good run, but I think this is my last Christmas. I don't know if I'll be around for the next one. You'll have to carry on and celebrate without me." Initially, her candor took me aback, but after two decades I came to believe she was invincible. It still seems incredible that such a vibrant spirit is gone, but whenever I think of her, I smile as I recall the wonderful memories. And that's exactly the same attitude Dottie had throughout her life.

# Filmography

The following films are listed in the order of release.

There were two other actresses named Dorothy Lee. One appeared in a couple of features for the Fox Film Corporation, *Her Elephant Man* (1920) and *Skirts* (1921), in addition to four comedy shorts starring Chester Conklin, also for Fox. The other Dorothy Lee co-starred in three Art Mix westerns—*Salt Lake Trail, Paths of Flame* and *The Man from the Rio Grande*, all released in 1926—for Denver Dixon Productions, and the drama *Sweeping Against the Winds* (filmed in 1928, released in 1930) for Victor Adamson Productions.

*Julius Sizzer* (1931) and *Full Coverage* (1931), RKO Pathé two-reel comedies starring Benny Rubin, have been listed in past Dorothy Lee filmographies, but it's actually Gwen Lee who appears in them.

## *Take Me Home* (1928)

*Director:* Marshall Neilan. *Story and screenplay:* Harlan Thompson, Grover Jones, Thomas J. Cizer, Ethel Doherty. *Titles:* Herman J. Mankiewicz. *Cinematography:* J. Roy Hunt. *Film editor:* Otto [Otho] Lovering.

*Cast:* Bebe Daniels (Peggy Lane), Neil Hamilton (David North), Lilyan Tashman (Derelys Devore), Doris Hill (Alice Moore), Joe E. Brown (Bunny), Ernie [Ernest] Woods (Al Marks), Marcia Harris (Landlady), Yvonne Howell (Elise), Janice MacLeod [Janet McLeod] (Betty), Dorothy Lee (Chorus girl).

Released October 13, 1928, by Paramount Pictures. 60 minutes.

*Synopsis:* Chorus girl Peggy Lane falls in love with David North, a simple country boy who aspires to be a magician, and introduces him to the bright lights of Broadway.

"Lightly seasoned backstage picture void of a definite punch.... Just a program picture.... None of the players leaves a mark beyond the named principals and [Joe E.] Brown, who could have stood building for added strength."—*Variety*

*Comments:* Dorothy's first movie role was an unbilled bit as a member of the chorus. She also appeared in a brief scene opposite Bebe Daniels, with whom she would co-star in *Rio Rita* (1929) and *Dixiana* (1930).

Joe E. Brown had a supporting comic-relief role in *Take Me Home*. Although Joe and Dorothy didn't share any key scenes in this picture, they would appear together in *Local Boy Makes Good*, one of Brown's starring comedies for Warner Brothers, three years later.

At this writing, there are no known surviving prints of *Take Me Home*.

## *Syncopation* (1929)

*Director:* Bert Glennon. *Producer:* Robert T. Kane. From Gene Markey's novel *Stepping High*. *Dialogue:* Gene Markey. *Adaptation:* Frances Agnew. *Dialogue supervisor:* Bertram Harrison. *Assistant directors:* Basil Smith, Fred Uttal. *Executive producer:* Joseph I. Schnitzer. *Cinematography:* George Webber, Dal Clawson. *Additional cinematography:* Frank Landi. *Settings:* Clark Robinson. *Film editors:* Paul Maschke, Edward Pfitzenmeier. Sound recorded by RCA Photophone System.

*Songs:* "Do Something" and "I'll Always Be in Love with You" by Bud Green, Sammy Stept and Herman Ruby; "Jericho" by Leo Robin and Richard Myers; "Mine Alone (My Inspiration Is You)" by Herman Ruby and Richard Myers; "Ah, Sweet Mystery of Life" by Victor Herbert; "Tin Pan Parade" by Léo Delibes.

*Cast:* Fred Waring's Pennsylvanians (Themselves), Barbara Bennett (Fleurette "Flo" Sloane), Bobby Watson (Benny Darrell), Morton Downey (Lew Lewis), Dorothy Lee (Peggy), Verree Teasdale (Rita Eliot), Ian Hunter (Alexander Winston), Osgood Perkins (Jake Hummel), Mackenzie Ward (Sylvester Cunningham), Leon Barté (Ramo Artino), Tom Brown (Bellhop).

Released March 24, 1929, by RKO Radio Pictures. (Premiered March 3, 1929.) 82 minutes.

*Synopsis:* Adagio dance team Benny Darrell and his wife Flo Sloane are hired by millionaire playboy Alexander Winston to appear at his nightclub. The ambitious Flo leaves poor Benny when she becomes romantically involved with the debonair Winston. Flo doesn't fare well with another dance partner. Worse yet, Winston reveals himself to be a cad who's only interested in a fling, not marriage. A sadder but wiser Flo returns to Benny, and they resume their union and their act.

"Those who revel in jazz bands and in stories of hoofers who become separated from their fair partners through the financial machinations of the smooth-voiced, good-looking men about Park Avenue and Broadway, may find this a jovial, melodious production. Others who want something more subtle or polished will hardly enjoy the ramifications of the narrative, although they may be entertained by Fred Waring's Pennsylvanians."—*New York Times*

*Comments:* Dorothy's assertion that her charm outweighed her performing inexperience was never so evident as it is in *Syncopation*. Her bubbly personality is engaging enough to get her through some rough patches (though most of those are technical in nature) and her performance provides a good indication of how lively she must have been on stage. The film itself, however, is clumsily executed, encapsulating the flaws inherent in many of the earliest talkies: tinny sound recording, static editing, leaden pacing, non-existent camera movement, maudlin plot twists and stilted acting.

Ironically, it's Dorothy and singer Morton Downey, the two cast members with the least amount of acting experience, who give the most enjoyable performances, perhaps because they're the least self-conscious. Their characters (a cabaret singer and his flapper girlfriend) exist on the sidelines of the overwrought storyline, so they're free to wander in and out, unburdened by the melodramatics that weigh everyone else down.

The other actors come across hammy (not in a good way), sullen or unsure of themselves. Ian Hunter seems particularly ill at ease, which is in sharp contrast to the smooth, erudite performances he would give in *A Midsummer Night's Dream* (1935), *The Adventures of Robin Hood* (1938), *Tower of London* (1939), *Strange Cargo* (1940), *Northwest Frontier* (a.k.a. *Flame Over India*, 1959) and a host of other pictures. Barbara Bennett did not enjoy the same success in movies as her sisters Joan and Constance did, and based on her work in *Syncopation*, that's not surprising. On the subject of relatives, Osgood Perkins, who plays a theatrical agent, was the father of actor Anthony Perkins.

Bobby Watson never established himself in leading-man roles, but he found steady employment as a character actor. (He turns up briefly in Wheeler and Woolsey's *Hips, Hips, Hooray!*, as a gay choreographer.) Watson's career took an unusual turn when he was repeatedly cast as

Adolf Hitler, essaying both comical and serious portrayals of Der Fuehrer in *The Devil With Hitler* (1942), *Hitler — Dead or Alive* (1942), *That Nazty Nuisance* (1943), *The Hitler Gang* (1944), *The Miracle of Morgan's Creek* (1944), *The Whip Hand* (1951; his scenes were deleted), *The Story of Mankind* (1957), *On the Double* (1961) and *The Four Horseman of the Apocalypse* (1962). Watson attained movie immortality as the diction coach in the "Moses Supposes" number in *Singin' in the Rain* (1952).

## *Rio Rita* (1929)

*Director:* Luther Reed. *Producer:* William LeBaron. Based on Florenz Ziegfeld's *Rio Rita* by Guy Bolton and Fred Thompson. *Adaptation:* Luther Reed. *Music:* Harry Tierney. *Lyrics:* Joseph McCarthy. *Musical director:* Victor Baravalle. *Cinematography:* Robert Kurrle. *Art director:* Max Rée. *Dialogue director:* Russell Mack. *Cimini Grand Chorus director:* Pietro Cimini. *Original music:* Max Steiner. *Orchestrator:* Roy Webb. *Photographic effects:* Lloyd Knechtel. *Dance staging:* Pearl Eaton. *Chief sound recorder:* Hugh McDowell, Jr. *Film editor:* William Hamilton. *Associate film editor:* Pandro S. Berman. *Color photography:* Technicolor process.

*Songs:* "Rio Rita," "The Kinkajou," "The Ranger Song (March of the Rangers)," "Down By the River of My Dreams (River Song)," "You're Always in My Arms (But Only in My Dreams)," "If You're in Love, You'll Waltz," "Are You There?," "I Can Speak Español," "Following the Sun Around," "I'm Out on the Loose Tonight," "Over the Boundary Line" and "Sweetheart, We Need Each Other" by Harry Tierney and Joseph McCarthy.

*Cast:* Bebe Daniels (Rita Ferguson), John Boles (Capt. Jim Stewart), Bert Wheeler (Chick Bean), Robert Woolsey (Ed Lovett), Dorothy Lee (Dolly Bean), Don Alvarado (Roberto Ferguson), Georges Renavent (General Ravenoff), Helen Kaiser (Katie Bean), Eva Rosita (Carmen), Lita Chevret (Showgirl), Raymond Maurel (Singer), Richard Alexander (Gonzales), Fred Burns (Wilkins), Sam Nelson (McGinn), Stanley "Tiny" Sanford (Louie Davalos), Clyde McClary (Louie's henchman), Charles Stevens (José), Sammy Blum (Café owner), Fred Scott, Hank Bell, Bud Osborne, Ben Corbett, Bud McClure, Thomas C. Smith (Texas Rangers), Nick De Ruiz (Padrone), Blue Washington (Fremont bank robber), Clyde McClary (Henchman), Robert Livingston (Dancer), Elias Gamboa (Mexican), the Pearl Eaton Girls, the Pietro Cimini Grand Chorus.

*Production dates:* June 26–July 20, 1929. Released October 6, 1929, by RKO Radio Pictures. 135 minutes.

*Synopsis:* Texas Ranger Jim Stewart falls in love with Rita Ferguson, a.k.a. Rio Rita, a señorita whose brother Roberto may very well be the notorious bandit known as "The Kinkajou." General Ravenoff also has designs on Rita, and makes Rita believe Jim will arrest Roberto. After spurning Jim, Rita agrees to marry Ravenoff in order to save her brother.

Meanwhile, bootlegger Chick Bean has married a chorus girl named Dolly, only to be notified by his shifty attorney Ed Lovett that the divorce from Katie, the previous Mrs. Bean, is not final. To his chagrin, Chick has to delay consummating the union until the legal matter can be straightened out. The situation flummoxes the unsuspecting Dolly.

Ravenoff stages a lavish wedding ceremony but before he can marry Rita, Jim comes to the rescue and reveals Ravenoff to be the Kinkajou. Roberto turns out to be a member of the Mexican Secret Service, Chick is free to be with Dolly after Katie falls for Ed Lovett, and Rita and Jim, not wishing to waste a good ceremony, tie the knot.

"A picture full of entertainment and polish for the masses and the classes.... In casting, the picture is perfect." — *Variety*

*Comments:* At this writing, it is a little difficult to properly evaluate *Rio Rita* since the version currently in circulation is missing more than a half-hour's worth of footage. (It was whittled down for a 1932 reissue; the Warner Archive DVD edition runs 102 minutes.) Based on what does exist, however, it's clear that it was (and is) one of the best early Hollywood musicals, superior to such efforts as *Sunnyside Up*, *The Cocoanuts*, *Hallelujah*, *The Love Parade* and even *The Broadway Melody*, which won the Best Picture Academy Award for that year. (Also in 1929, Fox Films tried to capitalize on the success of *Rio Rita* by casting J. Harold Murray, who played Capt. Jim Stewart in the Broadway production of *Rio Rita*, in the operetta *Married in Hollywood*, which featured Walter Catlett and Tom Patricola as Wheeler and Woolsey-esque comedy relief.)

For an early sound production, *Rio Rita* is technically ambitious and holds up remarkably well, with smooth performances by leads Bebe Daniels and John Boles. Operating on the periphery of the main story, Bert and Bob are seen to great advantage — their effortless rapport makes it seem as though they had been a team much longer than their two-year stage partnership — and it's no surprise that this one film launched their screen careers with a bang. Thanks to Bert's coaching, Dorothy's performance marks a considerable improvement over her debut in *Syncopation*, and their duet "Sweetheart, We Need Each Other" is a show-stopping blend of tender vocalizing and broad physical comedy.

For years, circulating copies of *The Cuckoos* and *Dixiana*, two subsequent Wheeler and Woolsey films, also had missing footage but these titles have since been fully restored. We can only hope a similar fate awaits *Rio Rita*.

Associate film editor Pandro S. Berman would later become a high-profile producer whose credits included *Cockeyed Cavaliers* (1934), *Top Hat* (1935), *Stage Door* (1937), *The Hunchback of Notre Dame* (1939), *Rio Rita* (the 1942 remake), *National Velvet* (1944), *The Picture of Dorian Gray* (1945), *Father of the Bride* (1950), *Blackboard Jungle* (1955) and *Jailhouse Rock* (1957).

## *The Cuckoos* (1930)

*Director:* Paul Sloane. *Producer:* William LeBaron. Based on the musical play *The Ramblers* by Guy Bolton, Bert Kalmar and Harry Ruby. *Adaptation:* Cyrus Wood and (uncredited) Roscoe "Fatty" Arbuckle. *Associate producer:* Louis Sarecky. *Cinematography:* Nick Musuraca. *Musical director:* Victor Baravalle. *Art direction:* Max Rée. *Dance staging:* Pearl Eaton. *Photographic effects:* Lloyd Knechtel. *Sound recording:* John Tribby. *Film editor:* Arthur Roberts. *Color photography:* Technicolor process.

*Songs:* "Down in Mexico," "Oh! How We Love Our Alma Mater," "All Alone Monday," "I Love You So Much," "Wherever You Are," "I'm a Gypsy," "Dancing the Devil Away," "Good-Bye," "California Skies" and "Tomorrow Never Comes" by Bert Kalmar and Harry Ruby.

Two Kalmar and Ruby songs written for the film, "Knock Knees" and "Looking for the Lovelight in Your Eyes," went unused, along with a third song, "If I Were a Traveling Salesman" by Joe Burke and Al Dubin.

*Cast:* Bert Wheeler (Sparrow), Robert Woolsey (Professor Cunningham), Dorothy Lee (Anita), Jobyna Howland (Fannie Furst), Hugh Trevor (Billy Shannon), June Clyde (Ruth Chester), Ivan Lebedeff (Baron de Camp), Marguerita Padula (Gypsy queen), Mitchell Lewis (Julius), Raymond Maurel (Gypsy singer), Lita Chevret (Slot machine señorita), Kalla Pasha (Hot-headed cowboy), Harry Semels, Bob Kortman (Amorous gypsies), Hector V. Sarno (Tamale vendor).

*Working titles: Radio Ramblers* and *Radio Revels. Production dates:* January 27–February 28, 1930. Released May 4, 1930, by RKO Radio Pictures. 97 minutes.

*Synopsis:* At a Mexican resort frequented by American tourists, Fannie Furst is trying to convince her niece Ruth Chester to marry the debonair Baron de Camp, but Ruth only has eyes for aviator Billy Shannon. Phony fortune-teller Professor Cunningham and his assistant Sparrow wander onto the scene; Billy falls in love with Anita, a pretty American girl who has been raised by gypsies, which incurs the wrath of gypsy leader Julius, who wants Anita for himself.

Unbeknownst to everyone at the resort, Baron de Camp is a scoundrel who is in league with Julius. When Ruth refuses to marry the baron, she is kidnapped by Julius and his band of gypsies. Billy, Sparrow and the Professor come to Ruth's rescue and deliver her safely back to Aunt Fannie.

"Utterly mad slapstick done in the traditional manner of musical comedy.... Wheeler and Woolsey are as low a pair of comics as you could wish for. Dorothy Lee adds considerable ginger." — *Hollywood Magazine*

*Comments:* The Cuckoos owes more to the early Marx Brothers movies *The Cocoanuts* (1929) and *Animal Crackers* (1930) than it does to the lavishly produced *Rio Rita*, in that it's more like a photographed stage play than a fully realized motion picture. That, however, is an asset; more than any other film, *The Cuckoos* documents what Wheeler and Woolsey were like on the Broadway stage. Many of their comedy routines and musical numbers unfold as they would have on stage, with a few cinematic flourishes tossed in. The nonsensical plot, the delightful score by Kalmar and Ruby, and the theatrical performances (with all the emphatic posturing and accentuated pauses) complete the illusion of watching a typical Broadway musical-comedy of the era. This may be one of the reasons why Bert Wheeler regarded this as one of the team's best efforts.

The version of *The Cuckoos* syndicated to television in the late 1950s was missing the film's three Technicolor sequences, all musical numbers: Bert and Bob's "Good-Bye," Dorothy's "Dancing the Devil Away" and the finale which reprised "I Love You So Much." This footage has since been restored, and today this entertaining time capsule can be seen in its full glory.

## *Dixiana* (1930)

*Director:* Luther Reed. *Producer:* William LeBaron. *Story and dialogue:* Anne Caldwell. *Adaptation:* Luther Reed. *Cinematography:* J. Roy Hunt. *Musical director:* Victor Baravalle. *Orchestrations:* Max Steiner. *Dance staging:* Pearl Eaton. *Assistant director:* Frederick Fleck. *Photographic effects:* Lloyd Knechtel. *Sound recording:* Hugh McDowell, Jr. *Film editor:* William Hamilton. *Color photography:* Technicolor process.

*Songs:* "Dixiana," "Mr. and Mrs. Sippi," "Here's to the Old Days," "My One Ambition Is You," "A Lady Loved a Soldier," "Guiding Star," "A Tear, a Kiss, a Smile," "I Am Your Baby Now" and "Life Is a Card Game" by Harry Tierney and Anne Caldwell.

*Cast:* Bebe Daniels (Dixiana Caldwell), Bert Wheeler (Pee Wee), Robert Woolsey (Ginger Dandy), Everett Marshall (Carl Van Horn), Dorothy Lee (Nanny), Joseph Cawthorn (Cornelius Van Horn), Jobyna Howland (Birdie Van Horn), Ralf Harolde (Royal Montague), Bill Robinson (Specialty dancer), Edward Chandler (Blondell), George Herman (Contortionist), Raymond Maurel (Cayetano), Bruce Covington (Colonel Porter), Eugene "Pineapple" Jackson (Cupid).

*Production dates:* March 24–April 26, 1930. Released September 4, 1930, by RKO Radio Pictures. 99 minutes.

*Synopsis:* In New Orleans during the 1840s, Hippodrome circus performer Dixiana Caldwell falls in love with plantation heir Carl Van Horn. Carl brings his fiancée, along with her circus cohorts Pee Wee and Ginger Dandy, home to meet his parents. Birdie Van Horn, Carl's mother, finds out about Dixiana's circus background and calls off the engagement.

Dixiana, Pee Wee and Ginger Dandy go to work at a gambling house run by no-account Royal Montague, who has always had designs on Dixiana. Pee Wee and Ginger both become smitten with Nanny, a fickle Southern belle who can't choose between them. To exact revenge on the Van Horns, Dixiana sets up Carl in a crooked card game, in exchange for Montague's promise that she will be named Mardi Gras Queen. But Dixiana, still in love with Carl, double-crosses Montague and saves Carl from a rigged duel. With Montague's treachery revealed, Dixiana and Carl are reunited, while Pee Wee gets Ginger out of the way so he can make time with Nanny.

"This screen operetta [is] a grand spectacle.... [Y]ou will be charmed by this." — *Photoplay*

*Comments: Dixiana* was RKO's woefully misfired attempt to follow up the success of *Rio Rita*. Despite one of Bert and Dorothy's best duets, 'My One Ambition Is You," and a specialty number by the legendary Bill "Bojangles" Robinson, it is strictly for Wheeler and Woolsey completists, and even they will find it a chore to sit through. Where *Rio Rita* was an entertaining blend of music and comedy, *Dixiana* is weighed down with the sort of lugubrious plotline common in several film musicals of the period (*Say It with Songs, Puttin' on the Ritz, Glorifying the American Girl, Melody Lane*).

In January 1930, RKO took out trade advertisements to announce that *Dixiana* would be shot in the new 63.5mm "Natural Vision" widescreen process, to back up the studio's claim that it would be "built to top *Rio Rita*." However, those grandiose plans were abandoned and *Dixiana* was shot and released in the standard 35mm gauge.

When *Dixiana* was syndicated to television in the late 1950s, the print ran only 78 minutes and was missing the entire Technicolor finale, which left the plot unresolved. The film was eventually restored to its full glory. It is amazing that so much effort was expended on such a creaky museum piece.

*Dixiana* is one of three Wheeler and Woolsey films that has fallen into public domain (*Half Shot at Sunrise* and *Hook Line and Sinker* are the other two), meaning the copyrights have lapsed so it can be marketed by any distributor that wishes to do so. Because of this, *Dixiana*, one of the weakest (and, for the longest time, one of the rarest) Wheeler and Woolsey efforts, is now one of their most accessible titles. Like *The Gorilla* (1939) with the Ritz Brothers, *At War with the Army* (1950) with Martin and Lewis, and *Utopia* (a.k.a. *Atoll K*, 1951) with Laurel and Hardy — three other comedies that have lapsed into public domain — *Dixiana* is hardy representative of the comedy team at their finest.

In the mid–1980s, Dorothy declined the opportunity to sit through *Dixiana* (the truncated version) but she did insist on watching the "My One Ambition Is You" number, which she always singled out as her favorite duet with Bert Wheeler.

## *Half Shot at Sunrise* (1930)

*Director:* Paul Sloane. *Producer:* William LeBaron. *Story:* James Ashmore Creelman. *Dialogue:* Anne Caldwell, Ralph Spence. *Additional material:* Roscoe "Fatty" Arbuckle (uncredited). *Cinematography:* Nick Musuraca. *Musical director:* Max Steiner. *Scenery and costumes:* Max Rée. *Dance staging:* Mary Read. *Sound recording:* Hugh McDowell, Jr. *Film editor:* Arthur Roberts.

*Songs:* "Whistling the Blues Away" and "Nothing But Love" by Harry Tierney and Anne Caldwell. Cut from final release version: "Kiss Me, Cherie," "Riviera Moon" and "On Parade."

*Cast:* Bert Wheeler (Tommy Turner), Robert Woolsey (Gilbert Simpkins), Dorothy Lee (Annette Marshall), George MacFarlane (Colonel Marshall), Edna May Oliver (Mrs. Marshall), Leni Stengel (Olga), Hugh Trevor (Lt. James Reed), Roberta Robinson (Eileen Marshall), John Rutherford (MP sergeant), Eddie de Lange, Charles Sullivan (Military policemen), Elisha H. Calvert (General Hale), Alan Roscoe (Captain Jones), The Tiller Sunshine Girls (Specialty dancers), Rolfe Sedan, André Cheron (Waiters), William Bechtel (Restaurant patron).

*Production dates:* June 30–August 8, 1930. Released October 4, 1930, by RKO Radio Pictures. 78 minutes.

*Synopsis:* In 1918, AWOL American soldiers Tommy Turner and Gilbert Simpkins mischievously cavort all over Paris, to the frustration of their commanding officer, Colonel Marshall, and the pair of dogged MPs on their trail. The colonel has additional headaches: His nagging wife is suspicious about his association with a sultry siren named Olga (Leni Stengel), and his two daughters, Annette and Eileen, can't hide their attraction to the opposite sex. Annette in particular is boy crazy and she becomes enamored with Tommy, while Gilbert makes time with Olga.

Annette steals secret orders from Lt. Reed, Eileen's boyfriend, and gives them to Tommy and Gilbert, so they can deliver it to General Hale at the front lines and become heroes in the process. At the battlefront, Gilbert volunteers Tommy for a deadly assignment, then looks on in horror when Tommy is caught in an explosion. Gilbert rushes to save Tommy and discovers he's okay after all — as is the MP sergeant who's been chasing them all over Paris!

Armistice is declared and the colonel is prepared to have Tommy and Gilbert face a firing squad, until the boys inform the colonel that what they thought were secret orders was actually a love letter from Olga. With Tommy and Gilbert holding the upper hand, the colonel reluctantly lets them off the hook.

"A high grade laugh program.... The cross fire and talk carry laughs throughout. This is pie for Wheeler and Woolsey, right in their comedy alley, with the situations the same.... Dorothy Lee is quite lively, playing as usual opposite Wheeler."—*Variety*

*Comments:* One of the best of the early Wheeler and Woolsey films, *Half Shot at Sunrise* captures Bert, Bob and Dorothy at their high-intensity peak. While they would go on to make more polished movies, the trio was rarely as uninhibited as they are here. After this, Dorothy's character would be toned down considerably, as she became less of a frisky flapper and more of a sedate ingénue. In *Half Shot at Sunrise*, she's allowed to be just as funny as the boys and she takes full advantage of it by delivering a playfully energetic performance.

Due to its public-domain status, *Half Shot at Sunrise* became the most widely distributed Wheeler and Woolsey title on the DVD market and even turned up in collections of serious World War I–themed movies.

In later years, Dorothy enjoyed watching *Half Shot at Sunrise* more than most other Wheeler and Woolsey pictures because her character reminded her of the flapper roles she played on stage, prior to her movie career.

## *Hook Line and Sinker* (1930)

*Director:* Edward Cline. *Producer:* William LeBaron. *Associate producer:* Myles Connolly. *Screenplay and dialogue:* Tim Whelan, Ralph Spence. *Story:* Tim Whelan and uncredited James Ashmore Creelman and Wallace Smith. *Assistant director:* Fred Fleck. *Cinematography:* Nick Musuraca. *Musical director:* Max Steiner. *Scenery and costumes:* Max Rée. *Sound recording:* Hugh McDowell, Jr. *Film editor:* Archie F. Marshek.

*Cast:* Bert Wheeler (Wilbur Boswell), Robert Woolsey (J. Addington Ganzy), Dorothy Lee (Mary Marsh), Ralf Harolde (John Blackwell, a.k.a. Buffalo Blackie), Jobyna Howland (Rebecca Marsh), Natalie Moorhead (Duchess Bessie Von Essie), Hugh Herbert (House detective), George F. Marion Sr. (Bellboy), Stanley Fields (Max McKay), William Davidson (Duke of Winchester, a.k.a. Frank Dukette), Larry McGrath (Izzy), Ben Hendricks, Jr. (Spudoni), G. Pat Collins (Motorcycle cop), Robert MacKenzie (Detective who apprehends the Duchess), Ethan Laidlaw (Blackwell henchman), Frank Mills (Blackwell henchman), Lynton Brent (Dukette henchman), Florence Wix (Hotel party guest).

*Production dates:* October 1–November 4, 1930. Released December 26, 1930, by RKO Radio Pictures. 75 minutes.

*Synopsis:* Wilbur Boswell and J. Addington Ganzy, a pair of glib insurance salesmen, meet Mary Marsh, who is on the run from her mother's constant pressuring to wed crooked attorney John Blackwell. Mary's uncle has left her the rundown Hotel Ritz De La Riviera and the boys (Wilbur in particular) decide to help her renovate the establishment. Touting the place as a resort playground for the wealthy and entitled, they attract a gullible high-society crowd — along with assorted gangsters who plot to get their hands on the guests' jewelry, stored in the hotel safe.

Mary's mother Rebecca brings Blackwell to the hotel, hoping to change her daughter's mind. Blackwell realizes he's out of the picture entirely when Mary falls for Wilbur and Rebecca becomes smitten with J. Addington, so he calls in his henchmen to bump off the unsuspecting duo. During a nocturnal shootout, the rival thugs only manage to eliminate each other. Wilbur and J. Addington emerge victorious, through no effort of their own.

"[The film] drew loud and fairly continuous laughter.... The comedians deliver their pleasantries with rapid-fire precision, sometimes with unwarranted enthusiasm."—*Variety*

*Comments: Hook Line and Sinker* is better suited for those who have already acquired a taste for Wheeler and Woolsey movies rather than as an introduction for the uninitiated. Bert and Bob (and Dorothy) have still not completed their transition from stage performers to film actors, but their established rapport makes some of the weak material seem funnier than it actually is. A good supporting cast — including Jobyna Howland (as Mary's mother), Hugh Herbert (an ineffectual house detective), George F. Marion (a decrepit bellboy) and Stanley Fields (a bombastic gangster) — helps considerably.

*Hook Line and Sinker* is a public-domain title that has been marketed by various DVD distributors. Unfortunately, some of these editions have been taken from an inferior-quality dupe of an edited TV print, obliterating whatever virtues this modest little film has.

## *Screen Snapshots* (1931)

*Director:* Ralph Staub. *Producer:* Harry Cohn.

*Cast:* Bert Wheeler, Robert Woolsey, Dorothy Lee, Sue Carol, Jack Mulhall, Harry Tierney (Themselves).

Released 1931 by Columbia Pictures. 9 minutes.

*Synopsis:* Composer Harry Tierney plays "Let's Pretend We're Sweethearts," his new composition (co-written with Benee Russell) for an assembled group of stars.

*Comments: Screen Snapshots* was a long-running (1924 to 1958) series of one-reel shorts that offered informal glimpses of Tinseltown stars at work and at play. While Bert and Bob made various appearances (together and separately) in these type of behind-the-scenes films — such as Tiffany Pictures' *The Voice of Hollywood* and Paramount's *Hollywood on Parade* series — this is Dorothy's only known appearance in one of them.

Songwriter Harry Tierney co-wrote the scores for the Wheeler and Woolsey pictures *Rio Rita, Dixiana* and *Half Shot at Sunrise.*

## *The Stolen Jools* (1931)

*Director:* William McGann. *Producer:* Pat Casey. *Production supervisor:* E.K. Nadel. *Story and screenplay:* Al Boasberg, Edwin J. Burke, Arthur Caesar, Howard Green, Percy Heath, Henry Myers, Edgar Allan Woolf.

*Cast (as themselves, unless noted):* Eddie Kane (Inspector Kane), Stan Laurel, Oliver Hardy (Assistant detectives), Norma Shearer, Maurice Chevalier, Joe E. Brown, Joan Crawford, Wallace Beery (Police sergeant), Buster Keaton (Policeman), Edward G. Robinson, Irene Dunne, Bert Wheeler, Robert Woolsey, Our Gang [Matthew "Stymie" Beard, Mary Ann Jackson, Bobby "Wheezer" Hutchins, Norman "Chubby" Chaney, Allen "Farina" Hoskins, Dorothy "Echo" DeBorba, Shirley Jean Rickert, Pete the dog], Loretta Young, Douglas Fairbanks, Jr., William Haines, Gary Cooper (Newspaper editor), Warner Baxter (The Cisco Kid), Dorothy Lee, Richard Dix, Jack Oakie, Fay Wray, Bebe Daniels, Ben Lyon, Winnie Lightner, Barbara Stanwyck, Frank Fay, Edmund Lowe, Victor McLaglen, El Brendel (Swedish waiter), Mitzi Green, George E. Stone, George Sidney, Charlie Murray (Hotel clerks), Fifi D'Orsay, Polly Moran (Norma Shearer's housekeeper), Charles "Buddy" Rogers, Stuart Erwin, Eugene Pallette, Richard "Skeets" Gallagher, Wynne Gibson (Reporters), Charles Butterworth ("Louise Fazenda"), Lowell Sherman, Hedda Hopper (Norma Shearer's friend), Claudia Dell (Actress), George "Gabby" Hayes (Hank the projectionist), Little Billy Rhodes (Billy the delivery boy), Jack Hill, J. Farrell MacDonald (Policemen), Robert Ames, Bert Lytell.

*British title: The Slippery Pearls. Production date:* Late February–March 7, 1931. Released April 4, 1931, by Paramount Pictures and National Screen Service. 18 minutes.

*Synopsis:* After a wild celebration at the Screen Actors Annual Ball, Norma Shearer discovers that her jewels have been stolen and hires Inspector Kane to solve the crime. Kane doggedly tracks down every possible suspect, encountering "more prominent stars than have ever before appeared in any one feature," to use the film's own introduction.

"An amusing piece of work.... Collections for the N.V.A. charity were made in all the theatres where this picture was on view. At the Capitol [Theatre] the baskets of bills and coins were brought to the stage by dancing girls and emptied into a large receptacle." —*New York Times*

*Comments: The Stolen Jools* was presented by National Variety Artists and distributed free to theaters by Paramount Pictures and National Screen Service, to help raise funds for the N.V.A.'s tuberculosis sanitarium in Saranac Lake, New York. No one at the time could appreciate the irony that a fund-raising short for respiratory diseases was produced in cooperation with a tobacco company, Chesterfield cigarettes. ("This is Chesterfield's contribution to the fine relief work of the N.V.A.")

Some of Hollywood's biggest stars donated their time to appear in this film, and it's a testament to Dorothy's popularity that she was included alongside such luminaries as Shearer, Maurice Chevalier, and Joan Crawford. But with so many people to accommodate within a two-reel running time, most of the cameos come and go in the blink of an eye. Dorothy's scene is one of the briefest star turns, lasting less than ten seconds: As she's sitting on a porch swing with an unidentified young man, Dorothy sings a couple lines of "I Love You So Much" from *The Cuckoos*. Inspector Kane pops in and says, "Oh, Miss Lee, I'd like to ask you...." "I know," Dorothy interjects, "you want my autograph," as she grabs his notepad. Fade out.

With such an overflowing celebrity cast, it isn't surprising that *The Stolen Jools* doesn't offer much beyond its novelty factor. However, it is surprising to learn that *seven* uncredited writers contributed to the flimsy screenplay. The material throughout has an off-the-cuff, ad-lib quality, and it's doubtful there were many — if any — retakes. Despite this, there are amusing contributions by Laurel and Hardy (in a memorable bit involving a collapsing automobile) and Wheeler and Woolsey (who enthusiastically reprise their slapping routine from *Rio Rita*).

In England, *The Stolen Jools* was released by RKO in 1932 under the title *The Slippery Pearls*, as part of the studio's Masquers Club comedy series. After its initial release, *The Stolen Jools* remained unseen for years until 1976 when Blackhawk Films, an Iowa-based distributor, offered 16mm prints for sale to the home-movie market. To avoid problems concerning music-rights issues, Blackhawk excised footage involving songs, even though no complete song numbers were performed in the film. As a result, Dorothy's already-limited footage was further truncated, along with other musical footage featuring Maurice Chevalier and Warner Baxter. Since then, the musical footage has been restored, although the Blackhawk version is the one that seems to turn up more frequently. All available editions are missing the final scene, with Bert Lytell making a plea to the audience for donations.

Like many long-unseen movies that have fallen into the public domain, *The Stolen Jools* is a staple of DVD collections built around p.d. titles.

## *Cracked Nuts* (1931)

*Director:* Edward F. Cline. *Producer:* William LeBaron. *Associate producer:* Douglas MacLean. *Screenplay:* Al Boasberg, and uncredited Douglas MacLean. *Dialogue:* Ralph Spence, Al Boasberg. Based on the short story "A Growing Concern" by Welford Beaton. *Cinematography:* Nicholas Musuraca. *Original music:* Max Steiner. *Music orchestrator:* Paul Marquardt. *Scenery and costumes:* Max Rée. *Sound recording:* Hugh McDowell, Jr. *Film editor:* Arthur Roberts.

*Song:* "Dance and Let the World Dance with You" by Harry Tierney and Ray Egan.

*Cast:* Bert Wheeler (Wendell Graham), Robert Woolsey (Zander Ulysses Parkhurst, a.k.a. Zup), Dorothy Lee (Betty Harrington), Edna May Oliver (Aunt Minnie Van Varden), Leni Stengel (Queen Carlotta), Stanley Fields (General Bogardus), Boris Karloff (Boris), Frank Thornton (Revolutionist), Ben Turpin (Cross-eyed Ben), Harvey Clark (King Oscar), Frank Lackteen (Assassin), Bud Geary (Footman), Edward Peil, Sr. (King's officer), Wilfred Lucas (Minister),

George Periolat (Royal advisor), Buster Brodie (Royal humidor), Robert Thurston (Royal lighter), Eric Mack (Royal ashtray), Eugene Burr (Royal toothpick), Mike Lally (Member of royal guard), Nick Bolin (Orchestra leader).

*Working title:* Assorted Nuts. *Production dates:* November 24–December 23, 1930. Released April 18, 1931, by RKO Radio Pictures. (New York opening: April 5, 1931.) 64 minutes.

*Synopsis:* Wendell Graham and Betty Harrington are hopelessly in love, but Betty's imperious Aunt Minnie looks upon Wendell as a lazy idiot and forbids her niece to have anything to do with him. To prove his worth, Wendell finances a revolution in the kingdom of El Dorania, planning to become the king after the current ruler is overthrown. Unbeknownst to Wendell, his old buddy Zander Ulysses Parkhurst ("Zup" for short) has won the El Doranian crown in a crap game.

When Wendell, Betty, and Aunt Minnie arrive in El Dorania, Wendell and the newly crowned King Zup argue over who the rightful ruler is, unaware that General Bogardus and his revolutionaries are plotting to assassinate whoever assumes the throne. To appease Bogardus and his crew, Wendell okays Zup's assassination — he will be killed by a bomb dropped from a plane — but takes measures to remove the explosive devices so his pal will emerge unharmed. However, the pilot repairs the bombs, so Zup is still in peril. A bomb misses Zup and the resulting explosion unleashes an oil gusher that brings financial solvency to El Dorania.

"A clever farce that deserves a better title.... Mr. Woolsey is excellent and Mr. Wheeler does splendidly as Graham. He also dances and sings with the comely Dorothy Lee.... Miss Oliver, as usual, makes the most of her role." — *New York Times*

*Comments: Cracked Nuts* is amusing enough but the sluggish pace and some dry stretches prevent it from becoming the wacky political farce it aspires to be. (It pales in comparison to *Diplomaniacs* [1933], one of the Wheeler and Woolsey films Dorothy did not appear in.) Bert and Bob are featured in separate subplots for the first half of the picture, before meeting face to face in El Dorania. These solo scenes may have paved the way, consciously or not, for their solo efforts: Bert's *Too Many Cooks* and Bob's *Everything's Rosie*, which were also released in 1931.

Dorothy's participation is limited to playing a standard-issue supporting ingénue role (Edna May Oliver gets whatever good lines weren't handed to Bert and Bob), though she and Bert perform a memorable song-and-dance number, "Dance and Let the World Dance with You." After that, Dorothy fades into the background until her fleeting reappearance at the conclusion. (The finale was revised and reshot, which accounts for her disappearance.)

In later years, Dorothy had zero interest in viewing *Cracked Nuts* in its entirety, but she adored her duet with Bert and had a video copy of the sequence (compiled with other Wheeler and Woolsey musical numbers) that she watched often.

## *Laugh and Get Rich* (1931)

*Screenplay and Director:* Gregory La Cava. *Producer:* William LeBaron. *Story:* Douglas MacLean. *Additional dialogue:* Ralph Spence. *Cinematography:* Jack MacKenzie. *Scenery and costumes:* Max Rée. *Sound recording:* John E. Tribby. *Film editor:* Jack Kitchin.

*Cast:* Edna May Oliver (Sarah Cranston Austin), Hugh Herbert (Joseph Austin), Dorothy Lee (Alice Austin), Russell Gleason (Larry Owens), John Harron (Bill Hepburn), Charles Sellon (Biddle), George Davis (Mr. Vincentini), Robert Emmett Keane (Mr. Phelps), Maude Fealy (Miss Teasdale), Louise Mackintosh (Cassandra "Cassie" Palfrey), Lita Chevret (Party guest), Wade Boteler (Detective Flannery), Herbert Prior (J.C. Pennypacker), Ivan Lebedeff (Count Dimitriff), Alan Roscoe (Mr. Fetherstone), Edmund Mortimer (Mr. Bellweather), Broderick O'Farrell (Art dealer), Rochelle Hudson (Miss Jones), John Elliott, Phillips Smalley (Dinner guests), Arline Judge (Alice's sympathetic friend), Joyce Davis.

*Working title:* Room and Board. Released April 20, 1931, by RKO Radio Pictures. (New York opening: March 27, 1931.) 72 minutes.

*Synopsis:* Sarah Cranston Austin does the best she can to cope with her husband Joseph and their daughter Alice. Joe, a "chronic loafer," is content to sit back and spin tall tales while his wife works hard running their small-town boarding house. Sarah would prefer that Alice go out with a nice young man like Bill Hepburn, instead of the seemingly directionless Larry Owens, an inventor whose latest creation, the Whistling Valve, allows motorists to "hear" when air is leaking from tires. Joe thinks Larry is really onto something, and they become business partners. Joe is also supportive of one of their boarders, Mr. Vincentini, a struggling artist obsessed with painting pictures of cows.

When another boarder, Mr. Phelps, offers Joe a chance to buy shares in oil stock, Joe secretly grabs Sarah's hard-earned savings and makes an investment. Sarah discovers the cash missing, and when she accuses Mr. Vincentini of theft, Joe confesses. Then Bill, whom Alice has been dating to make Larry jealous, is exposed as a petty crook.

Just as the entire Austin family seems to have hit rock bottom, the oil stocks pay off big time and the Austins are wealthy. Yet they learn material gain is no guarantee for personal happiness, and their foray into high society runs dry when the oil well does, leaving them flat broke once again. Their fortunes take another upswing when a rubber company purchases the exclusive rights to the Owens-Austin Whistling Valve, and Mr. Vincentini, their last remaining boarder, lands a job with a dairy company, painting cows on advertising signs.

"A pleasant little comedy, distinguished by the performance of Edna May Oliver. Dorothy Lee figures in a youthful romance, which is only one of more sub-plots than is profitable to recall."—*New York Times*

*Comments:* Although *Laugh and Get Rich* was promoted as Dorothy Lee's first starring film (she was given top billing on the promotional materials), she receives third billing in the film's credits, after the two real lead performers Edna May Oliver and Hugh Herbert. Conceptually, Herbert's idle-dreamer character is not unlike the ones W.C. Fields played in *So's Your Old Man* (1926) and *Running Wild* (1927), which were also directed by Gregory La Cava. But *Laugh and Get Rich* is too somber for its own good, and even moments that are intended to be uplifting are oddly joyless. Herbert's peccadilloes are treated a little too realistically to be humorous; when he invests his wife's money without telling her, his well-intentioned actions come off as irresponsible and foolhardy.

Considering that *Laugh and Get Rich* was intended as a breakthrough showcase for Dorothy, it's unfortunate that she gives such a wooden performance here, indicating she received little coaching or guidance from La Cava, whose handling of actors was usually adept—as it was in two of his finest films, *My Man Godfrey* (1936) and *Stage Door* (1937).

## *Too Many Cooks* (1931)

*Director:* William A. Seiter. *Producer:* William LeBaron. *Associate producer:* Douglas Mac-Lean. Based on the play *Too Many Cooks* by Frank Craven. *Screenplay:* Jane Murfin. *Cinematography:* Nick Musuraca. *Scenery and costumes:* Max Rée. *Sound recording:* P.J. Faulkner, Jr. *Film editor:* Arthur Roberts.

*Cast:* Bert Wheeler (Albert Bennett), Dorothy Lee (Alice Cook), Rosco [Roscoe] Ates (Mr. Wilson), Robert McWade (Uncle George Bennett), Sharon Lynn (Ella Mayer), Hallam Cooley (Frank Andrews), Florence Roberts (Mrs. Cook), Clifford Dempsey (Michael J. Cook), Ruth Weston (Minnie Spring), George Chandler (Cousin Ned), Kathrin Clare Ward (Aunt Louise), Dorothea Wolbert (Aunt Emma), Bill Scott (Louis), Erville Alderson (Max Simpson), Alfred P. James (Uncle Walter), Lewis Sargent (Joe), Harry Watson (Jimmy), Billy Watson (Jimmy's brother).

*Production dates:* February 28–March 22, 1931. Released July 18, 1931, by RKO Radio Pictures. 77 minutes.

*Synopsis:* Albert Bennett's careful plans to build a dream home for himself and his fiancée

Alice Cook are undermined by Alice's pesky relatives. As the bickering escalates, the lovebirds separate but Albert completes the construction anyway, then puts the house up for sale. The couple eventually reconciles, as Albert's Uncle George buys the home and gives it to them for a wedding present.

"[An] amusing, innocuous little picture for the masses when the masses aren't too particular.... Nothing excepting the acting mainly by Wheeler and Miss Lee rises above the humdrum."—*Variety*

*Comments:* Having Bert and Dorothy play realistic characters for a change was an intriguing idea that might have succeeded had they not been saddled with a dreary property like *Too Many Cooks*. Considering neither one had any enthusiasm for the project (they both thought it was terrible), Bert and Dorothy give earnest performances but it's all for naught. The main problem is that the setbacks heaped upon Bert's character provoke irritation rather than amusement, and it isn't long before the viewer becomes just as exasperated as he does. Moviegoers expecting lighter fare from this pair must have been severely disappointed by the drab mood of the picture, which is unredeemed by the inevitable happy ending.

## *Caught Plastered* (1931)

*Director:* William A. Seiter. *Producer:* William LeBaron. *Associate producer and Story:* Douglas MacLean. *Adaptation and dialogue:* Ralph Spence, and (uncredited) Jane Murfin. *Additional dialogue:* Eddie Welch. *Cinematography:* Jack MacKenzie. *Scenery and costumes:* Max Rée. *Sound recording:* P.J. Faulkner, Jr. *Film editor:* Jack Kitchin.

*Song:* "I'm That Way About You, After All" by Victor Schertzinger.

*Cast:* Bert Wheeler (Tommy Tanner), Robert Woolsey (Egbert G. Higginbotham), Dorothy Lee (Peggy Morton), Lucy Beaumont (Mother Talley), Jason Robards (Harry Waters), Charles B. Middleton (Flint), DeWitt Jennings (Chief H.A. Morton), Josephine Whittell (Miss Newton), James Farley (Trolley conductor), Bill Scott (Clarke), Grace Hayle (Overweight customer), Arthur Housman (Drunk counter patron), Nora Cecil (Miss Loring), Lee Moran (Drunk).

*Working title: Full of Notions. Production dates:* May 18–June 9, 1931. Released August 9, 1931, by RKO Radio Pictures. 68 minutes.

*Synopsis:* Tommy Tanner and Egbert G. Higginbotham, unemployed vaudevillians, meet Mother Talley, a sweet old lady whose dilapidated drug store is about to be seized for debts by crooked businessman Harry Waters. The boys take over the store and turn it into a booming success, which infuriates Waters, who intended to use the place for his covert bootlegging operation. Waters is also sore that Peggy Morton, daughter of the local police chief, has fallen for Tommy.

Waters plots with a bootlegger named Clarke to sell the store a special brand of lemon syrup which, unbeknownst to Tommy and Egbert, is spiked with alcohol. When the drug-store customers get roaring drunk, Waters notifies the police chief, who raids the establishment. But Peggy coaxes her father to search Clarke's residence, where they find Clarke in the cellar with his bootleg goods. In the meantime, Waters convinces Mother Talley that she is ruined and buys the drug store for a song. Elated, Waters goes to see Clarke. When Tommy, Egbert, Peggy and the police chief overhear Waters boasting to Clarke of his crime, the crooks are apprehended, the sale of the store is cancelled, and the boys pick up where they left off.

"No romance and possessing slight action. Most chatter of a wisecracking nature, some of it new and much of it old. Only the Wheeler-Woolsey experience in handling gags saves the film from utter mediocrity. Miss Lee cannot handle dramatics with her voice against her before she starts."—*Variety*

*Comments:* Slight but entertaining, *Caught Plastered* has enough funny set pieces to (almost) disguise the fact that this is essentially a two-reel comedy short padded out to feature length. Bert and Bob are particularly effective in a scene where they try to cheer up Mother Talley by performing an impromptu vaudeville routine, complete with wheezy jokes ("What's the difference between a Scotsman and a cocoanut?" "You can get a drink out of a cocoanut") and a soft-shoe dance.

By now, Bert, Bob and Dorothy were functioning like a well-oiled machine and their genial camaraderie goes a long way to compensate for the thinness of the material.

## *Local Boy Makes Good* (1931)

*Director:* Mervyn LeRoy. Suggested by the play *The Poor Nut* by J.C. and Elliott Nugent. *Adaptation:* Robert Lord, Raymond Griffith, Ray Enright. *Cinematography:* Sol Polito. *Second cameramen:* Thomas Brannigan, Mike Joyce. *Assistant cameramen:* Robert Mitchell, Thomas Riddell. *Vitaphone Orchestra conductor:* David Mendoza. *Original music:* David Mendoza. *Orchestrations:* Oscar Potoker. *Art direction:* Jack Okey. *Film editor:* Jack Killifer. *Gowns:* Earl Luick. *Sound:* Charles David Forrest.

*Cast:* Joe E. Brown (John Augustus Miller), Dorothy Lee (Julia Winters), Ruth Hall (Marjorie Blake), Edward Woods (Spike Hoyt), Edward J. Nugent (Wally Pierce), Wade Boteler (Doc), John Harrington (Coach Jackson), William Burress (Colonel Small), Maude Eburne (Maid), Lee Phelps (Assistant coach), Curtis Benton (Announcer at track meet), Edward Hearn (Relay caller), Allan Lane (Runner with bad knee).

Released October 27, 1931, by Warner Brothers–First National Pictures. 67 minutes.

*Synopsis:* John Augustus Miller, a meek botany student who works at the Ohio University book store, spends his time writing secret love letters to psychology student and beauty contest winner Julia Winters. John doesn't have the nerve to mail any of his correspondence, but when one letter is accidentally dispatched, an excited Julia shows up only to discover that he is not the collegiate track star he claimed to be. But John's inferiority complex intrigues Julia and she goads him when he does get the opportunity to participate in a relay race.

Julia's interest in John doesn't sit well with Spike Hoyt, her jealous boyfriend, and Marjorie Blake, a book store clerk who loves John for what he is, not what he's pretending to be. When John falters during the important track meet, Julia turns her back on him, while Marjorie offers him support — and a shot of rubbing alcohol. John's victory makes him realize that Marjorie, not Julia, is the girl meant for him.

"It has laughs if no punch.... Dorothy Lee and Ruth Hall are the femme interest and turn in moderate performances. However, it's all Brown and the farce has a fair share of speed." —*Variety*

*Comments:* This indifferent Joe E. Brown vehicle offered Dorothy a change-of-pace role, as a self-centered beauty who is not quite the dream girl Brown imagined her to be. It's an interesting departure for her and she clearly relishes the opportunity to play something other than a standard-issue ingénue. Yet it's not enough to offset the elements that don't work. Too much time is spent trying to build Brown's nebbishy character into a sympathetic figure; in the process he's rendered ineffectual rather than appealing, so it becomes difficult for the viewer to root for him.

## *Peach-O-Reno* (1932)

*Director:* William A. Seiter. *Producer:* William LeBaron. *Supervisor:* John E. Burch. *Original story:* Tim Whelan and (uncredited) Louis A. Sarecky and Bert Wheeler. *Adaptation and dialogue:* Ralph Spence, Tim Whelan, Eddie Welch. *Cinematography:* Jack MacKenzie. *Musical director:* Max Steiner. *Scenery and costumes:* Max Rée. *Sound:* George D. Ellis. *Film editor:* Jack Kitchin. *Camera operators:* William H. Clothier, Eddie Pyle.

*Song:* "Niagara Falls to Reno" by Richard Whiting, Grant Clarke and Harry Akst.

*Cast:* Bert Wheeler (Wattles), Robert Woolsey (Julius Swift), Dorothy Lee (Prudence Bruno), Zelma O'Neal (Pansy Bruno), Joseph Cawthorn (Joe Bruno), Cora Witherspoon (Aggie

Bruno), Sam Hardy (Judge Jackson), Mitchell Harris (Ace Crosby), Arthur Hoyt (Wattles and Swift's secretary), Josephine Whittell (Mrs. Doubleday-Doubleday, a.k.a. The Vamp), Monty Collins (Courtroom snack vendor) Eddie Kane (Courtroom radio announcer), Harry Holman (Counselor Jackson #2), Frank Darien (Counselor Jackson #3), Olaf Hytten (Croupier), Gordon [Bill] Elliott (Juror). Deleted from final release print: Lita Chevret.

*Working titles:* Six Weeks in Reno; Renovated in Reno; and Wedding Rings of Reno.

*Production dates:* September 28–October 14, 1931. Released January 1, 1932, by RKO Radio Pictures. (New York opening: December 23, 1931.) 63 minutes.

*Synopsis:* As Joe and Aggie Bruno celebrate their silver anniversary, a harmless remark by Joe snowballs into a full-blown row. Seeking a divorce, the couple heads to Reno, Nevada, where Wattles and Swift reign supreme as the town's leading divorce lawyers. Swift takes Aggie's case and Wattles takes Joe's, just as the Brunos' daughters Prudence and Pansy show up to try to stop the divorce proceedings. Ace Crosby, an ornery thug and gambler, arrives with one goal in mind: to kill Wattles for handing his (Crosby's) wife's divorce.

At the stroke of 6 P.M., with the flip of a switch, the Wattles and Swift law firm is transformed into the Wattles and Swift casino. Desks and book cases are converted into gambling tables and bars, male staffers are now waiters and croupiers, and page girls become chorus girls and hostesses. Wattles disguises himself as the "Widow Hanover," Joe Bruno's co-respondent; the masquerade also allows Wattles to hide in plain sight from vengeful Ace Crosby.

After Aggie switches her allegiance to a rival law firm, the divorce trial is set in motion. The courtroom takes on a boxing-arena atmosphere, complete with a cheering crowd and a bombastic radio announcer. Wattles and Swift play mercilessly upon the sympathies of the judge, jury and spectators, and all are in tears by the time the duo is through with their melodramatics (Wattles plays "Hearts and Flowers" on a violin while Swift addresses the jurors). Joe and Aggie reconcile, and Wattles and Swift marry Prudence and Pansy.

"Bert Wheeler and Robert Woolsey furnish a good deal of rowdy fun. There are some painful puns and a few good lines in this effusion.... Let it be known that silly as are some of the episodes, old as are many of the jokes, [*Peach-O-Reno*] served its purpose by promoting heaps of merriment among an audience yesterday afternoon."—*New York Times*

*Comments:* One of the best Wheeler and Woolsey vehicles, *Peach-O-Reno* was the funniest, most assured comedy the team made up to that point. Far more character- and plot-driven than their previous starring vehicles, it blends visual and verbal humor expertly, mixing wisecracks and double entendres with zany sight gags.

With the focus on Bert, Bob, and a host of supporting players, Dorothy has little to do. Her main contribution is her delightful duet with Bert, "Niagara Falls to Reno." Otherwise, she's relegated to the sidelines in this one, despite her third-billed position.

## *Girl Crazy* (1932)

*Director:* William A. Seiter. *Director of retakes:* Norman Taurog (uncredited). *Executive producer:* David O. Selznick. *Producer:* William LeBaron. From the musical comedy *Girl Crazy* by John McGowan and Guy Bolton. *Adaptation:* Herman J. Mankiewicz. *Screenplay:* Tim Whelan. *Dialogue:* Eddie Welch, Walter de Leon. *Musical director:* Max Steiner. *Additional new music:* George Gershwin and (uncredited) Max Steiner. *Cinematography:* J. Roy Hunt. *Assistant cameramen:* Willard Barth, Charles Burke, George E. Diskant, Harold E. Wellman. *Camera operators:* Russell Metty, Eddie Pyle, Edward Henderson, Harry J. Wild. *Scenery and costumes:* Max Rée. *Sound:* Hugh McDowell, Jr. *Film editor:* Arthur Roberts. *Choreography ("I Got Rhythm" number):* Busby Berkeley (uncredited).

*Songs:* "Bidin' My Time," "I Got Rhythm," "But Not for Me" and "You've Got What Gets Me" by George and Ira Gershwin. ("Embraceable You," also written by the Gershwins, was filmed but deleted from the final cut.)

*Cast:* Bert Wheeler (Jimmy Deegan, "The Taxi Driver"), Mitzi Green (Tessie Deegan, "His Sister"), Robert Woolsey (Slick Foster, "The Gambler"), Kitty Kelly (Kate Foster, "His Wife"), Eddie Quillan (Danny Churchill, "The Hero"), Arline Judge (Molly Gray, "The Heroine"), Dorothy Lee (Patsy, "The Gal of the Golden West"), Brooks Benedict (George Mason, "The New York Villain"), Stanley Fields (Lank Sanders, "The Arizona Heavy"), Lita Chevret (Mary), Crispin Martin [Chris-Pin Martin] (Pete), Nat Pendleton (Motorcycle cop), Monty Collins (Custerville bartender), Alfred Cooke (San Luz bartender), Josefina Ramos, Esther Garcia (San Luz señoritas), High Eagle (Eagle Rock), Dick Curtis (Cowboy giving directions), Frank Ellis, Ethan Laidlaw, Jim Mason, Artie Ortega, Bob Reeves (Custerville cowboys), Max Steiner and the RKO orchestra ("The Orchestra" in the opening credits). Contrary to some accounts, Lon Chaney, Jr., does not appear in the final release version.

*Production dates:* December 15, 1931–January 12, 1932. Retakes: Mid-February–February 28, 1932. Released March 27, 1932, by RKO Radio Pictures. (New York premiere: March 24, 1932.) 74 minutes.

*Synopsis:* Manhattan playboy Danny Churchill is sent by his father to the rural western town of Custerville, Arizona, where it is hoped that Danny will curb his skirt-chasing ways. Instead, Danny opens a dude-ranch casino and fills it with showgirls to attract clientele. When Danny hires Slick Foster and his wife Kate to help operate the casino, Slick cons taxi driver Jimmy Deegan into taking them from Chicago to Arizona. Jimmy's little sister Tessie tags along.

Danny falls for Custerville postmaster Molly Gray, while Jimmy becomes smitten with Patsy, a cowgirl. Lank Sanders, an outlaw who runs a rival gambling joint, decides to run for sheriff so he can close down Danny's casino. But Jimmy runs against Lank and winds up winning the election — and incurring Lank's wrath.

After witnessing Danny's interaction with some showgirls, Molly heads to Mexico with city slicker George Mason. Danny follows Molly south of the border, accompanied by Slick, Jimmy, Kate, Patsy and Tessie. Lank and his henchman Pete are in hot pursuit. Danny and Molly untangle their romantic complications, while Kate and Patsy get Slick and Jimmy to settle down.

"If you don't go to see this picture you will miss a lot of your favorites — Bert Wheeler, Robert Woolsey, Dorothy Lee, clever Mitzi Green, Eddie Quillan, debonair Ivan Lebedeff [*where is he in this movie?*], Arline Judge and many more." —*Photoplay*

*Comments: Crazy Quilt* would have been a more appropriate title for this film, given its checkered production history. The first cut was completed under the supervision of producer William LeBaron and direction of William Seiter. Then David O. Selznick, who succeeded LeBaron, insisted upon retakes that up-ended the structure and content of the original. A number of scenes were dropped — including much of Dorothy's footage — and replaced with new, inferior material directed by Norman Taurog. In an effort to "improve" things, Selznick only created a mess.

As a result, *Girl Crazy* is an odd blend of very funny comedic set pieces and flat-footed musical numbers. Bert and Bob's timing is especially sharp and their energy is infectious. Yet the beautiful George and Ira Gershwin score is butchered by ruinous renditions and presentations. "I Got Rhythm" and "But Not for Me" are two prime casualties; the former is poorly warbled by Kitty Kelly while Eddie Quillan and Arline Judge talk their way through the latter. "Bidin' My Time" is tossed away in an offhand manner; it isn't even sung by any of the principals. "You've Got What Gets Me," a Bert-Dorothy duet allegedly written for the picture (it was actually recycled from a rejected Broadway tune), emerges by default as the best musical interlude in the picture.

Mitzi Green reprises "But Not for Me" as an excuse for her to imitate Bing Crosby, Roscoe Ates, George Arliss and Edna May Oliver. The imitations are uncanny (her takes on Arliss and Oliver are hilarious) but the potential of the song is again squandered. Plus, the three-minute routine stops the story dead in its tracks.

If *Girl Crazy* hadn't been tampered with, it would have ranked with the best Wheeler and Woolsey comedies. As is, it's a frustrating reminder of what could have been.

The film went unseen for decades after its initial release because it was eclipsed by (and legally tied up because of) MGM's 1943 remake starring Mickey Rooney and Judy Garland. Thanks to the efforts of Miles Kreuger and his Institute of the American Musical, the original resurfaced in 1973 as part of a "Gershwin on Film" series at the New York Cultural Center. (It was intended to open the series but the restoration took longer than anticipated and it wound up as the closing attraction.)

*Girl Crazy* was eventually made available in the 16mm format by Films Incorporated, a movie-rental organization. In the 1980s, Dorothy was given the opportunity to see it but she refused. Though she usually expressed interest in revisiting her musical numbers, she even took a pass on watching "You've Got What Gets Me" because the bitter memories of what Selznick did to the production still lingered. She said bluntly, "I don't know how much time I've got left, but I'm not going to waste any of it sitting through that dog again."

## *Mazie* (1933)

*Director and producer:* Dallas M. Fitzgerald. *Story:* Henry Day. *Continuity and dialogue:* Frank W. Gay. *Cinematography:* Milton Moore, Friend R. Baker. *Sound recording:* W.C. Smith. *Editing:* S. Edwin Graham. *Settings:* Educational Pictures.

*Cast:* Dorothy Lee (Mazie), John Darrow (Boyd Kenton), LeRoy Mason (Paul Barnes), Kay [Katherine] Ellis (Edith Stone), Walter Miller (Jason Steele), Lee Moran (Mike McCann), Gladden James (Crook), William H. Strauss (Mr. Webber), Connie Elliott (Irene Murphy), Henry Hall (Café customer), Sammy Blum, Cornelia Kellogg.

*Production date:* September 1932. Released by Plymouth Pictures Corporation. 63 minutes.

*Synopsis:* After her father steals from his investment company and then commits suicide, Edith Stone goes into seclusion to protect her sweetheart, Paul Barnes. She hides out at a cheap boarding house where she befriends Mazie, the most popular waitress at Webber's Café. Mazie gets Edith a job at the café, while Mazie borrows some of Edith's clothes and tries to emulate her classy new friend. When Edith tells Mazie all about her situation with Paul, Mazie decides to take Edith down to the high-society resort where Paul is staying and straighten things out. Edith is recognized by Jason Steele, her father's business partner, who tries to find out where she's living, but by this time Edith and Mazie have already taken off on their vacation. Mazie helps Edith reunite with Paul, and it is revealed that Steele murdered Edith's father and made it look like a suicide. Mazie finds true love with Boyd Kenton, a wealthy friend of Paul's.

"Pleasant and inconsequential tale that won't cause any complaints, but which won't draw any too much attention."—*The Exhibitor*

*Comments: Mazie* was the most obscure production that Dorothy was ever involved with. Produced by Plymouth Pictures Corporation, it was filmed at the Metropolitan Studios in Fort Lee, New Jersey. For Plymouth's debut effort, company president Dallas M. Fitzgerald served as the director.

Dorothy wound up suing Plymouth Pictures and Fitzgerald for her back salary, which served as an omen for the extremely limited—and mostly undocumented—distribution it received. It was marketed on a "States' Rights" basis (sold on a territorial basis) to independent film exchanges.

After fading from view almost immediately, *Mazie* resurfaced in the early 1950s when an obscure distribution company called Samart Pictures released 16mm prints to television and rental markets. For some strange reason, Samart renamed it *Sweet Poison*, a title that had absolutely nothing to do with the actual film.

## *A Preferred List* (1933)

*Director:* Leigh Jason. *Producer:* Lou Brock. *Story and screenplay:* Tom Lennon, Walter Weems. *Original music:* Roy Webb. *Film editor:* Edward Mann.

*Cast:* Dorothy Lee, Chick Chandler.

*Working title: The Preferred List.* Released October 6, 1933, by RKO Radio Pictures. 20 minutes.

*Synopsis:* A political satire with musical numbers.

*Comments:* This was the first entry in RKO's "Headliner" series of musical-comedy shorts. The cast delivered rhyming dialogue in song, as in the "Musical Novelty" musical shorts produced by Columbia Pictures. (*A Preferred List* is often mistakenly listed as a Columbia production.) Studio press releases indicated this would be the first in a series of Dorothy Lee-Chick Chandler two-reelers. It was nominated for an Academy Award for Best Short Subject (Comedy). Ken Murray may also appear in the film.

## *Take a Chance* (1933)

*Directors:* Monte Brice and Laurence Schwab. *Producer:* Laurence Schawb, in association with William Rowland and Monte Brice. Based on the play *Take a Chance* by B.G. DeSylva, Laurence Schwab, Sid Silvers, Nacio Herb Brown, Richard Whiting, Vincent Youmans and E.Y. Harburg. *Director of musical numbers:* Bobby Connolly. *Cinematography:* Joseph Valentine and (uncredited) William O. Steiner. *Costumes:* Charles Le Maire. *Film editor:* Robert R. Snody. *Sound:* C.A. Tuthill.

*Songs:* "It's Only a Paper Moon" by Harold Arlen, E.Y. Harburg and Billy Rose; "Eadie Was a Lady" by B.G. DeSylva, Nacio Herb Brown and Richard Whiting; "I Did It With My Little Ukulele" by Jay Gorney and E.Y. Harburg; "Night Owl" by Herman Hupfeld; "New Deal Rhythm" by Roger Edens and E.Y. Harburg; "Come Up and See Me Sometime" by Louis Alter and Arthur Swanstrom; "Should I Be Sweet (or Hot)?" by Vincent Youmans and B.G. DeSylva; "Rise 'n' Shine" by Vincent Youmans and B.G. DeSylva; "So Do I" by Vincent Youmans and B.G. DeSylva. *Dropped during production:* "You're an Old Smoothie" by B.G. DeSylva, Nacio Herb Brown and Richard Whiting.

*Cast:* James Dunn (Duke Stanley), Cliff "Ukulele Ike" Edwards (Louie Webb), June Knight (Toni Ray), Charles "Buddy" Rogers (Kenneth Raleigh), Lillian Roth (Wanda Brill), Dorothy Lee (Consuelo Raleigh), Lilian Bond (Thelma Green), Lona Andre (Miss Miami Beach), Robert Glecker (Mike Caruso), Charles Richman (Andrew Raleigh), Harry Shannon (Bartender), George McKay (Steve the stage manager), Vivian Vance ("Eadie Was a Lady" backup singer), Mildred Webb (Chorus girl), Enrico Caruso, Jr. Deleted from final release print: Marjorie Main (Delegate from Arizona). Contrary to other sources, Shirley Temple did not portray the little girl who says "Down with spinach" in a deleted scene from the "New Deal Rhythm" number.

*Production dates:* late July–August 1933. Released November 25, 1933, by Paramount Pictures. 82 minutes.

*Synopsis:* Carnival workers Duke Stanley, Louie Webb and Toni Ray head to New York to follow Wanda Brill, Duke's no-nonsense ex-girlfriend, who wants to make a splash in the "Big Puddle." The trio finds work at Mike Caruso's Place, a Greenwich Village night spot specializing in entertainment, gambling and fleecing the patrons. Wanda lands a featured role in *Humpty Dumpty*, a stage revue set to open on Broadway, and introduces Toni to the show's writer-director Kenneth Raleigh, a millionaire's son. After hearing Toni sing, Kenneth offers her a role, a gesture that doesn't sit well with Thelma Green, the show's leading lady.

Through Toni, Duke and Louie invade high society but they soon revert to their old carny ways, which threatens Toni's romance with Kenneth. But the boys redeem themselves when they, along with Ken's ditzy sister Consuelo, fill in for injured actors during the play's opening night performance. The audience mistakes their stumblebum antics for inspired lunacy and the show becomes a hit.

*Comments:* Considering all of the talent involved in this project, *Take a Chance* is a crushing disappointment on just about every level. As an East Coast production (shot at the Eastern Service Studios in New York), it's not as technically slick as the movies coming out of Hollywood during the same period. Despite some fairly ambitious musical numbers, several passages have the paltry look of a Poverty Row effort rather than the gloss of a major-studio release.

The humor is never as funny as it aims to be, and the energy of the cast only serves to magnify how shallow the material is. Dorothy is handed one running gag — performing her snake-hips routine for anyone who'll stand still long enough to watch her — and the joke wears out its welcome because she's given little else to do. June Knight and Charles "Buddy" Rogers try their best, but only James Dunn, Cliff "Ukulele Ike" Edwards and Lillian Roth manage to emerge relatively unscathed from the oppressive mediocrity. In fact, Dunn, Edwards and Roth are featured in the film's best musical numbers. Edwards warbles "I Did It With My Little Ukulele," an enjoyable novelty tune detailing his adventures as a castaway on an uncharted desert island. (The number incorporates an elaborate flashback sequence that is one of the few highlights of the picture.) Edwards and June Knight sing separate choruses of "Night Owl" while Dunn performs a spirited dance routine with a group of chorines. Roth does a fine rendition of "Eadie Was a Lady" and an all-too-brief version of "Come Up and See Me Sometime."

Typical of the film's botched creative judgment was the decision to jettison the majority of "New Deal Rhythm," an elaborate production number celebrating President Franklin D. Roosevelt's National Recovery Administration. It was one of the best numbers devised for *Take a Chance*— perhaps the most ambitious one — yet it only appears in a truncated form in the final cut. (The entire number was released as a separate one-reel short that same year, under the title *New Deal Rhythm*.)

## *Plane Crazy* (1933)

*Director:* Roy Mack. *Story:* Eddie Moran, Cyrus Wood. *Cinematography:* Edwin DuPar. *Ensembles:* Paul Florenz.

*Songs:* "I Feel I'm Safe with You," "Make You Feel at Home," "Pretty Face" and "As Long as the Ganges Flows" by Cliff Hess.

*Cast:* Dorothy Lee (Dottie), Arthur and Morton Havel (Jack and Bill), Brook Allen (Freddie Richman), Catherine Field ("Ganges" singer), Stone & Vernon Foursome (Specialty dancers).

*Working title: Plane Fools. Production date:* August 1933. Released December 23, 1933, by Warner Brothers Pictures. 20 minutes.

*Synopsis:* Seeking a surefire publicity stunt, small-time aviators Jack and Bill decide to stage a phony around-the-world flight. Plane-crazy Dottie overhears their scheme and takes part in their charade. When they arrive in New York, Dottie is hailed as the first stowaway to circle the globe. At a reception held in their honor, the trio spins tall tales about their exciting, tune-filled adventures in foreign lands.

*Comments:* The flimsy plot is merely an excuse for a series of songs and dances, including Dorothy's cute duet with Brook Allen, "I Feel I'm Safe with You." Lively performances (Dottie appears to be having a grand time throughout), slick production values, and perky ensemble numbers make *Plane Crazy* the sort of whimsical, charmingly shapeless concoction that could only have been created during the early 1930s.

## *Signing 'Em Up* (1933)

*Cast (as themselves):* Bert Wheeler, Robert Woolsey, Dorothy Lee, Bruce Cabot, Pert Kelton, Sydney Jarvis.

*Production date:* October 31, 1933. Released in December 1933, by RKO Radio Pictures. 4 minutes.

*Synopsis:* Bert and Bob wander around the RKO studio lot, trying to get pledge signatures for the NRA (National Recovery Administration), President Franklin D. Roosevelt's industry-regulation bureau for economic recovery. After encounters with Bruce Cabot and Pert Kelton, the boys join Dorothy for an outdoor scene directed by Sydney Jarvis.

*Comments:* Dorothy appears briefly in this NRA promotional short that's pretty brief to begin with. During the final moments, Bert and Bob are filming a dangerous stunt in which Dorothy is supposed to come to their rescue. When the end-of-the-day whistle sounds, she and the entire crew quickly depart, leaving the boys trapped in a perilous situation.

## *Hips, Hips, Hooray!* (1934)

*Director:* Mark Sandrich. *Executive producer:* Merian C. Cooper. *Associate producer:* H.N. Swanson. *Screenplay:* Bert Kalmar, Harry Ruby, Edward Kaufman. *Story:* Bert Kalmar, Harry Ruby. *Dance direction:* Dave Gould and (uncredited) Hermes Pan. *Cinematography:* David Abel. *Photographic effects:* Vernon Walker. *Musical director:* Roy Webb. *Art direction:* Van Nest Polglase, Carroll Clark. *Costumes:* Walter Plunkett. *Special effects supervisor:* Harry Redmond, Sr. *Sound recorder:* P.J. Faulkner, Jr. *Sound cutter:* George Marsh. *Film editor:* Basil Wrangell.

*Songs:* "Keep Romance Alive" and "Keep on Doin' What You're Doin'" by Bert Kalmar and Harry Ruby; "Tired of It All," another Kalmar and Ruby song, was written for the film but not used.

*Cast:* Bert Wheeler (Andy Williams), Robert Woolsey (Dr. Dudley), Ruth Etting (Herself), Thelma Todd (Amelia Frisby), Dorothy Lee (Daisy Maxwell), George Meeker (Armand Beauchamp), Phyllis Barry (Madame Irene), James Burtis (Detective Sweeney), Matt Briggs (Detective Epstein), Spencer Charters (Mr. Clark), June Brewster (Clark's secretary), Elise Cavanna (Miss Pilot, radio announcer), Dorothy Granger (Miss Cole), Bobby Watson (Dance director), Marion Byron (Enthusiastic flavored-lipstick girl), Jean Carmen, Patricia Parker (Flavored-lipstick girls), Carlyle Moore, Jr. (Assistant), Stanley Blystone (Madame Irene Cosmetics race car driver), Otto Fries, Walter James (Mountaineers), Alfred P. James (Mule driver), Nat Carr (Gas station proprietor), Joe Marba (Pool room proprietor), Lee Shumway (Policeman), Doris McMahon (Frisby's maid), True Boardman (Radio announcer).

*Production dates:* October 17–November 16, 1933. Released February 2, 1934, by RKO Radio Pictures. 68 minutes.

*Synopsis:* Andy Williams and Dr. Dudley, street peddlers hawking flavored lipsticks, lure customers away from the Maiden America Beauty Products business stationed across the street, despite the pretty model, Daisy Maxwell, demonstrating products in the Maiden America showroom window. Andy becomes smitten with Daisy and offers to peddle her cosmetics in order to compensate her for the revenue she's lost. Due to pressure from the police, the boys wind up giving the merchandise away but Daisy is convinced that they're super-salesmen and encourages her boss, Amelia Frisby, to have a meeting with the duo.

Commandeering a gullible businessman's office, Andy and Dudley make enough of an impression on Amelia to prompt her to offer a merger. As he dashes out of the office, Dudley inadvertently grabs a satchel filled with valuable securities. The businessman, Mr. Clark, hires private detectives Epstein and Sweeney to retrieve his securities and arrest the culprits.

Unbeknownst to Amelia, her sales manager, Armand Beauchamp, is feeding company secrets to rival cosmetics manufacturer Madame Irene. When he discovers that Andy and Dudley are the ones being sought for the theft, Beauchamp steals the securities immediately after the boys realize their error. Unable to make restitution, Andy and Dudley flee town.

Amelia enters Maiden America in the Cross-Continental Motor Classic auto race, hoping to win the prize money that will salvage her failing company. On the road, Andy and Dudley elude the pursuing detectives by hopping into the Maiden America car, which was abandoned by crooked drivers working in cahoots with Beauchamp, and suddenly find themselves participating in the race. After a wild ride, loaded with setbacks and detours, they cross the finish line and win the competition, just as Amelia informs Epstein and Sweeney that Beauchamp is guilty and has already been apprehended. With that burden lifted, Andy and Dudley are free to settle down with Daisy and Amelia.

"To keep the croggy plot on its feet the familiar Wheeler and Woolsey antics are worked overtime. That they're always surrounded by lookers is quite an aid to their comedy."—*Variety*

*Comments:* For those unfamiliar with Wheeler and Woolsey, *Hips, Hips, Hooray!* may be the best place to start because it encapsulates all the virtues of their finest movies: bright performances, snappy patter, entertaining song-and-dance routines and elaborate and inventive sight gags. (The race-car finale is one of the funniest sequences from any of their pictures.) Plus, it's a sterling example of the sort of risqué, pre–Code filmmaking that would soon disappear from the screen.

This was Dorothy's favorite Wheeler and Woolsey film, the one she had no problem watching multiple times in its entirety. In later years, for the few personal appearances she would make, this is the picture she preferred to have screened in conjunction with those events.

## *Cockeyed Cavaliers* (1934)

*Director:* Mark Sandrich. *Executive producer:* Pandro S. Berman. *Associate producer:* Lou Brock. *Screenplay:* Edward Kaufman, Ben Holmes. *Additional dialogue:* Ralph Spence, Grant Garrett. *Cinematography:* David Abel. *Photographic effects:* Vernon Walker. *Musical director:* Roy Webb. *Art direction:* Van Nest Polglase, Carroll Clark. *Costumes:* Walter Plunkett. *Sound:* P.J. Faulkner, Jr. *Film editor:* Jack Kitchin.

*Songs:* "(We Went Hunting) And the Big Bad Wolf Was Dead," "Dilly Dally" and "News" by Will Jason and Val Burton.

*Cast:* Bert Wheeler (Bert), Robert Woolsey (Bob), Thelma Todd (Lady Genevieve), Dorothy Lee (Mary Ann), Noah Beery (Baron), Robert Grieg (Duke of Weskit), Henry Sedley (Baron's friend), Franklin Pangborn (Town crier), Alfred P. James (Squire Dale, Mary Ann's father), Billy Gilbert (Golden Boar Inn landlord), Jack Norton (King's physician), Snub Pollard (Physician's aide), Kate Price (Nora), Kewpie Morgan (Andrew), Frank Mills (Bell ringer), Charlie Hall (Coach driver), Kit Guard (Stable boy), Frank Baker.

Although they are referred to as "Bert" and "Bob" in the cast listing, the names of Wheeler and Woolsey's characters are unspecified in the actual film.

*Production dates:* March 29–April 24, 1934. Released June 29, 1934, by RKO Radio Pictures. 72 minutes.

*Synopsis:* In 17th century England, itinerant peasants Bert and Bob get into trouble because of Bert's involuntary bouts of kleptomania. They are rescued from pillory by a plucky young lad who is, unbeknownst to them, actually a plucky young lady named Mary Ann who has disguised herself as a boy to avoid a pre-arranged marriage to the undesirable Duke of Weskit (Robert Grieg). At the Golden Boar Inn, Bert's kleptomania once again gets them into hot water, and the boys switch clothes with two drunken ("cockeyed") guests who turn out to be the king's physician and his aide.

Mistaken for the king's emissaries, Bert, Bob and Mary Ann are escorted to the duke's home, where his niece, Lady Genevieve, and her husband, the baron, also reside. After Bert and Bob cure the duke's insomnia, they are treated like royalty. Bert falls in love with Mary Ann once she reveals her true identity and Bob dallies with the beautiful Genevieve. The jealous baron finds out about the affair, but restrains himself because he believes Bob is under the protection of the king.

Mary Ann forgoes her masquerade to save her father from the duke's wrath, and the baron discovers the interlopers aren't who they're pretending to be. A wild boar ("The Black Devil") is terrorizing the countryside and a reward of 5,000 sovereigns is offered for its capture. Bert and Bob manage to bring the boar back alive and the reward money allows both Mary Ann and Lady Genevieve to gain their freedom.

"A bright Wheeler and Woolsey comedy with a fair quota of laughs and eclipsing their previous releases." — *Variety*

*Comments:* Generally considered to be the best Wheeler and Woolsey comedy, *Cockeyed Cavaliers* has the shapeliest structure of all their vehicles, with a sturdy storyline supporting the lively comic set pieces and infectious musical numbers. It also provides Dorothy with what is arguably her best role in a W&W picture. She's more integral to the plot than she had been in some of the previous films and her character reflects the tomboy aspects of the real Dorothy. Once again, Thelma Todd is a welcome addition to the cast, and her engaging performance turns the endearing triumvirate into a delightful quartet.

*Cockeyed Cavaliers* offers several highlights, chief among them the enjoyable "Dilly Dally" song-and-dance number with Bert, Bob, Dorothy and Thelma, and the climactic boar chase that evokes visual comedy at its finest.

Dorothy liked *Cockeyed Cavaliers* well enough to own a videotape of it, but she tended to watch individual scenes rather than sit through the entire film. Eventually she had the "Dilly Dally" musical number copied to a tape that had some of her other numbers, and she preferred to view this collection of highlights instead.

## *If This Isn't Love* (1934)

*Director:* Leigh Jason. *Producer:* Lee Marcus.

*Song:* "If This Isn't Love" by Will Jason and Val Burton.

*Cast:* Dorothy Lee, Walter Wolfe [Walter Woolf King], Hazel Forbes, Eddie Kane, Keye Luke.

*Production date:* June 1934. Released September 28, 1934, by RKO Radio Pictures. 22 minutes.

*Synopsis:* An entry in RKO's "Musicomedies" series, showcasing the talents of Dorothy Lee and Walter Wolfe.

*Comments:* Billed as "A Radio Musical Comedy," *If This Isn't Love* was promoted with colorful poster art and a song sheet. Some of the trade journals mistakenly listed it as a Ruth Etting short. (Etting was starring in a series of RKO musical two-reelers at the time.) In his subsequent films, Walter Wolfe would be billed as Walter Woolf King; his best-known roles were in the Marx Brothers comedies *A Night at the Opera* (1935) and *Go West* (1940), and in Laurel & Hardy's *Swiss Miss* (1938).

Lee Marcus also produced seven Wheeler and Woolsey films, including two that co-starred Dorothy, *The Rainmakers* (1935) and *Silly Billies* (1936).

## *School for Girls* (1935)

*Director:* William Nigh. *Producer:* M.H. Hoffman. *Screenplay and screen story:* Albert DeMond. *Story* "Our Undisciplined Daughters" by Reginald Wright Kauffman. *Associate producer:* M.H. Hoffman, Jr. *Production manager:* Rudolph Flothow. *Cinematography:* Harry Neumann. *Film editor:* Mildred Johnston.

*Cast:* Sidney Fox (Annette Eldridge), Paul Kelly (Garry Waltham), Lois Wilson (Miss Cartwright), Lucille LaVerne (Miss Keeble), Dorothy Lee (Dorothy Bosworth), Toby Wing (Hazel Jones), Dorothy Appleby (Florence Burns), Lona Andre (Peggy), Russell Hopton (Elliott Robbins), Barbara Weeks (Nell Davis), Kathleen Burke (Gladys Deacon), Anna Q. Nilsson (Dr. Anne Galvin), Purnell Pratt (Inspector Jameson), Robert Warwick (Governor), William Farnum

(Charles Waltham), Charles Ray (Duke), Mary Foy (Miss Gage), Dawn O'Day [Anne Shirley] (Catherine Fogarty), Myrtle Stedman (Mrs. Winters), Eddie Kane (Ted), Gretta Gould (Mrs. Smoot), George Cleveland (Reeves), Helene Chadwick (Larson), Helen Foster (Eleanor), Fred Kelsey (detective), Edward LeSaint (Judge), Harry Woods (Detective), Jack Kennedy (Hansen).

*Production dates:* Late June–early July 1934 (at RKO Radio Pictures Studio). Released February 19, 1935, by Liberty Pictures Corporation. 66 minutes. (Some sources state 73 minutes.)

*Synopsis:* Found guilty of a crime she didn't commit, Annette Eldridge is sent to a reform school run by Miss Keeble, a sadistic head matron. Garry Waltham, a member of the visiting committee, believes in Annette's innocence and attempts to get her paroled.

"Smooth but rather tedious film, which will interest mildly.... [O]ld-fashioned type of a yarn without definite plan and made largely for the propaganda angle. Chief value is the presence in the cast, many of them fleetingly, of a string of recognizable names. Sidney Fox suffers from an artificially written role and also from the more natural conduct of some of the other girls."
— *Variety*

*Comments:* Despite being ruled with an iron fist, the reform school depicted in *School for Girls* is one of those cinematic criminal institutions where the inmates are left unguarded for stretches at a time, or at least when it's convenient for the plot. Whatever its shortcomings, the film treats '30s movie buffs to glimpses of some of the prettiest starlets of the era cast as reform-school inmates.

The cast also included a relatively unknown actress named Dawn O'Day whose next film role was the lead in *Anne of Green Gables*, RKO's adaptation of the L.M. Montgomery novel. RKO convinced O'Day to change her name to Anne Shirley, which was the name of the character in the novel and the film, and she would continue to use the name professionally for the remainder of her career. *Anne of Green Gables* was released before *School for Girls*, so Liberty Pictures was able to capitalize on the popularity of the RKO film by taking existing posters and pasting an attachment over Dawn O'Day's name: "Anne Shirley, '*Anne of Green Gables*.'"

## *In the Spotlight* (1935)

Also known as *Broadway Brevities: In the Spotlight*

*Director:* Joseph Henabery. *Producer:* Sam Sax. *Cinematography:* Ray Foster. *Musical director:* David Mendoza. *Film editor:* Bert Frank.

Songs: "It Pays to Advertise," "Powder Puff" and "I Love Shoes" by David, Hess, and Green; "Dancing Silhouettes" by Hess and Mendoza.

*Cast:* Hal LeRoy (Hal), Dorothy Lee (Dorothy), Herb Warren, Bob Simmons.

*Production date:* October 1934. Released March 30, 1935, by Warner Brothers Pictures. 20 minutes.

*Synopsis:* Dorothy, the daughter of a shoe manufacturer, is returning by ship from a trip abroad when she sees Hal, a shy deckhand, dancing. She invites him to an advertising exhibition sponsored by her father's company, and makes him appear with her in a floor show.

*Comments:* Produced at the Vitaphone Studios in Brooklyn, this was an entry in Vitaphone's "Broadway Brevities" series. Dancer Hal LeRoy starred in a few of these musical shorts, opposite leading ladies such as Betty Hutton, Toby Wing, and June Allyson.

## *Without Children* (1935)

*Director:* William Nigh. *Producer:* M.H. Hoffman. *Screenplay:* Gertrude Orr. Based on the short story "Eyes of Youth" by Mrs. Wilson Woodrow [Nancy Mann Waddel Woodrow]. *Associate producer:* M.H. Hoffman, Jr. *Production manager:* Rudolph Flothow. *Cinematography:* Harry Neumann. *Musical director:* Abe Meyer. *Film editor:* Mildred Johnston. *Sound recording:* Richard E. Tyler (recorded by RCA Victor System at RKO-Pathé Studios).

*Songs:* "Man About Town" by Marcella Freedman; "Auf Wiedersehn" by Eberhard Storch. English lyrics by John Sexton and John Turner.

*Cast:* Marguerite Churchill (Sue Cole), Bruce Cabot (David F. Cole), Evelyn Brent (Shirley Ross), Reginald Denny (Phil Graham), Dorothy Lee (Carole Cole), William Janney (David "Sonny" Cole), Dickie Moore (Sonny as a child), Cora Sue Collins (Carole as a child), Lillian Harmer (Frieda), Joan Woodbury (Secretary).

*Working title: Penthouse Party.*

*Production dates:* August 24–early September 1934. Released April 15, 1935, by Liberty Pictures Corporation. 60 minutes. (Running time often listed as 77, 81 or 85 minutes.) Re-released by Republic Pictures in February 1936 as *Penthouse Party*.

*Synopsis:* Sue and David Cole get divorced due to David's affair with Shirley Ross. As a single parent, Sue indulges their children, Carole and Sonny, who become spoiled and undisciplined adolescents. Family friend Phil Graham, a successful businessman, wants to marry Sue, but she's still carrying a torch for her ex. To Sue's dismay and Phil's consternation, Carole develops a crush on Phil, who rejects her advances.

Sue decides to teach her children a lesson by behaving as irresponsibly as they do. She and Phil go partying every night, which provides fodder for newspaper gossip columns. An irate Sonny threatens to confront Phil, but his gun accidentally discharges, seriously wounding Carole. When David, now living in Europe, hears the news about his children, he leaves Shirley for good and rushes back to his family.

"Story is convincing enough in its essentials but could have proven better screen material in different hands ... Dorothy Lee and William Janney are okay as the grown-up children." —*Variety*

*Comments: Without Children* turned out to be one of Dorothy's better low-budget melodramas. Her role as an insouciant playgirl allowed her to exhibit the humor and "pep" she displayed in her earlier Wheeler and Woolsey movies. Though Dorothy was the first to admit that she was no great shakes as a dramatic actress, here she delivers a fine, well-modulated performance, especially in her scenes opposite Reginald Denny and William Janney. Her flirty rendition of "Man About Town" captures the essence of her character: a callow young lady who thinks she's a sophisticated woman.

## *The Curtain Falls* (1935)

*Director:* Charles Lamont. *Producer:* George R. Batcheller. *Story:* Karl Brown. *Cinematography:* M.A. Andersen. *Sound recorder:* Pete Clark. *Assistant director:* Melville Shyer. *Art director:* Edward Jewell. *Film editor:* Roland Reed. *Supervisor:* Lon Young.

*Cast:* Henrietta Crosman (Sarah Crabtree, a.k.a. Aunt Hetty), Dorothy Lee (Dorothy Scorsby), William Bakewell (Barry Graham), Natalie Moorhead (Katherine "Kitty" Scorsby), Holmes Herbert (John Scorsby), John Darrow (Allan Scorsby), Edward [Eddie] Kane (Taggart), Dorothy Revier (Helene Deveridge), Jameson Thomas (Martin Deveridge), Aggie Herring (Mrs. McGillicuddy), William Benge (Butler), Fern Emmett (Maid), Jack Shutta, Al Bridge (Wrecking company employees), Bryant Washburn (MacArthur), Lloyd Ingraham (Lansing), Tom Ricketts (Hotel manager), Bess Flowers (Secretary), Jane Keckley, Edward LeSaint, Lafe McKee, Robert [Bobby] Burns (Seven Eleven Club maitre d'), Alexander Pollard.

*Production dates:* September 7 to mid–September 1934 (at RKO Radio Pictures Studio). Released May 1935 by Chesterfield Motion Picture Corporation. 67 minutes.

*Synopsis:* Broke and homeless, elderly Sarah Crabtree, the greatest stage actress of her era, tries to get in touch with the wealthy Lady Henrietta Scorsby, an old friend who was once a fellow actress. But when Lady Scorsby is reported missing, Crabtree decides to impersonate her. Gaining admittance to the spacious home of John Scorsby, her long-lost "nephew," the feisty impostor proceeds to straighten out the tangled lives of the privileged family: John, who's facing financial ruin; his wife Katherine, who is having an affair with Martin Deveridge, a family friend; daughter Dorothy, whose romance with true love Barry Graham unravels when she attempts to woo Martin away from her mother; and son Allan, a playboy saddled with gambling debts.

"Story is rather weak in its telling but stacks up stronger than numerous dual billers. Trouping by Henrietta Crosman is largely responsible. Considerable production value.... [C]reditable work by Holmes Herbert, Natalie Moorhead, John Darrow, Dorothy Lee — well cast, for a change, as the young daughter — and Jameson Thomas." — *Variety*

*Comments:* While this melodrama is never really convincing (for one thing, "Aunt Hetty" pulls off her masquerade with ridiculous ease), Henrietta Crosman's engaging performance smoothes over several of the rough patches. Like the character she plays here, Crosman had been a leading stage actress for years, specializing in grande-dame roles. Her most prominent film role was the lead in *Pilgrimage* (1933), directed by John Ford.

Dorothy once again plays an ingénue role, but this time with a slight twist: She nearly sacrifices her own happiness in order to save her parents' marriage. This subplot makes her otherwise standard-issue character a little more interesting, although Dorothy and other cast members take a back seat to the 72-year-old Crosman, who dominates the picture.

Director Charles Lamont is best known for his comedies, which include Buster Keaton shorts for Educational, Three Stooges shorts for Columbia, and Universal features such as *Hit the Ice* (1943), *Ma and Pa Kettle* (1949), *Abbott and Costello Meet the Invisible Man* (1951), *Abbott and Costello Go to Mars* (1953), *Ma and Pa Kettle at Home* (1954), *Abbott and Costello Meet the Mummy* (1955) and *Francis in the Haunted House* (1956).

## *The Old Homestead* (1935)

*Director:* William Nigh. *Producer:* M.H. Hoffman. *Story, continuity and dialogue:* W. Scott Darling. Based on the novel by John Russell Corvell and the play by Denman Thompson. *Associate producer:* M.H. Hoffman, Jr. *Production manager:* Rudolph Flothow. *Cinematography:* Harry Neumann. *Musical arrangements:* Howard Jackson. *Film editor:* Mildred Johnston. *Sound recording:* Harold Bumbaugh (recorded by RCA Victor System at RKO-Pathé Studios).

*Songs:* "Moonlight in Heaven" by John [Jack] T. Scholl and Louis Alter; "Plow Boy" by J. Keim Brennan and Ted Snyder; "Love Me Ever" by George Waggner, Howard Jackson, and Jack Bennett; "Somehow I Knew" by Harry Tobias, Neil Morey, and Charles Rosoff; "Harlem Nasty Man" by George Waggner and Howard Jackson; "Old Age Pension" by Manny Stone; "Way Out There," "Happy Cowboy" and "That Old White Mule of Mine" by Bob Nolan; "Old Rover" by Tim Spencer; "Honey Dat I Love So Well" by Harry Freeman. Additional songs and music by the Sons of the Pioneers.

*Cast:* Mary Carlisle (Nancy Abbott), Lawrence Gray (Bob Shackelford), Dorothy Lee (Elsie Wilson), Willard Robertson (Uncle Jed), Eddie Nugent (Rudy Nash), Lillian Miles (Peggy), Fuzzy Knight (Lem), Eddie Kane (Mr. Wertheimer), Harry Conley (J. Wilberforce Platt), The Sons of the Pioneers [Verne Spence, Bob Nolan, Roy Rogers, Hugh Farr], Sally Sweet ("Nasty Harlem Man" vocalist), George Lloyd (Elsie's husband), Alec Craig.

*Production dates:* Mid- to late February 1935. Released August 10, 1935, by Liberty Pictures Corporation. 73 minutes.

*Synopsis:* Bob Shackelford, an unassuming country boy who loves to vocalize, works on his Uncle Jed's farm, along with five farmhands who also provide musical accompaniment. His sweetheart Nancy arranges for Mr. Wertheimer, a New York talent scout, to see the boys perform. Wertheimer is duly impressed and signs them up for his radio program, *The Old Homestead Hour.* Everyone — including Nancy and Uncle Jed — heads to New York City, where sudden fame inflates Bob's ego. To complicate matters, Rudy Nash, a popular radio crooner, becomes smitten with Nancy, while a jealous Elsie Wilson, another radio vocalist, makes a play for Bob.

And good old Uncle Jed gets involved with a brassy gold digger named Peggy. Nancy and Bob soon learn that they were both much happier leading simpler lives on the farm.

"An unpretentious romance of farm and city life which manages to please but doesn't have the class nor the punch to essay choice engagements. Makes good company for another feature on double bills.... While the story charts no original paths in screenland and the dialog makes no pretensions to brilliance, on the whole it isn't difficult to take.... [It's] a clean innocuous picture with fairly good music and production stature."—*New York Times*

*Comments:* With its stay-in-your-own-backyard cautionary message, *The Old Homestead* was squarely aimed at small-town and rural patronage. The idea that Bob could become a huge radio star overnight stretches credulity, but the popularity that the Sons of the Pioneers enjoy in the film reflects their real-life success — only they didn't wind up back on the farm. This production is quite polished by Poverty Row standards and provides a good showcase for the Sons of the Pioneers; the group would continue to make movies and recordings.

Despite receiving third billing, Dorothy's participation is limited. She does get to sing a pleasant tune, "Somehow I Knew." Otherwise, the plot focuses on the two romantic leads, with much of the screen time devoted to the songs.

Former actor George Waggner, who co-wrote two of the songs in *The Old Homestead*, became a director in 1938 and had a prolific career in movies and television. He is best remembered for directing the horror classic *The Wolf Man* (1941).

## *The Rainmakers* (1935)

*Director:* Fred Guiol. *Associate producer:* Lee Marcus. *Screenplay:* Grant Garrett, Leslie Goodwins. *Story:* Albert Treynor, Fred Guiol. *Additional material:* Stanley Rauh. *Cinematography:* Ted McCord. *Musical director:* Roy Webb. *Original music:* Roy Webb. *Orchestrators:* Gene Rose, Maurice De Packh. *Art direction:* Van Nest Polglase, Feild M. Gray. *Costume design:* Walter Plunkett. *Special effects supervisor:* Harry Redmond, Sr. *Special effects:* Vernon Walker. *Sound effects:* Walter Elliott. *Sound:* George D. Ellis. *Film editor:* John Lockert.

*Song:* "Isn't Love the Grandest Thing?" by Louis Alter and Jack Scholl.

*Cast:* Bert Wheeler (Billy), Robert Woolsey (Roscoe Horne), Dorothy Lee (Margie Spencer), Berton Churchill (Simon Parker), George Meeker (Orville Parker), Frederic [Frederick] Roland (Henry Spencer), Edgar Dearing (Kelly), Clarence Wilson (Dennis P. Hogan), Edward LeSaint, Jack Richardson (Engineers), Harry Bernard, Leo Sulky (Firemen), Billy Dooley, Harry Bowen (Switchmen), Eddie Dunn (Dispatcher), Peggy Waters (Hogan's secretary), Robert McKenzie, Lon Poff, Ed Brady, Eddie Sturgis, Frank Moran (Farmers), Eddie Borden, George Magrill, Charles Dorety (Hobos), Jack Curtis (Railroad man), Billy Bletcher (Angry townsman at council meeting), Bill Wolfe, Donald Kerr, Don Brodie, Billy Engle, Robert Graves, Frank Hammond, Pat Harmon, Edward Hearn, John Ince, Warren Jackson, Joe Marba, Nelson McDowell (Townsmen).

*Original script title: Silver Streak. Production dates:* July 17–August 16, 1935. Released October 25, 1935, by RKO Radio Pictures. 78 minutes.

*Synopsis:* Roscoe Horne — "Roscoe the Rainmaker" — and his new assistant Billy arrive in Lima Junction, California, where, at the request of banker Henry Spencer, they intend to end the drought that has been crippling this farming community. Roscoe and Billy immediately clash with wealthy landowner Simon Parker, who is trying to cheat local farmers out of their properties via a shady deal involving the construction of a flume (a chute for carrying water).

While Roscoe plans to demonstrate his patented Magno-Magnetizer cloudburst-producing machine, Orville Parker, Simon's equally crooked son, steals the magnet from the device and disables it. A large crowd is needed for Roscoe's machine to function properly; he arranges to have two old locomotives collide in a spectacular fashion, which attracts a huge turnout. But the engineers refuse to start the engines because that dynamite has been placed in the tender to guarantee a spectacular explosion. Unaware of the dynamite, the boys decide to take over the engineering duties themselves. Billy inadvertently sends his locomotive in reverse, prompting Roscoe to try to catch him. A harrowing train chase ensues, during which the dynamite is discovered in Billy's tender. Roscoe saves Billy, the dynamite is safely detonated, and the locomotives head back to their starting point.

In the meantime, Margie has recovered the stolen magnet and the rainmaking machine is restored to working order. As Roscoe and Billy hop out of the cabs in the knick of time, the trains collide and the resulting smash-up unleashes a downpour.

"The first 50 minutes are too slow, too talky and too lacking in inventiveness to save 20 minutes of runaway train stuff.... May appeal mildly to their fans." — *Variety*

*Comments:* The Rainmakers represents Dorothy's last noteworthy appearance in a Wheeler and Woolsey picture. Her scenes with the boys are charming — their interaction is as strong as ever — and she performs one of her best duets with Bert, "Isn't Love the Grandest Thing?"

At times *The Rainmakers* has the feel of a two-reel comedy stretched to feature length, with scenes too languidly paced to be fully effective. Nevertheless, it's an underrated effort, with enough funny moments to compensate for some undeniable dry spots. The train chase compares favorably to the similar climax in the Marx Brothers' *Go West* (1940) and it remains one of the best-remembered set pieces from any Wheeler and Woolsey film.

Wheeler and Woolsey fans are divided on their opinions regarding *The Rainmakers*. Some dismiss it as one of the team's weaker endeavors, while others rank it just a notch below their best comedies. Nearly fifty years after the film was initially released, Dorothy was persuaded to watch it, presumably for the first time. She deemed it "not bad," which, coming from her, was high praise. However, she was thrilled to see her duet with Bert: "I always loved that number but I could never remember which movie we did it in. That was the best part of the picture for me."

## *Silly Billies* (1936)

*Director:* Fred Guiol. *Associate producer:* Lee Marcus. *Screenplay:* Al Boasberg, Jack Townley. *Story:* Thomas Lennon, Fred Guiol. *Assistant director:* Jean Yarbrough. *Cinematography:* Nick Musuraca, J. Roy Hunt. *Musical director:* Roy Webb. *Orchestrators:* Gene Rose, Clarence Wheeler. *Art direction:* Van Nest Polglase, Feild M. Gray. *Special effects:* Vernon Walker. *Sound:* John E. Tribby. *Film editor:* John Lockert.

*Song:* "Tumble On Tumble Weed" by Dave Dryer and Jack Scholl.

*Cast:* Bert Wheeler (Roy Banks), Robert Woolsey (Dr. Philip "Painless" Pennington), Dorothy Lee (Mary Blake), Harry Woods (Hank Bewley), Ethan Laidlaw (Mr. Trigger), Chief Thunderbird (Chief Cyclone), Delmar Watson (Martin), Dick Alexander (John Little), Maurice Black (Bandit with toothache), Leo Willis, Ivan Christie (Bandits), Richard Powell (Stagecoach driver), Nelson McDowell (Horse trader), Blanche Rose (Stagecoach passenger), Willie Best ("Excitement"), Edward Hearn (Mark, Martin's father), Dick Elliott (Mayor Culpepper), Stanley Blystone (Cavalry captain), Frank Hammond (Barker), Jim Thorpe (Medicine man), Chief Thundercloud, Phillip Armenta, Carl Mathews (Indians), Anna Demetrio (Princess Humming Bird), John "Blackie" Whiteford (Settler), Tommy Bond (Young boy), Joan Breslau (Young girl), Jerry Tucker (Young boy at camp), Harry Bernard (Prospector), Jack Rice (Cavalry officer), Lafe McKee, Mabel Forrest, Olin Francis, Ivar McFadden, Jack Curtis (Pioneers), Georgia O'Dell, Allen Sears, John Ince, Jane Keckley, Joe Marba.

*Working title:* The Wild West. *Production dates:* December 5, 1935–January 3, 1936. Released March 20, 1936, by RKO Radio Pictures. 64 minutes.

*Synopsis:* "Painless" dentist Dr. Philip Pennington, his assistant Roy Banks and schoolmarm Mary Blake are among the stagecoach passengers heading west to Little Town. The townsfolk have been gripped by the Gold Rush fever of 1850 and everyone is pulling up stakes and heading for gold territory. The boys set up shop in what they are led to believe is a prime location, only to later discover that the populace has moved on and they're the only ones left in town.

Dr. Pennington and Roy learn that the citizens will be slaughtered by Indians, an ambush set up by Hank Bewley (Harry Woods), the leader of Little Town's wagon train. The pair catches up with the caravan to warn the people of impending doom, but the finger of suspicion is pointed directly at them. They save the day during an Indian attack, handily dispatching the marauders by using a slingshot to fire dental sponges soaked in chloroform.

"May appeal to dyed in the wool W&W fans, but not even they are apt to regard it as one of the comedians' best. Draggy all the way and the gags are preposterous and stretched far too long.... Dorothy Lee has rather less to do than usual."—*Variety*

*Comments: Silly Billies* was the last and weakest of the thirteen feature-length films Dorothy made with Bert and Bob. Despite the slick production values and first-rate cinematography, the film is done in by a poor script and slack direction. The climactic Indian attack, which should have been the highlight of the picture, lacks the punch of previous comic finales, and even Bert and Dorothy's duet is a wasted opportunity.

Native American athlete Jim Thorpe, the first person ever to win Olympic medals for both the decathlon and pentathlon, appears in *Silly Billies* as a medicine man. Thorpe was stripped of his Olympic medals when it was learned he had played professional baseball; he went on to pursue a career in baseball, football and basketball. During the Great Depression, he fell upon hard times and took a variety of odd jobs, including bit roles in movies, usually playing Indians. He was the subject of the biopic *Jim Thorpe—All American* (1951), with Burt Lancaster in the lead role. The International Olympic Committee restored Thorpe's titles in 1983, thirty years after his death.

## *Twelve Crowded Hours* (1939)

*Director:* Lew Landers. *Producer:* Robert Sisk. *Screenplay:* John Twist. *Story:* Garrett Fort, Peter Ruric. *Contributor to story treatment:* Joe Bigelow. *Production executive:* Lee Marcus. *Cinematography:* Nicholas Musuraca. *Musical director:* Roy Webb. *Art Direction:* Van Nest Polglase. *Associate art director:* Albert D'Agostino. *Gowns:* Renié. *Special effects:* Vernon L. Walker. *Sound:* Hugh McDowell, Jr. *Film editor:* Harry Marker.

*Cast:* Richard Dix (Nick Green), Lucille Ball (Paula Sanders), Allan Lane (Dave Sanders), Donald MacBride (Sgt. Detective Joe Keller), Cyrus W. Kendall (George Costain), John Arledge (Red), Granville Bates (James McEwen), Bradley Page (Tom Miller), Dorothy Lee (Thelma), Addison Richards (Berquist), Murray Alper (Louie Allen), John Gallaudet (Jimmy), Joseph de Stephani (Rovitch a.k.a. Mr. Itch), Anthony Warde (Jerry Miller), Lee Van Atta (Copyboy), Kay Sutton (Miss Martin), Jack Rice (Professor Busby), Blue Washington (First bartender), Edgar Dearing (Second bartender), Emory Parnell (Doorkeeper), Mike Lally (Henchman), Greta Meyer (Mama Rovitch), Edmund Cobb (Pool hall proprietor), Stanley Blystone (Patrolman), George Davis (Gus the French waiter), Eleanor Hansen (Mary the hatcheck girl), Richard Clarke (Police driver), Dorothy Lovett (Cigarette girl), Bruce Sidney (Headwaiter), Ray Turner (Redcap).

*Production dates:* Late November–December 1938. Released March 3, 1939, by RKO Radio Pictures. (New York opening: February 24, 1939.) 64 minutes.

*Synopsis:* Over the course of twelve hectic hours, newspaper reporter Nick Green tries to expose a numbers racket run by ruthless crime lord George Costain. Nick's investigation is hampered by his rocky relationship with his sweetheart Paula Sanders, who thinks he framed her recently paroled brother.

"As the crime-busting reporter out to smash the policy ring (again), [Richard Dix] skips nimbly from peril to peril, covering the ground so fast that we hardly had a chance to see the familiar landmarks whisk by.... Mr. Dix is used to such slam-bang melodramatic stuff, Lucille

Ball plays it with just the appropriate air of somnambulism and Mr. [Cyrus W.] Kendall, as the heavy, is obviously to the manner born." —*New York Times*

*Comments:* This so-so newspaper yarn focuses squarely on its star, Richard Dix, with all the other cast members clearly in support. Cyrus W. Kendall gives a properly menacing performance as the villain of the piece, but for second-billed Lucille Ball, it was just another thankless assignment during her tenure as an RKO contract player.

In her first film in three years (and marking her return to RKO), Dorothy has a minor supporting role as Thelma, the switchboard operator at the newspaper office. In her brief scenes she primarily appears opposite comic-relief John Arledge, who had been one of her co-stars in a stage production of *She Loves Me Not*.

## *S.O.S. Tidal Wave* (1939)

*Director:* John H. Auer. *Associate producer:* Armand Schaefer. *Screenplay:* Maxwell Shane, Gordon Kahn. *Original story:* James Webb. *Production manager:* Al Wilson. *Cinematography:* Jack Marta. *Musical director:* Cy Feuer. *Additional music:* William Lava, Paul Sawtell, Joseph Nussbaum. *Art direction:* John Victor Mackay. *Supervising editor:* Murray Seldeen. *Film editor:* Ernest Nims.

*Cast:* Ralph Byrd (Jeff Shannon), George Barbier (Uncle Dan Carter), Kay Sutton (Laurel Shannon), Frank Jenks (Peaches Jackson), Marc Lawrence (Melvin Sutter), Dorothy Lee (Mabel), Oscar O'Shea (Mike Halloran), Mickey Kuhn (Buddy Shannon), Ferris Taylor (Clifford Farrow/Stanley Morgan), Donald Barry (Curley Parsons), Raymond Bailey (Roy Nixon), Forrest Taylor (James Ross), Lloyd Ingraham (Doctor), John Dilson (Appleby), Dave Willock (Page boy), Richard Cramer (Butch), Lynton Brent (Teletype operator), George Turner (Chester), Mickey Daniels (Messenger boy), Gino Corrado (Barber), Lew Davis (TV watcher), Rex Lease (Ambulance attendant), Robert J. Wilkie (Man in TV studio), Roy Barcroft (Lunch counter patron), Harrison Greene (Panicked citizen), Ben Taggart (Police officer), Hooper Atchley, Thomas Carr, Roy Darmour, George Montgomery, Crane Whitley, Elizabeth Valentine, Landers Stevens.

*Working title and British title: Tidal Wave. Production dates:* April 14–April 26, 1939. Released June 2, 1939, by Republic Pictures. 62 minutes.

*Synopsis:* Crusading television-newsreel reporter Jeff Shannon sets out to expose Clifford Farrow, a mayoral candidate whose campaign is being managed by Melvin Sutter, a ruthless racketeer. Sutter and his gang threaten the lives of Shannon's family and friends; when Farrow's corrupt background is publicly revealed, Sutter tries to keep voters away from the polls by broadcasting phony footage of a massive tidal wave inundating New York City.

"A synthetic quickie.... The tidal wave is simply tagged onto the picture as a convenient method of winding up a childish yarn about a mayoral race, a crooked candidate and a television reporter." —*New York Times*

*Comments:* This low-budget melodrama utilized the spectacular special-effects footage from Admiral Productions' *Deluge* (1933), an independent production distributed by RKO. In an era long before slick computer-generated images, Ned Mann (miniature model construction), Russell E. Lawson and Billy Williams (special effects photography) created scenes of apocalyptic destruction: the Empire State Building crumbling, Manhattan submerged, ships washed away.

In 1939 Republic Pictures acquired these cataclysmic scenes and fashioned a story around the footage. Taking a cue from the real-life public panic that ensued during Orson Welles's radio broadcast of *The War of the Worlds* the previous year, the screenwriters used the medium of television as the central theme of the picture.

Although commercial television wouldn't become commonplace until after World War II, *S.O.S. Tidal Wave* depicts TV as already being a part of everyday life: Members of the general public who don't own television sets can watch it at a variety of business establishments, which explains why Jeff Shannon is such a well-known media figure about town. (Oddly, the medium of radio takes a backseat to television in this tale.)

Republic was known for its serials, and the storyline here is prone to the same lapses in logic and continuity that you'd find in the average chapterplay. Since it's never made clear where the central action is taking place, it's open to conjecture as to how close (or far) the setting is from New York City. Judging from the terrified reaction of the local citizenry, it can't be too far away. In a convenient plot contrivance, everyone immediately falls for the tidal-wave hoax — because if they didn't, the story would have nowhere to go. Speaking of contrivances, Melvin Sutter and his gang are able to get their hands on the tidal-wave footage in virtually no time at all, thanks to a movie-rental outfit called Horror Films Incorporated (!).

The lead actors essay their roles as best they can, given the circumstances, with Ralph Byrd making a good, stalwart hero and Marc Lawrence appropriately menacing as the villain. Dorothy, in her last significant film role, plays Frank Jenks's long-suffering girlfriend. They make an unlikely pair but they establish a good rapport and provide some welcome (and much-needed) comic relief.

Movie buffs will recognize several character actors who make fleeting appearances, including Mickey Daniels, who was seen in numerous silent-era Our Gang comedies. Donald Barry, who plays mob henchman Curley Parsons, would later star in B-Westerns and serials billed as Don "Red" Barry. Former stuntman George Montgomery would soon become a high-profile contract player at 20th Century–Fox. Television would play a key role in the career of character actor Raymond Bailey (seen here as newspaper executive Roy Nixon), who became a familiar face to generations of TV viewers as wily bank president Milburn Drysdale on *The Beverly Hillbillies* (1962–1971).

*S.O.S. Tidal Wave* is unevenly paced, with an abundance of overly talky, dialogue-driven passages and intermittent bursts of action leading up to the stock footage-laden climax. Despite its poor reputation, however, the film is not entirely without interest and is best enjoyed when approached with lowered expectations.

Ever the cost-conscious operation, Republic would re-use the *Deluge* footage in two of their serials: *Dick Tracy vs. Crime. Inc.* (1941) and *King of the Rocketmen* (1949).

In 1952 a syndicated package of Republic features was marketed to local TV stations by Hollywood Television Service, a subsidiary of Republic. The selections (65 titles in all) were re-edited to fit one-hour time slots, allowing for commercial breaks. *S.O.S. Tidal Wave* was trimmed to a 53-minute running time.

For decades *Deluge* was considered a lost film, until an Italian-dubbed, English-subtitled version was made available to the home-video market through Wade Williams's Englewood Entertainment in 2000. During the years prior to its rediscovery, *Deluge* acquired a near-mythic reputation that it couldn't possibly have lived up to ... and it didn't.

## *Laddie* (1940)

Also known as *Gene Stratton-Porter's Laddie*.

*Director:* Jack Hively. *Producer:* Cliff Reid. *Screenplay:* Bert Granet, Jerry Cady; based on the novel by Gene Stratton-Porter. *Cinematography:* Harry Wild. *Original music:* Roy Webb. *Additional music:* Cyril J. Mockridge. *Orchestrators:* Gene Rose, Maurice De Packh, George Parrish, Charles Maxwell. *Art direction:* Van Nest Polglase. *Associate art director:* Carroll Clark. *Costumes:* Renié. *Sound recording:* Richard Van Hessen. *Special effects:* Vernon L. Walker. *Film editor:* George Hively.

*Cast:* Tim Holt (Laddie Stanton), Virginia Gilmore (Pamela Pryor), Joan Carroll ("Little Sister" Stanton), Spring Byington (Mrs. Stanton), Robert Barrat (John Stanton), Miles Mander (Charles Pryor), Esther Dale (Sarah), Sammy McKim (Leon Stanton), Joan Brodel [Joan Leslie] (Shelley Stanton), Martha O'Driscoll (Sally Pryor), Rand Brooks (Peter Dover), Mary Forbes (Anna Pryor), Peter Cushing (Robert Pryor), Dorothy Lee (Bridesmaid).

Released October 18, 1940, by RKO Radio Pictures. 69 minutes.

*Synopsis:* In a small Indiana farming community of the 1870s, Laddie Stanton falls in love with Pamela Pryor, the daughter of a newly arrived English landowner who disapproves of her interest in someone of lower social standing. In time, Laddie proves his worth by mending the strained relationship between the stern father and his estranged son.

"Despite its dated background and old-fashioned and simple story-telling technique, picture stills retains a sufficient hominess in its leisurely unfolding to be acceptable fare."—*Variety*

*Comments:* The semi-autobiographical Gene Stratton-Porter novel had been filmed twice before, in 1926 (by Film Booking Offices of America, a.k.a. FBO) and 1935 (by RKO). In this adaptation, Dorothy had an uncredited bit role as a bridesmaid. The film also marked early cinematic appearances by future stars Joan Leslie (billed as Joan Brodel) and Peter Cushing (as Charles Pryor's estranged son).

## *Repent at Leisure* (1941)

*Director:* Frank Woodruff. *Producer:* Cliff Reid. *Screenplay:* Jerry Cady. *Story:* James Gow, Armand d'Usseau. *Cinematography:* Nicholas Musuraca. *Original music:* Arthur Lange, Nathaniel Shilkret, Frank Tours, Edward Ward. *Art Direction:* Van Nest Polglase. *Associate art director:* Albert D'Agostino. *Gowns:* Renié. *Special effects:* Vernon L. Walker. *Sound:* John E. Tribby. *Film editor:* Harry Marker.

*Cast:* Kent Taylor (Richard Hughes), Wendy Barrie (Emily Baldwin/"Emily Smith"), George Barbier (Robert Cornelius "R.C." Baldwin), Thurston Hall (Jay Buckingham), Charles Lane (Clarence Morgan), Nella Walker (Sally Baldwin), Rafael Storm (Prince Paul Stephanie), Ruth Dietrich (Miss Flynn), Cecil Cunningham (Mrs. Morgan), "Snowflake" [Fred] Toones (Rufe), Michael Dunaway (Robert Cornelius "Bobby" Hughes), Dorothy Lee (Miss Lewis), George Chandler (Bus conductor), Georgia Backus (Nurse), Virginia Vale (Elevator operator), Jack Briggs (Phil the stock boy), Charles Coleman (Jerome the butler), Wanda Cantlon (Salesgirl), Jane Patten (Richard's secretary), Hooper Atchley (Floorwalker), Paul Le Pere, Barbara Burke (Clerks), Jack Gargan (Store employee), Norman Mayes (Porter), Eddie Arden (Messenger).

*Production dates:* Late January to mid–February 1941. Released April 4, 1941, by RKO Radio Pictures. 66 minutes.

*Synopsis:* Emily Baldwin, daughter of department store magnet R.C. Baldwin, breaks off her engagement to the fortune-hunting Prince Paul Stephanie and sets out to find if there's "some decent men left in the world." She meets and becomes attracted to Richard Hughes, a humble clerk at her father's store, but she keeps her real identity a secret. When flagging sales forces the firing of all single male employees, Richard asks Emily to pose as his wife, so he can keep his job. The charade spins out of control after the "married" couple adopts a baby to further the illusion of domestic bliss. Richard rises to the position of store manager, still unaware that Emily is the boss's daughter. When the truth is finally revealed, Richard breaks up with Emily and, adding insult to injury, goes to work for R.C.'s arch-rival, leaving Emily and her father to resort to desperate measures to win him back.

"This moderately budgeted program number, despite its falling to pieces for a finish, provides sufficient interest."—*Variety*

*Comments:* The overwhelming financial and critical success of Frank Capra's *It Happened One Night* (1934) resulted in scores of imitations and knock-offs, none of them capturing the magic of the original. *Repent at Leisure* begins as a blatant copy, as an impetuous young lady leaves her titled fiancé and runs off to find true love. Then the film strikes out in a different direction—or *directions*, as it twists and turns through screwball-comedy territory, with added touches of melodrama and knockabout slapstick. Not all of the ingredients mesh well, but deft performances by Wendy Barrie, Kent Taylor, George Barbier and a strong supporting cast compensate for the lack of cohesion.

Dorothy makes a fleeting, unbilled appearance as Miss Lewis, a flirtatious salesgirl who tells Richard, "If I wasn't going steady, I'd marry you myself." It was an ignominious note on which to end her association with RKO, where she had once been one of the studio's highest-profile contract stars.

## *Roar of the Press* (1941)

*Director:* Phil Rosen. *Producer:* Scott R. Dunlap. *Screenplay:* Albert Duffy. *Original story:* Alfred Block. *Cinematography:* Harry Neumann. *Assistant director:* Allen Wood. *Recording engineer:* Karl Zint. *Technical director:* E.R. Hickson. *Production manager:* C.J. [Charles] Bigelow. *Musical director:* Edward Kay. *Film editor:* Jack Ogilvie.

*Cast:* Jean Parker (Alice Williams), Wallace Ford (Wally Williams), Jed Prouty (Gordon MacEwan), Suzanne Kaaren (Angela Brooks), Harland Tucker (Harry Brooks), Evalyn Knapp (Evalyn), Robert Frazer (Louis Detmar), Dorothy Lee (Frances Harris), John Holland (Robert Mallon), Maxine Leslie (Mabel Leslie), Paul Fix (Sparrow McGraun), Betty Compson (Thelma Tate), Matty Fain (Nick Paul), Eddie Foster (Fingers), Charles King (Lt. Homer Thomas), Frank O'Connor (Lt. Jim Hall), Dennis Moore (Toughy), Robert Pittard (Tim the newsboy), Byron Foulger (Eddie Tate), Donald Kerr (Red Keane), Lester Dorr (Switchboard operator), Mildred Shay (Helen), Pat Gleason (Jim Leslie), Jack Cheatham, Lynton Brent, Jack Perrin (Reporters), I. Stanford Jolley (Pedestrian who finds note), Charles McMurphy (Policeman).

*Working title: Widows of the Press. Production dates:* Mid- to late March 1941. Released April 18, 1941, by Monogram Pictures Corporation. 71 minutes.

*Synopsis:* Even when he's on his honeymoon, hot-shot newspaper reporter Wally Williams is still being handed assignments by his editor, Gordon MacEwan. Other reporters' wives caution Wally's new bride Alice that she's now "a widow of the press." During a murder investigation, Wally and Alice tangle with a ring of fifth-column saboteurs.

"A synthetic conception of a daring reporter in action.... Nearly all plot elements seem quaintly familiar, except done so much better in previous films."—*Variety*

*Comments:* In this slow-moving comedy-mystery with deliberate overtones of *The Front Page*, Dorothy had a two-minute scene as Frances Harris, Wally's jilted sweetheart. Monogram press materials touted this as Dorothy's "comeback" but it could hardly be called that.

## *Too Many Blondes* (1941)

*Director:* Thornton Freeland. *Associate producer:* Joseph G. Sanford [Joseph Gershenson]. *Screenplay:* Maxwell Shane, Louis S. Kaye. *Original story:* Maxwell Shane. *Cinematography:* Milton Krasner. *Musical director:* Charles Previn. *Music arranger:* Walter O'Keefe. *Incidental music:* Frank Skinner. *Art Direction:* Jack Otterson. *Associate art director:* Richard H. Riedel. *Set decorations:* R.A. [Russell] Gausman. *Gowns:* Vera West. *Assistant director:* Vernon Keays. *Sound supervisor:* Bernard B. Brown. *Sound technician:* William Hedgcock. *Film editor:* Bernard W. Burton.

*Songs:* "Whistle Your Blues to a Bluebird," "Don't Mind If I Do" and "Let's Love Again" by Milton Rosen and Everett Carter; "The Man on the Flying Trapeze" by Alfred Lee and George Leybourne (although the credits list Walter O'Keefe as the composer).

*Cast:* Rudy Vallee (Dick Kerrigan), Helen Parrish (Virginia "Ginny" Kerrigan), Lon Chaney Jr. (Marvin Gimble), Jerome Cowan (Ted Bronson), Shemp Howard (Ambrose Tripp), Iris Adrian (Hortense Kent), Eddie Quillan (Wally Pelton), Irving Bacon (Mr. Twitchell), Jeanne Kelly [Jean Brooks] (Angie DuValle), Paco [Francisco] Moreno (Luis Garvanza/"Garbonza"), Gus Schilling (Elevator operator), Dorothy Lee (Lorene LaRue), Carmela and Jose Cansino (Dancers), Dinorah [Dinora] Rego ("Chick-a-Boom" singer), Humberto Herrera and Orchestra, Marek Windheim (Cousin Manuel), Eddie Bruce (Ken Atterbury), Paul McVey (Mr. Talbot), Charles Trowbridge (John V. Barton), Ethelreda Leopold (Barton's secretary), Joey Ray (Chris

Jackson), Janet Warren (Sophie Deltz), Jolly Rowlings (Smiley), Douglas Evans (UBC radio announcer), Jerry Mandy (Bartender), Eddie Coke (Usher), Guy D'Ennery (Croupier), Joe Recht (Messenger), Paul Ellis (Hotel clerk), Gene O'Donnell, Reid Kilpatrick (Announcers), James Conaty, Edmund Mortimer (Nightclub patrons), Catherine Winter (Salesgirl), Kernan Cripps (Gate official), Milton Kibbee (Brakeman), Jasper Weldon (Porter), Ernest Wilson (Red cap).

*Production dates:* April 2 to mid–April 1941. Released August 1, 1941, by Universal Pictures. 60 minutes.

*Synopsis:* Dick and Virginia Kerrigan, two-thirds of a singing trio known as "The Bluebirds," agree to stay married until they can save up enough money for a divorce. Dick doesn't want to break up with Virginia, but she no longer trusts him because there have been too many blondes in his life, despite his assurances that they're all "old professional friends." Complicating these delicate marital negotiations is the third Bluebird, Ted Bronson, who's smitten with Virginia.

"Too little entertainment.... [It] sputters and stutters due to inadequacies in both the story and the script. Nothing direction nor cast can do about it — the basic material just isn't there." — *Variety*

*Comments:* This was one of several inexpensive musical-comedies churned out by Universal during this period. Occasionally, the assembly line concocted a noteworthy effort, such as the mega-hit *Buck Privates* (1941) starring Abbott & Costello and the Andrews Sisters. More often than not, however, the results were quick, painless, and eminently forgettable — which perfectly sums up *Too Many Blondes*.

Crooner Rudy Vallee enjoyed great popularity with his recordings and radio program, yet he had difficulty achieving similar success in motion pictures — though he would prove himself to be a marvelous character comedian in Preston Sturges's *The Palm Beach Story* (1942). Unfortunately, *Too Many Blondes* doesn't give Vallee the same opportunity to shine. Vallee's low-key personality often came across less than dynamic in front of a movie camera, and the inclusion of an audience-sing along rendition of "The Man on the Flying Trapeze" (with lyrics printed onscreen during the chorus) may have been an attempt on his part to connect directly with the audience.

There's barely enough plot to propel this one-hour film, but there's no shortage of activity, with a half-dozen musical interludes tossed into the mix and a supporting cast brimming with seasoned comedians and character actors. For Helen Parrish, Lon Chaney Jr. and Jerome Cowan, this was just another assignment to fulfill contractual obligations, and they display more enthusiasm than their cardboard roles warrant. Shemp Howard, Iris Adrian, and Eddie Quillan deliver lively performances, carrying on as though they actually had quality material to work with.

In her final film appearance, a 29-year-old Dorothy plays Lorene LaRue, one of Vallee's blonde "friends." She's flip and funny, and her two brief scenes are over with much too quickly.

# Chapter Notes

## Chapter 3

1. A fictionalized account of Edwards' career was presented in the 1939 movie *The Star Maker* starring Bing Crosby as "Larry Earl."

2. When Woolsey left the Broadway production of *Rio Rita* six months into the run, he was replaced by Catlett. Woolsey later rejoined the show and also repeated his role for the film adaptation.

3. Although Fay Wray had appeared in a number of films at this point in her career — notably *The Street of Sin* (1927) and *The Wedding March* (1928) — she would achieve movie immortality for her role in *King Kong* (1933).

4. RKO issued a press release saying that the project was "postponed indefinitely" but didn't offer any follow-up announcements. Referencing outdated publicity blurbs, some fan magazines referred to the never-made *Babes in Toyland* as Dorothy's "latest release." In 1933, producer Hal Roach brought the rights to *Babes in Toyland* and it was fashioned into a vehicle for Stan Laurel and Oliver Hardy. Released as *Babes in Toyland* (1934), the film was reissued over the years under the alternate titles *March of the Wooden Soldiers* and *Revenge Is Sweet*. It has been remade twice (in 1961 and 1986). Since the operetta had no plot, these remakes have reworked the storyline of the Laurel and Hardy film.

5. On August 11, 1930, Dorothy recorded "My One Ambition Is You" for RCA Victor, with composer Harry Tierney accompanying her on the piano. The recording was not released commercially.

## Chapter 4

1. Arbuckle ranked among the screen's most popular comedians until 1921 when he became the center of one of Hollywood's most notorious celebrity trials. He was accused of raping an actress named Virginia Rappe, and her death triggered a scandal that ruined his career. Although he was eventually acquitted, the negative publicity rendered him unemployable as a performer and he worked behind the scenes for several years. He began appearing in movies again in 1932, and was on the verge of a comeback when he died the following year.

## Chapter 5

1. The film was referred to as *Peach O'Reno* in the press materials and copyright records but the onscreen title is *Peach-O-Reno*.

2. An uncredited Busby Berkeley choreographed the bizarre presentation of "I Got Rhythm," which incorporates swirling spotlights, undulating cacti, a bouncing stuffed owl and a swaying bison head. Perhaps these touches were added to take the viewer's mind off of Kitty Kelly's ghastly vocalizing.

## Chapter 6

1. Although Dorothy received third billing in the cast list at the end of *Girl Crazy*, she was billed seventh in the opening credits and billed fourth in publicity materials.
2. Built in the 1920s, the Harold Lloyd Estate consisted of a 44-room mansion with a tennis court and a golf course.
3. The Hearst Castle was like a kingdom unto itself, with tennis courts, gardens and a private zoo. It had 56 bedrooms, 61 bathrooms, 19 sitting rooms, indoor and outdoor swimming pools, a hilltop patio and a movie theater. Orson Welles used it as the inspiration for Charles Foster Kane's opulent mansion in *Citizen Kane* (1941).
4. "Pooch" was a reference to a life-size stuffed toy dog that Fred gave to Dorothy; she was seen posing with the gift in numerous publicity shots.

## Chapter 7

1. A dictation routine with Robert Woolsey and Dorothy Granger in *Hips, Hips, Hooray!* was another jettisoned bit from *Duck Soup*. It was originally scripted for Groucho and Zeppo Marx.
2. *Cockeyed Cavaliers* and *Hips, Hips, Hooray!* were the first Wheeler and Woolsey pictures to adequately establish "good sound" for Dorothy's voice. In the early talkies, her voice was recorded at a higher pitch that made her sound "squeaky"—something that affected many film actors of the era. Now her voice could be heard as it actually sounded in real life.
3. *She Loves Me Not* was adapted for the screen twice: Miriam Hopkins played Curley Flagg in *She Loves Me Not* (1934), and Sheree North played the role in *How to Be Very, Very Popular* (1955).

## Chapter 8

1. *Radio City Revels* was a property waiting in the bullpen for Bert and Bob after *High Flyers*. When it became obvious that Bob would never be able work again, *Radio City Revels* went into production with Milton Berle and Jack Oakie in the roles intended for Bert and Bob.
2. In 1941, Warner Brothers produced two service comedies that came close to capturing the style, if not the content, of the Wheeler and Woolsey films. *You're in the Army Now* paired bumbling Jimmy Durante with bespectacled wise-guy Phil Silvers for a catalogue of military antics not unlike the kind Bert and Bob would have indulged in. Closer still was *Navy Blues*, with Jack Haley as a baby-faced patsy and Jack Oakie as his loudmouth pal. Their interaction is very similar to Bert and Bob's, and their comic duet "When Are We Going to Land Abroad?" would have been perfectly suited for Wheeler and Woolsey.

## Chapter 9

1. Some claimed that the attack on Pearl Harbor, which occurred three days after the opening, and America's resulting entry into World War II further hurt ticket sales for a show in which the male lead gets killed during the War of 1812.
2. Bert repeated his stage and film role.
3. Dancer-actress Eleanor Norris married Buster Keaton in 1940. The marriage, his third, lasted until his death in 1966.
4. Actor Wayne Morris (*Paths of Glory*, *Kid Galahad*, *I Wanted Wings*) served as a Navy fighter pilot during World War II and was awarded four Distinguished Flying Crosses and two Air Medals.
5. Bert's role in *Las Vegas Nights* (1941) marked his last appearance in a feature film. He ended his screen career by starring in a pair of comedy shorts for Columbia Pictures, *Innocently Guilty* (1950) and *The Awful Sleuth* (1951).

## Chapter 11

1. Dorothy remained connected to Fred Waring through one of his sons, whom she occasionally had lunch with, and maintained a friendship with Peter T. Kiefer, the coordinator of Waring's estate.

# Bibliography

## Books

Adamson, Joe. *Groucho, Harpo, Chico, and Sometimes Zeppo: A History of the Marx Brothers and a Satire on the Rest of the World.* New York: Simon & Schuster, 1973.

Barrios, Richard. *A Song in the Dark: The Birth of the Musical Film.* Oxford: Oxford University Press, 1995.

Bradley, Edwin M. *The First Hollywood Musicals: A Critical Filmography of 171 Features, 1927 through 1932.* Jefferson, NC: McFarland, 1996.

Drew, William M. *At the Center of the Frame: Leading Ladies of the Twenties and Thirties.* Lanham, MD: Vestal Press, 1999.

Epstein, Lawrence J. *Mixed Nuts: America's Love Affair with Comedy Teams.* New York: Public Affairs, 2004.

Hischak, Thomas S. *The Rodgers and Hammerstein Encyclopedia.* Westport, CT: Greenwood, 2001.

Jenkins, Henry. *What Made Pistachio Nuts?: Early Sound Comedy and the Vaudeville Aesthetic.* New York: Columbia University Press, 1992.

Jewell, Richard B., with Vernon Harbin. *The RKO Story.* New York: Arlington House/Crown, 1982.

Keaton, Buster, with Charles Samuels. *My Wonderful World of Slapstick.* Garden City, NY: Doubleday, 1960.

Kreuger, Miles (editor). *The Movie Musical from Vitaphone to "42nd Street."* New York: Dover, 1975.

Liebman, Roy. *Vitaphone Films: A Catalogue of the Features and Shorts.* Jefferson, NC: McFarland, 2003.

Maltin, Leonard. *Movie Comedy Teams.* New York: Signet/The New American Library, 1970.

McCaffrey, Donald W. *The Golden Age of Sound Comedy: Comic Films and Comedians of the Thirties.* Cranbury, NJ: A.S. Barnes, 1973.

Miller, Don. *B Movies.* New York: Curtis Books, 1973.

Munn, Michael. *The Hollywood Murder Casebook.* New York: St. Martin's, 1987.

Neibaur, James L. *The RKO Features: A Complete Filmography of the Feature Films Released or Produced by RKO Radio Pictures, 1929–1960.* Jefferson, NC: McFarland, 1994.

Robinson, Jeffrey. *Teamwork: The Cinema's Greatest Comedy Teams.* New York: Proteus, 1982.

Skretvedt, Randy. *Laurel and Hardy: The Magic Behind the Movies.* Beverly Hills, CA: Moonstone Press, 1987.

Slide, Anthony. *The Vaudevillians: A Dictionary of Vaudeville Performers.* Westport, CT: Arlington House, 1981.

Springer, John, and Jack D. Hamilton. *They Had Faces Then: Superstars, Stars and Starlets of the 1930s*. Secaucus, NJ: Citadel Press, 1974.

Walker, Alexander. *The Shattered Silents: How the Talkies Came to Stay*. Great Britain: Elm Tree Books/Hamish Hamilton, 1978.

Watz, Edward. *Wheeler and Woolsey: The Vaudeville Comic Duo and Their Films, 1929–1937*. Jefferson, NC: McFarland, 1994.

## Articles

Albert, Katherine. "The Million Dollar Baby: One of the Prettiest, Brightest Things That Ever Happened in Hollywood — Little Dynamite Dorothy Lee!" *Photoplay* (April 1931).

Bell, Nelson B. "Film Funsters Take Reporter for Nice Ride." *The Washington Post* (January 15, 1934).

Brotherton, Jamie. "Bert Wheeler, Robert Woolsey and Dorothy Lee: An Unforgettable Team." *Classic Images* (September 1998).

_____. "Dorothy Lee: Farewell to the Stunning Beauty of the 1930's." *Big Reel* (September 1999).

_____. "Dorothy Lee: RKO's Brightest Star." *Big Reel* (July 1996).

_____, with William M. Drew. "Robert Woolsey: Zany Comic." *Classic Images* (July 2002).

Burke, Marcella. "Hollywood's Pet Starlet: Dorothy Lee Is Scampering Her Way to Success Just for the Fun of It." *Screen Play Secrets* (December 1930).

Byron, John. "She Packs a Wallop: Dorothy Lee Has Muscled Her Way into Stardom." *Silver Screen* (April 1931).

Carr, Constance. "Dot Dashes Along: Miss Lee's Young Life Has Been One Mad Rush Toward Stardom." *Screenland* (May 1931).

Collura, Joe. "Dorothy Lee: That Wheeler and Woolsey Girl." *Classic Images* (December 1994).

Drew, William M. "The Screwball Satirists: Wheeler and Woolsey." *American Classic Screen* (March/April 1978).

Fryxell, David. "Remember Dorothy? She Used to Be in the Movies." *Dubuque Telegraph-Herald* (September 1, 1982).

Glosson, William M. "When the Money Starts Rolling In." *Silver Screen* (December 1931).

Maltin, Leonard. "Wheeler and Woolsey." *Film Fan Monthly* #83 (May 1968).

Miller, Mark A. "Wheeler and Woolsey: Part One." *Filmfax* #29 (October/November 1991).

_____. "Wheeler and Woolsey: Part Two." *Filmfax* #30 (December 1991/January 1992).

Okuda, Ted. "Dorothy Lee Remembers Wheeler & Woolsey." *Classic Images* (March 1985).

_____. "Dorothy Lee: The Wheeler and Woolsey Girl." *Filmfax* #29 (October/November 1991).

_____. "Wheeler and Woolsey." *Classic Film Collector* (Spring 1978).

Page, Eleanor. "Dorothy Lee: A Collector's Item for Film Fans." *Chicago Tribune* (April 19, 1976).

Ramsey, Walter. "An Eye-Opener: Things Happen to People Who Meet and Talk to Dorothy Lee." *Motion Picture Classic* (November 1930).

Ray, Richard. "Miss Midget: A Close-up of the Little Girl — Dorothy Lee to You — Who's Known to Most of Hollywood as Midge." *Photoplay* (October 1930).

Simpson, Grace. "Lovers Propose." *Silver Screen* (May 1931).

# Index

Numbers in *italics* indicate Filmography entries.
Numbers in ***bold italics*** indicate photographs.

Abbott, Bud 48, 133
Abbott, George 94
Actors Equity Association 76
Allen, Gracie 9
Alvarado, Don 28
American Movie Classics 139
Ames, Leon 76
Amos 'n' Andy 44
Anderson, John Murray 94, 109, 114
Andre, Lona 92
Appleby, Dorothy 92
Appleton, Martha *see* O'Driscoll, Martha
Arbuckle, Roscoe "Fatty" 29, 40
Arledge, John 90, 91, 107
Ashe, Arthur 122
*Assorted Nuts see Cracked Nuts*
Astaire, Adele 66
Astaire, Fred 66, 87, 103, 104
*At the Center of the Frame: Leading Ladies of the Twenties and Thirties* 141
Ates, Rosco (Roscoe) 86
Atwater, A. G. 97, 101, 105, ***106***, 107–111, 115
Atwater, Donna 111, ***119***
Aylesworth, Merlin 67, 75

*Babes in Toyland* 32, 33, *179*
*Bad Girl* 55
Ball, Lucille 107
Ballard, Francis Drake "Pat" 32
Bankhead, Tallulah 81
Barrie, Sir James 69
Barry, Phyllis 84
Barrymore, Lionel 76
Beaumont, Lucy 56
Beery, Noah 88
Beery, Wallace 50
Bellamy, Ralph 76
*Benchwarmer* 116
Benedict, Brooks 66

Bennett, Barbara 16, 17
Bennett, Constance 16
Bennett, Joan 16
Berkeley, Busby 129, 131
Berle, Milton 93
Berle, Sadie 93
Bersbach, Betsy 115, 124, 141
Bersbach, Bill 115, 126
Bersbach, Brent 115, 141
Bersbach, Dick 113, 115
Bersbach, Frank John 115, 116, 123
Bersbach, Frank John, Sr. 115
Bogart, Humphrey 76
Boles, John 25, 28, 30
Bolton, Guy 29
Bond, Lilian ***78***
Boothe, Robert ***11***, 12, 18, 19
Borzage, Frank 55
*Bottoms Up see So This Is Africa*
Bradley, Estelle *see* Lamont, Estelle
Brady, Alice 76
Brice, Monte 78
Briggs, Matt 84
Briskin, Barney 77
*The Broadway Melody* 19
Brooke, Tyler 76
Brotherton, Jamie 139, 143, 144
Brown, Joe E. 12, 50, 59, ***60***, 61, 105, 108, 116
Brown, Margaret 46
Buka, Donald 118
Bundy, May Sutton 74
Burke, Edwin J. 55
Burke, Kathleen 92
Burns, George 9
Burtis, James 84
Byfield, Ernie 115

C & C Movietime 120, 121, 133, 134
Cabot, Bruce 86, 92
Cagney, James 76, 111

Calderini, Charles 123, 124, 126–129, ***130***, 136, 140, 141
Calderini, Eleanor 123
Caldwell, Anne 33, 46
Calvin, Henry 118
*The Campus Flirt* 51
Cantor, Eddie 21, 23, 75, 76
Carlisle, Mary 92, 93
Carol, Sue 46
Carson, Johnny 136
Catlett, Walter 22
*Caught Plastered* 56, ***58***, 59, *158*, *159*
Cavallo, John 139, 140
Cawthorn, Joseph 61, ***62***
Chandler, Chick 76, ***77***, 87
Chaney, Bess *see* Millsap, Bess
Chaney, Elizabeth 5, 44
Chaplin, Charlie 21, 74, 106, 136
Charisse, Cyd 10
*Check and Double Check* 44
*The Cherry Hunt* 47
Chesterfield Pictures 92
Chevalier, Maurice 50
Choos, George 12, 13
Churchill, Berton 76, 98
Churchill, Marguerite 92
Churchill, Winston 74
Clark, Bobby 29, 70, 83
Cline, Edward F. 44
Clyde, June 30, 41, 80, 90, 93, 113, 116, 124, ***125***, 136, 137
*Cockeyed Cavaliers* 87, 88, ***89***, 90, 98, 135, 140, *166*, *167*
Cocoanut Grove 75, 76
Collins, Monty 62
Columbia Pictures 70, 75
Compton, Joyce 45, 46
Cooley, Mrs. Charles 71, 72
Cooper, Gary 50, 76
Cooper, Merian C. 75, 83
Costello, Lou 48, 133
*The Cowboy Quarterback* 108

183

# Index

Cox, Bill 118, 119
Cox, Lee 118
*Cracked Nuts (Assorted Nuts)* 39, 44, 46–48, **47**, **49**, 50, 58, 59, *155*, *156*
Craven, Frank 53
Crawford, Joan 10, 50
Crosby, Bing 41, 116, 117
*The Cuckoos* **31**, 32, 33, 39, 41, 44, 50, 83, 87, *150*, *151*
Cugat, Xavier 76
Curran, Homer 90
*The Curtain Falls* 92, 101, *169*, *170*

*Dance Band* 93
Daniels, Bebe 12, 24, 25, 28, 30, 32, 33, 50, 51
Davies, Marion 74
Davis, George 51, **52**
Day, Doris 10
Dee, Frances 46
de Lange, Eddie 37
Dell, Claudia 71
Delmar, Viña 55
*Deluge* 108, *175*
DiCiccio, Pat 104, 105
Dickinson, Homer 9–11, 21, 86
*Diplomaniacs* 75
Dix, Richard 50, 107
*Dixiana* 12, 32–34, **35**, 44, 46, 83, 89, 108, 114, *151*, *152*
Downey, Morton **17**
Downey, Morton, Jr. 17
Drake, Alfred 110
Drew, William M. 141
Duffield, Betty 126
Duffield, Harriett 81, 100
Duffield, Marshall 71, **72**, 77, 80, 81, 91–93, 97, 98, 111, 126
Dumont, Margaret 30
Dunn, James 77–79
Dunne, Irene 32, 50, 87
Durante, Jimmy 70, 93

Eagan, Frank 6
Ebert, Roger 136
Educational Pictures 100
Edwards, Cliff "Ukelele Ike" 77–79
Edwards, Gus 21
*Eight Girls in a Boat* 81
Eilers, Sally 55
Ellis, Kay 73
Etting, Ruth 85
*Everything's Rosie* 53
Ewell, Tom 114

Fairbanks, Douglas 8
Fairbanks, Douglas, Jr. 8, 50
Fanchon and Marco (Fanny and Mike Wolff) 10–12, 30, 87
Faversham, Phillip 90
Faye, Alice 111

FBO (Film Booking Offices of America, Inc.) 16
Fidler, Jimmie 46, **47**, 54, 59, 70–72, 108, **109**, 116, 128
Fields, Stanley 44, 48, **65**, 66
Fields, W.C. 5, 23, 51, 53, 133
Film Booking Offices of America, Inc. *see* FBO
Fitzgerald, Dallas M. 72, 73
Flavin, Jimmy (James) 87
Flicker Buffs 134, 135
Flynn, Errol 111
*Follow the Fleet* 103, **104**
*Footlites* 70–72
Fox Studio *see* 20th Century–Fox
Francis, Noel 23
*Frat Heads* 86, 87
Frazee, Treva 118
*The Fred Waring Show* 118
Freeland, Thornton 80, 93, 113, 114, 136
*Full of Notions* see *Caught Plastered*

Gable, Clark 76
Garber, Dorothy **98**
Garber, Jan 97
Garland, Judy 66, 111
Gay, Alden 76
Gentile, Pietro 71
Gerswhin, George 64, 66
Gerswhin, Ira 64, 66
Gibson, Althea 121
Gilbert, Billy 88
Gillmore, Frank 76
*Girl Crazy* (1930 play) 64
*Girl Crazy* (1932) 64, **65**, 66, 67, 69, *160–162*
*Girl Crazy* (1943) 67
Gleason, James 76
Gleason, Russell 51
Glennon, Bert 16
*Good News* (1927 play) 13, 63
Gould, Dave 15
Grable, Betty 69, 95
Grae, Margaret Kudner *see* Wheeler, Betty
Grafton, Gloria 95
Grant, Cary 45
Grauman, Sid 76
Gray, Lawrence 93
Green, Bud 17
Green, Mitzi 50, **65**, 66
Grieg, Robert 88
Gries, Joseph 116
Guiol, Fred 99, 102

Haines, Sally 106
*Half Shot at Sunrise* 37, **38**, 40, 43, 48, 58, 73, 85, 98, *152*, *153*
Hall, Charlie 88
Hall, Ruth 59
Hamilton, Lloyd 101

Hammerstein, Oscar 114
Harding, Ann 76, 87
Hardy, Oliver 50, 105, 133, 136
Harlow, Jean 76
Harolde, Ralf 33, 42, 44, 46
Harris, Phil 76
Hart, Lorenz 94
Hartline, Mary 124
Havel, Arthur 80
Havel, Morton 80
Hayes, Grace 111
Hayes, Peter Lind 111
Healy, Mary 111
Hearst, William Hearst 74
Hecht, Ben 93
Held, John, Jr. 15
*Hello Yourself* 12, 13, 16–18, 24, 32, 37
*Hellzapoppin'* 70, 86
Hepburn, Katharine 87
Herbert, Hugh 42, 44, 51, **52**
Herbert, Victor 32, 33
Higgins, Wee-Wee 22
*High Flyers* 44, 105, 106
*Hips, Hips, Hooray!* 83, **84**, 85–89, 98, 134, *165*, *166*
*Hold 'Em Jail* 39, 65, 67, 69, 95
*Hollywood on the Air* 108, **109**
*Hook Line and Sinker* 42–44, 46, 50, 56, 59, *153*, *154*
Hope, Bob 116, 117
Hope, Edward 90
Hopton, Russell 90
*Howdy Doody* 117, 118
Howland, Jobyna 30, 42, 44
Hughes, Howard 76
Hunter, Ian 17
Hutton, Betty 75

*I Love Lucy* 79
*If I Was Rich* 55
*If This Isn't Love* 92, *167*
*In the Spotlight* 92, *168*

Jacquemot, Ray 118
Jarrett, Arthur 76
*The Jazz Singer* 16
Jenks, Frank 108
Jennings, DeWitt 56
Jessel, George 21
Johnson, Chic 70, 75, 86, 133
Johnston, Johnny 118
Jolson, Al 16, 74, 75
Jones, Allan 122
Judge, Arline **65**, 66
*Jumbo* 93–95, 109
*Just Imagine* 75, 135

Kaiser, Helen 28
Kalmar, Bert 29, 83–85
Kane, Eddie 50, 61
Karloff, Boris 48, 49, 76
Keaton, Buster 24, 25, 40, 50,

# Index

60, 70, 100, 101, 105, 106, 118, **119**, 120, 126, 127, 136, 180
Keaton, Eleanor (Eleanor Norris) 118, 119, 180
Keeler, Ruby 74, 75, 129, 131
Keith, Ian 76
Kelland, Clarence Buddington 70
Kelly, Gene 109–111
Kelly, Kitty **65**, 66
Kelly, Patsy 129
Kelton, Pert 86
Kennedy, John F. 115
*Kentucky Kernels* 92, 97, 98
King, Walter Woolf (Walter Wolfe) 92
Knight, June 77, 78

LaCava, Gregory 51
*Laddie* 113, *175, 176*
Lake, Alice 40
Lamont, Charles 92, 101
Lamont, Estelle (Estelle Bradley) 101
Landers, Lew 107
*Laugh and Get Rich* 39, 44, 51, **52**, 53, 55, 65, 73, 121, *156, 157*
Laughton, Charles 111
Laurel, Stan 50, 105, 133, 136
LeBaron, William 24, 29, 31, 64, 65, 76
Lebedeff, Ivan 30
Lee, Dixie 41
LeRoy, Hal 92, 118
LeRoy, Mervyn 60
Lewis, Jerry 133
Lewis, Mitchell 30
Liberty Pictures 92, 93
*Lights of New York* 16
Lindberg, Charles 74
Lindsay, Howard 90
Lloyd, George 110
Lloyd, Harold 22, 60, 74, 116, 136
*Local Boy Makes Good* 12, 59, **60**, 61, *158*
Lockhart, Gene 76
Logan, Ella 95
Loper, Don 110
Louise, Anita 53
Luciano, Charlie "Lucky" 105
Lugosi, Bela 76
Luke, Keye 92

MacArthur, Charles 93
MacFarlane, George 37
MacGregor, Edgar 90
MacLean, Douglas 51
Madison, Noel 76
Malcolm, Durie Kerr 115
Maltin, Leonard 133
Mankiewicz, Herman J. 64
March, Fredric 76
Marion, George, Sr. 42
Markey, Gene 16

Marshall, Everett 33
Martin, Crispin (Chris-Pin) **65**, 66
Martin, Dean 133
Marx, Groucho 21, 23, 30
Marx, Zeppo 85
The Marx Brothers 74, 83, 105, 108, 133
Mason, LeRoy 73
Matteson, Ruth 71
May, Ada 23, 25
Mayfair, Mitzi 79
*Mazie* 72, 73, *162*
McAteer, Dorothy 18
McCrea, Joel 45, 46
McCullough, Paul 29, 70, 83
McDonald, Grace 109, 110
McGuire, William Anthony 55
Meeker, George 84
Menjou, Adolphe 76
Merman, Ethel 64, 78
Metro-Goldwyn-Mayer 19, 44, 64, 111, 118
Miller, Charles 76
Miller, Mark A. 140
Mills, Virgie 140
Millsap, Bess 5–7, 12
Millsap, Homer C. 5, 7, 8, 59
Millsap, Marjorie Elizabeth (referencing Dorothy Lee's birth name) 5, **6, 7**, 8, 121
Millsap, Melissa 8, 137
Mitchell, Grant 76
Monogram Pictures 113
Montgomery, Robert 76
Moore, Grace 33
Moore, M.L. 5
Moorhead, Natalie 44
Moran, Tom 21, 22
Morgan, Kewpie 88
Morgan, Ralph 76
Morison, Patricia 118
Morris, Chester 76
Morris, Wayne 121
*Movie Comedy Teams* 133
Mowbray, Alan 76
Muir, Esther 75
*Mummy's Boys* 105
Muni, Paul 76
Murray, J. Harold 23
*Musical Comedy Time* 118
*My Wonderful World of Slapstick* 119
Mycroft, Walter C. 93
Myers, Richard 15

Nair, Evalyn 13, 14
Neilan, Marshall "Mickey" 12
*New Orleans (Sunny River)* 114
*The Nitwits* 95, 97, 98
*No, No, Nanette* (1971 revival) 129
Norris, Eleanor *see* Keaton, Eleanor
Norton, Jack 88
Nugent, Eddie **94**

Oakie, Jack 50, 76
O'Connor, John 18
O'Day, Nell 110
O'Driscoll, Martha 124, **125**
*Off Side* 51
Okuda, Ted 134, 144, 145
*The Old Homestead* 93, **94**, *170, 171*
Oldfield, Barney 5
Oliver, Edna May 14, 32, 39, 47, 48, 51, **52**
Olsen, Ole 70, 75, 86, 133
*On Again—Off Again* 44, 105
*One for the Money* 109, **110**, 114
O'Neal, Zelma 61, **62**, 63
Our Gang 50

Padilla, Marguerita 30
Pan, Hermes 88, 103
Pangborn, Franklin 88
Paramount Pictures 6, 12, 24, 64, 109
Parker, Patricia 77
Pathé Studio 16, 63
*Peach-O-Reno (Peach O'Reno)* 61, **62**, 63, 98, *159, 160*
Pendleton, Nat 76
Penner, Joe 108
Pennington, Ann 15
*Penthouse Party* see *Without Children*
*Peter Pan* 69
Petrie, Walter 23
*Plane Crazy* 80, *164*
Plunkett, Walter **89**
Plymouth Pictures Corporation 72, 73
Pollard, Snub 88
Powell, Dick 76
*A Preferred List* 76, **77**, *163*
The Pump Room 115

Quillan, Eddie **65**, 66

Radio Pictures *see* RKO Radio Pictures
*Radio Revels* 29, 31; *see also The Cuckoos*
*Radio Revels of 1929* 42
*Radio Revels of 1930* 42
*Rah Rah Daze* 32, 34, 35
*The Rainmakers* 97, 98, **99**, 100, 102, *171, 172*
*The Ramblers* 29, 83
Ray, Leah 76
Raye, Martha 75
Razzore, Bill "Razz" 47
Razzore, Honey 47
Reagan, Ronald 111, 116
Reed, Luther 26, 32, 83
Reed, Mignonne Park *see* Woolsey, Mignonne
Reisner, Charles 108
Renavent, George 28

185

# Index

*Repent at Leisure* 113, *176*, *177*
Republic Pictures 108
The Rhythm Boys 41
Richman, Charles **78**
*Rio Rita* (1927 Broadway production) 23
*Rio Rita* (1929) 3, 12, 20, 24–26, **27**, 28–34, 44, 50, 73, 83, 89, *149*, *150*
*Rio Rita* (1942) 150
*Rio Rita* (1950) 118
The Ritz Brothers 86, 111, 133
RKO Radio Pictures 19, 23, 24, 28, 29, 32–34, 36, 42, 44, 45, 50–53, 55, 58, 61, 64, 65, 67, 69, 70, 75–77, 83, 86, 87, 92, 97, 101–103, 107, 108, 113, 120, 121, 131, 136, 139
*The RKO Story* 136
*Roar of the Press* 113, *177*
Robards, Jason (Sr.) 56
Robin, Lee 15
Robinson, Bill "Bojangles" 34
Robinson, Edward G. 50, 76
Robinson, Jackie 121
Robinson, Roberta 39
Rodgers, Richard 94
Rogers, Charles "Buddy" 77, **78**, 93
Rogers, Ginger 63, 74, 87, 103
Rogers, Roy 93
Rogers, Will 46
Roland, Frederic 98
Romberg, Sigmund 114
*Room and Board* see *Laugh and Get Rich*
Rooney, Mickey 67
Roosevelt, Franklin D. 74
Rose, Billy 93, 94
Roth, Lillian 77, **78**, 79
Rothert, Harlow 7
Rothert, Lory 7
Roye, Virginia 116
Rubin, Samuel K. 133, 134
Ruby, Harry 29, 83–85
Russell, Jane 120, 124, **125**
Russell, Rosalind 76
Rutherford, Jack 37
Ryman, Lucille 90

Samuels, Charles 119
Sandrich, Mark 83, 85, 87, 88
Santa Maria, Nick 2
Schertzinger, Victor 58
Schneider, Todd 124
Schnitzler, Joseph 23
*School for Girls* 92, *167*, *168*
Schulberg, B.P. 63
Schwab, Laurence 78
Scott, Randolph 103, **104**
Screen Actors Guild 76
*Screen Snapshots* 154
Scrivens, Mae 101

Seiter, William A. 53, **54**, 64
Sellon, Charles 51
Selznick, David O. 64–67, 75, 87
Selznick, Lewis J. 64
*She Loves Me Not* 90, **91**, 107
Shearer, Norma 50
Sheffield, Reginald 71
Sheridan, Ann 111
*Show Boat* (1927 play) 14
*Show Boat* (1958 play) 122
*Signing 'Em Up* 85, *164*, *165*
*Silly Billies* 101, 102, **103**, 104, 105, 107, *172*, *173*
*Silver Streak* see *The Rainmakers*
*The Singing Fool* 16
Siskel, Gene 136
*The Slippery Pearls* see *The Stolen Jools*
Slye, Leonard see Rogers, Roy
Smith, C. Aubrey 76
Snyder, Marty ("Marty the Gimp") 85
*So This Is Africa* (*Bottoms Up*, *That's Africa*) 44, 75
*S.O.S. Tidal Wave* 108, *174*, *175*
*Speak Easily* 70
Spence, Ralph 51
Stanwyck, Barbara 50, 111
Starrett, Charles 76
Stengel, Leni 40, 48
*Stepping High* 16
Stept, Sam H. 17
Stevens, George 97, 98
*The Stolen Jools* (*The Slippery Pearls*) 50, *154*, *155*
Stone, George E. 87
Stuart, Gloria 76
Sully, Frank 76
*Sunny River* see *New Orleans*
Swanson, Gloria 8, 32
*Sweet Poison* 162; see also *Mazie*
*Syncopation* 16, *17*, 19, 20, 24, 26, *148*

Taft, Billy 69, 71
*Take a Chance* 77, **78**, 79, 93, *163*, *164*
*Take Me Home* 12, *147*
Talbot, Lyle 76
Talmadge, Natalie 24, 25, 101
Talmadge, Norma 8
Taurog, Norman 65
Tempest, Florence 9
Terry, Ethelind 23
*That's Africa* see *So This is Africa*
Thomson, Kenneth 76
The Three Stooges 75, 133
*Thumbs Up* 92
Tibbett, Lawrence 33
*Tidal Wave* see *S.O.S. Tidal Wave*
Todd, Thelma **84**, 85, 88, 104, 105
*The Tonight Show* 136

*Too Many Blondes* 113, 114, *177*, *178*
*Too Many Cooks* 53, **54**, 55, 121, *157*, *158*
Torres, Raquel 75, 85
Tracy, Spencer 76
Travis, June 124, **125**
Treadwell, Laura 90
Treen, Mary 35
Trevor, Hugh 30, 39
*Turned Loose in College* 51
Turner Classic Movies 139
Turpin, Ben 48
*Twelve Crowded Hours* 107, 121, *173*, *174*
20th Century–Fox (Fox Studio) 55
Tyres, John 118

Universal Pictures 25, 113

Vallee, Rudy 113, 114
Vance, Vivian 79
Vitaphone Studios 80, 92

WAIF (World Adoption International Fund) 120, 124, **125**, **127**, **128**, 129
Walgreen, Charles R., Sr. 106
Waring, Fred 12, 13, **14**, 16, 18, 19, 21, 24, 26, 32, 34, 35, 42, 46, 52, 53, 59, 69, 70, 80, 100, 111, 120, 126, 136
Waring's Pennsylvanians 12, 13, 15, 16, 19
Warner Brothers 16, 28, 70, 79, 108
Watson, Bobby 16
Watson, Homer 26, 27
Watz, Ed 140
Wayburn, Ned 22
Wayne, John 80, 81
WBKB-TV 120, 121
Webster, Ferris B. 80
Weissmuller, Johnny 76
West, Mae 62
West, Roland 105
Wheeler, Bert 2, 3, 15, 20–23, 25–30, 32–34, 37, **38**, 39–48, **49**, 50, 51, 53, **54**, 55, 57, **58**, 61, **62**, 63, 64, **65**, 66, 67, 69, 70, 75–77, 81, 83, **84**, 85–88, **89**, 90–93, 95, 97, 98, **99**, 100–102, **103**, 105–109, 116, 118, **121**, 122, 127, 128, 131, 133–136, 139, 148–162, 164–167, 171–173, 180
Wheeler, Betty (Margaret Kudner Grae) 21, 22, 107
*Wheeler and Woolsey: The Comic Vaudeville Duo and Their Films, 1929–1937* 140
White, Marjorie 75

# Index

Whiteman, Paul 13, 41, 93
*The Wild West* see *Silly Billies*
William, Warren 76
Wilson, Marie 108
Wing, Toby 92
Witherspoon, Cora 60
*Without Children* (*Penthouse Party*) 92, *168*, *169*
Wolfe, Rube 11
Wolfe, Walter see King, Walter Woolf
Wolff, Fanny and Mike see Fanchon and Marco
Wood, Cyrus 29
Woods, Edward 59
Woolsey, Mignonne (Mignonne Park Reed) 23
Woolsey, Robert 2, 3, 15, 22, 23, 25, 26, 28–30, 32–34, 37–48, **49**, 50, 51, 53, 54, 55, 57, **58**, 61, **62**, 63, 64, **65**, 66, 67, 69, 70, 75–77, 81, 83, **84**, 85–88, **89**, 90–93, 95, 97, 98, **99**, 100–102, **103**, 105–109, 116, 118, 121, 122, 128, 131, 133–136, 139, 148–156, 158–162, 164–167, 171–173, 180
World Adoption International Fund see WAIF
Wray, Fay 25, 50
Wrigley, P.K. 97
Wung, Ho Li 93
Wyman, Jane 111, 116
Wynn, Keenan 110

Young, Elizabeth 90
Young, Loretta 50, 111
Young, Robert 76

Ziegfeld, Florenz 14, 22, 23
*The Ziegfeld Follies* (1923 edition) 22